Towards a Romanian Silicon Valley?

Enikö Baga, Dr. phil., is a research associate at the Institute for Comparative Politics and International Relations at the Goethe University in Frankfurt/Main, Germany.

Enikö Baga

Towards a Romanian Silicon Valley?

Local Development in Post-Socialist Europe

Campus Verlag
Frankfurt/New York

Distribution throughout the world except Germany, Austria and Switzerland by

The University of Chicago Press
1427 East 60th Street
Chicago, IL 60637

Bibliographic Information published by the Deutsche Nationalbibliothek.
Die Deutsche Nationalbibliothek lists this publication in the Deutsche Nationalbibliografie; detailed bibliographic data are available in the Internet at http://dnb.d-nb.de.
ISBN 978-3-593-38126-8

Printed on acid free paper.
Printed in Germany

For further information:
www.campus.de
www.press.uchicago.edu

Contents

Introduction

The Romanian transformation process gradually uncovered phenomena of spatial and social polarisation within the country. These consisted primarily of historically constituted regional disparities, which gained in significance as a consequence of the country's reorientation within the international economic and political context. Migration phenomena, linking together strategies of social mobility and spatial relocation, further contributed to this picture.

Growing spatial and social disparities have represented a continuous challenge to Romanian governments. The decentralisation of the administration and the dismantling of the central redistribution apparatus became unavoidable under growing external and internal pressure. At the same time, there were fears that a precipitous or all-encompassing decentralisation would only reinforce existing disparities and would lead to a destabilisation of state power (Paradis 1998). Administrative reform was therefore implemented incrementally. It consisted of the creation of elected local government bodies (1991–1992), assignment of independent financial means to them (1998), and continuous extension of their competences *vis-à-vis* the state administration structures (1991–2001).

These measures did not cause the regulatory capacity of the central state to implode, as some may have feared, but they did result in the dismantling of the former authoritarian administrative structures. Thus new spaces for public action emerged in which local and central, state-based, and civic actors could freely interact. Different actors used these spaces in different ways. In some cases, one could witness the establishment of patron-client systems on the local level; in others, the emergence of new, more citizen-oriented policy patterns. However, a clear distinction between these two patterns of policy-making is only possible on the analytical level. Political thinking and action must be viewed as being contextualised. Contextualisations, in their turn, are determined not only by objective, so-called

»hard« constraints, but they are also influenced by subjective, or »soft«, factors. External conditions, like the specific pattern of integration into global exchange relations or the national transformation regime, are equally important as identity discourses and ways in which the actors perceive and interpret external conditions. Against this background, my thesis investigates the extent to which the actors and institutions emerging on the local level during the transformation process are able to trigger and sustain processes of local development. Explanatory approaches result from the analysis of the interplay between two groups of multidimensional factors. The first group consists of the socialist and pre-socialist structural legacy, taking into account the political, economic, social, and cultural dimensions. The second group of factors refers to the new political, economic, social, and cultural dynamics triggered by post-socialist integration into both European and global political and economic networks.

My analysis considers two levels of this interplay. The major level of analysis remains the national transformation regime. On the one hand, it sets the general legal and institutional, but also the economic and social, frameworks for developments on subordinate levels. On the other hand, it also provides the cognitive framework for the understanding, description, and analysis of local and regional politics and society. Subsequently, the analysis focuses on the interplay between the specific legacy of a particular locality and the – centrally mediated – impact of global tendencies on it. At this point, my analysis refers to Eisenstadt's assumption that specific features of the local structural legacy influence the patterns of its integration into larger political and economic contexts (Eisenstadt 1998). However, one should not forget that throughout this whole process the central state maintains its key position in acting as a mediator between the local and the global. Mediation is legislative in nature. The existence or non-existence of specific legislation regulating local-global interactions, the possibilities for influential actors to influence policy-making directly through »state capture« (Hellman/Kaufmann 2001), as well as the persistence of urban regimes based on bureaucratic allocation of state property (Chelcea/Latea 2000) shape the framework for interaction between local and transnational actors.

By choosing the city of Timisoara for the empirical study, my aim is to investigate the extent to which it is possible to create a »local path to development« in a rather development-unfriendly environment. The historically created »cultural premises« of Timisoara's structural legacy differ in considerable dimensions from the nationally dominant ones. Timisoara's pre-socialist historical development path and the city's experience of modernisation (Eisenstadt 1998: 12) show significant differences from the dominant patterns of Romanian national development. Consequently, one might assume that Timisoara's integration into global political and economic networks may develop alternative dynamics. Two arguments contradict this assumption. First, »cultural premises« may prove to have little explanatory value when confronted with hard factors like economic rationalities or geo-political interests. Second, Timisoara's historically created »cultural premises« themselves may have changed, both as a consequence of socialist uniformisation policies and of the integration process itself. In spite of a »Western identity« claimed by the Timisoara elites, integration with »the Western world« may prove less smooth than one might expect, as integration turns out to possess its specific ambivalences. Opportunities for local development therefore arise from the institutionally supported abilities of the local elites to combine structural legacies with opportunities for integration in a way that benefits the local community.

This lead question is operationalised through a series of subordinate questions. Are the centrally dominant institutionalisation patterns simply reproduced on the local level, or is there still room for manoeuvre for local actors? Does interference from the central state on the local level remain an »external« constraint for local action, or does it also influence the cultural logic of action on the local level, thus becoming an »internal« constraint? Do local actors possess sufficient resources and competences of their own, or do they act as a mere transmission belt for the central authorities? Which are the resources that enable local actors to develop institutionalisation patterns different from those promoted by national politics? Can local identity function as a relevant symbolic resource in this respect?

In addition to the questions focussing on interactions between the national and the local levels, questions about local-local interactions arise. To what extent do local elites act in the interest of the whole community, and to what extent do they serve their own interests? How does the local community deal with the opportunities as well as the disruptions created through global and European integration? What is the function of local identity in this respect? Do new patterns of local participation emerge? Do certain population segments tend to remain excluded?

Both the empirical material and a considerable part of the theoretical framework of the thesis are based on the work conducted by the author within the framework of the research project »Local and Regional Development Policy: Actors and Institutions in Hungary, Poland, Romania, and Ukraine«, coordinated by Prof. Dr. Melanie Tatur of the Institute for International Relations and Comparative Policy Research at Johann Wolfgang Goethe University in Frankfurt am Main and funded by the Volkswagen Foundation.

Theoretical references

Path-dependency and institutional change

The concept of path-dependency is based on the theory of long duration (Braudel 1992), which assumes that underneath every historical event there are long-lasting structures at work. These structures of long duration influence present political action in a twofold way. They limit its scope to what is historically conceivable but also create opportunities for political mobilisation. Structures of long duration represent relatively stable links between certain realities and the masses, which persist over time. They can be detected in statistical records of economic and social macrostructures, in the civilisational impact of geographic conditions, and in mentalities and behaviour patterns that persist, although scholars frequently consider them to be irrational and therefore not amenable to perseverance. Considering these factors, history becomes a kind of »infrastructure« shaping social action (Braudel 1992: 57–61).

Institutions shape the everyday interactions between social actors and structures of long duration. They »consist of informal constraints and formal rules, and of their enforcement characteristics. Together they provide the rules of the game of human interaction« (North 1993: 245). As such they are located at the intersection between present and past. In a way similar to structures of long duration, institutions simultaneously facilitate and obstruct human action. Hence, they create predictability and social stability as well as an incentive structure for productivity and economic growth (North 1993: 245–247). As soon as an institutional incentive structure has become stable, it will be reinforced by the learning and adaptation processes of organised actors and by their historically derived, subjective interpretations and solutions for newly emerging questions.

However, North concedes that unintended consequences of actions as well as external influences and other factors, which his model does not take into consideration, can lead to a change of development paths. In his opinion, policy changes are most likely to lead to the modification of a development path through institutional change (North 1990: 112). Nevertheless, Putnam's research about the influence of civic traditions on the efficiency of political institutions in Italy (Putnam 1993) suggests that the successful political implementation of institutional change depends on historically accumulated social capital, i.e. on a form of a structure of long duration.

Socialism as an institutional substitute for liberal capitalist modernity

Socialism can also be understood as a path-dependent mode of institutionalisation. In what follows I adopt the perspective developed by Ken Jowitt. He regards socialism as a »modern amalgam« (Jowitt 1992: 120), conceptualising it as a specific response from peasant societies faced with the challenge of modernisation under the conditions of dependency.

Starting from Weber's distinction between the traditional, the charismatic, and the modern type of legitimacy of dominance, Jowitt considers Leninism to be a qualitatively novel form of dominance legitimised by the »charismatic impersonalism« of the Communist Party (Jowitt 1992: 125). The Communist Party is regarded as an »organisational hero« who succeeds in breaking up the patterns of peasant society by recombining »the fundamentally conflicting notions of individual heroism and organisational impersonalism« (Jowitt 1992: 3). This »party of a new type« therefore becomes »the unit designated as having extraordinary powers and being ›worthy‹ of loyalty and sacrifice« (Jowitt 1992: 1). The program corresponding to »the party of a new type« is the »correct line«, »a modern program understood and encompassed in neosacral terms« (Jowitt 1992: 10).

The Party has exclusive knowledge, scientific socialism, »as a grasp of inexorable, universal, and unilinear historical laws« (Jowitt 1992: 10), and serves a heroic cause, the transformation of society in accordance with the »historical laws of social development« (Jowitt 1992: 11). The Party fulfils its historical task with the help of the Party apparatus. The Party apparatus is a bureaucratic organisation consisting of disciplined cadres, but at the same time it also represents the exclusive circle of those committed to the heroic cause.

Although modern attitudes like individual responsibility, achievement as a central criterion for social mobility, and a sense of individual efficacy and control over events are also expected from Party members, they do not develop the same dynamics as in a capitalist bureaucratic system. Individualism is limited by the collective as a social form of organisation. An orientation towards gradual achievement is difficult to reconcile with the intrinsic heroic quality of Party membership. A reflexive and critical attitude towards social reality necessarily leads to a conflict with the notion of history as a display of »inexorable, universal, and unilinear historical laws« (Jowitt 1992: 18). Charismatic, traditional, and modern elements coexist in this understanding of socialism. Both charismatic and traditional orientations have a similar preference for personal, in contrast to abstract; and substantive, in contrast to formal, considerations. These characteristics enabled the Communist Party first to penetrate, and then to transform peasant societies. Traditional features that were »formally congruent with certain facets of a peasant-status society« therefore enabled the Party to gain acceptance in peasant societies and to recruit its membership from among the mobilised peasantry. However, the Communist Party's revolutionary fervour targeted not only the elite organisations, but also the institutional bases of peasant society. »In communist countries, the attack has typically taken the form of substituting organisational for social elites and formal organisations (e.g. the collectives) for social modes of economic production (e.g. the peasant village household)«, explains Jowitt (1992: 27). He goes on to argue that collectivisation represents »a particular means of undermining the peasant extended household and village – not so much as work units or social references, but rather as units and models of social, economic, and political power« (Jowitt 1992: 32).

Communist rule thus succeeds in breaking up the central institutional matrix of peasant societies. In spite of its antitraditional rhetoric, the socialist society it sought to build retained neotraditional features. The violent reorganisation of the whole of society based on the pattern of a single household – the arithmetical approach to the economy, the forceful incorporation of the individual into the politically organised collective – represent the reproduction of peasant mentalities on the systemic level.

If the charismatic moment proved most decisive for the period of break-through, neotraditional features gain relevance after the routinisation of the Party's charisma. Jowitt defines routinisation as a phenomenon occurring »when a charismatic organisation's leadership can no longer identify a compelling transformation task, define it [...], and mobilise significant sections of the organisation around both task and strategy« (1992: 141). The routinisation of the Party's charisma goes along with its inability or unwillingness to fulfil its heroic task, resulting in systemic corruption. The Communist Party retains its dominant position in society, and therefore membership in higher Party ranks remains attractive. However, the idea of providing it with a heroic aura shifted fundamentally to more concrete opportunities for personal enrichment.

Post-socialist transition as a path-dependent process

Based on an understanding of socialism as »fake«, »incomplete«, or »failed« modernisation, post-socialist transition has been analysed in terms of a systemic »re-boot« to the »correct« institutional matrix of modernity: a democratic political system and a market economy. From this perspective the reference model for both actors and analysts was an ideal of Western modernity, which served as a model for institutional design against which the development of post-socialist societies was measured (Dahrendorf 1990). Because the systemic change was expected to be realised through a new design of basic institutions, the political elites, who were in a position to deal with central issues like the adopting or changing of constitutions; the promulgation or revocation of laws; and decisions concerning the fate of state property, were regarded as the major actors of change. Referring to studies on democratic transitions in Southern Europe and South America, processes of institutional reconstruction and consolidation were analysed as depending mainly on the constellations of political elites and their linkages with population segments that could eventually be mobilised. The relation between authoritarian government and opposition, as well as the balance of power between »hard-liners« and »soft-liners« within both groupings, determined the modes of democratic breakthrough and the resulting choice of basic institutions (Linz/Stepan 1996; for the case of Romania Culic 2002).

From the very beginning, scholars working on Eastern Europe have pointed out that, in contrast to the classic cases of transition studies, the social structures of socialist societies were largely amorphous. They generated neither economic nor political interests to be aggregated and represented by political actors (Staniszkis 1991). There was no social control over the actions of political elites, who could therefore use the »dilemmata of simultaneity« according to their own short-term interests. Additionally, the high social costs of economic transformation were expected to create popular unrest. This was likely to lead to populist responses from the political elites, thus endangering the initial reform project (Offe 1994). This last expectation was contradicted by empirical evidence. For the initial phase of the reforms, social scientists have argued that the reform projects could be sustained both by insulating the reformist elites from popular pressures and by the predominance of forward-looking, interpretative »frames« that induced the »Promised Land-effect« in transition societies (Bönker 1995). For the consolidation phase, they expect that international pressure, together with the elites' willingness and ability to impose the reform project, will overcome the obstacles posed by the structural legacies of the past (Crawford and Lijphardt 1995).

In contrast to this perspective, which more or less took the possibility of institutional engineering for granted, a competing perspective emerged. Its advocates claimed that innovative institutional forms do not represent the outcome of either institutional engineering or an institutional vacuum but of the recombination of existing resources (Stark 1995). Contradicting the transitologists' position, David Stark argued that post-socialist states were not strong, but rather weak, and that the real power was vested in personal networks of influential officials who had already consolidated their positions during the period of the routinisation of Communist rule. Under these circumstances, Stark assumed that post-socialist transition cannot be regarded as a process following a clearly defined aim but rather as an innovative process of adaptation. It consisted of a series of qualitatively different transformation processes, which resulted from the introduction of new elements into the existing social order.

In the same line of argument, the Polish sociologist Jadwiga Staniszkis put forward an »evolutionary paradigm of precipitate change« (Staniszkis 1995). She attempted to explain the end of communism by »bring(ing) together evolutionary processes and the precipitate change effected in the logic of the system, combining the tendencies encoded within the contradictions of communism and its ›generative grammar‹ with phenomena incidental to that ›grammar‹ »(Staniszkis 1995: 20). She argues that the communist system not only generated its own implosion by requiring increasing efforts to preserve political control, but also – unintentionally – laid the foundation for the new order. This took place through unofficial liberalisation and the tolerance of a »second economy«, the very measures that were meant to stabilize the system. Frequently unaware of the process itself, the actors affected by these developments underwent a »learning process« that resulted in changes in both their interests and identities. The outcome of these processes therefore resulted in »non-continuity between the actions of individuals and the aggregate effect of many such actions« (Staniszkis 1995: 21).

After having outlined both the »continuities in change« and the »change in continuity«, the question arises whether the post-communist order represents a reproduction of the Western model of modernity, or whether it generates »structures and mechanisms of a specifically individual nature« (Staniszkis 1995: 31). In a subsequent comparison, Staniszkis targets three different dimensions of modernity: the economy, social structure, and political system. With regard to the economy, she finds that the post-communist order differs from the capitalist model by not only allowing for but also requiring various hybrid forms of ownership to emerge as a precondition for global competitiveness. The outcome is a growing segmentation between the domestic sector and the internationalised one, resulting in a diversion of resources from the former to the latter. However, the two sectors also share common interests related to institutional and financial stability and can therefore be integrated by state policies. As far as social structure is concerned, the developments in post-socialist societies differ from those observed at the advent of modernity. Instead of the emergence of a large middle class, one can witness a polarisation between an oligarchy consisting of interwoven networks of political decision-makers, holders of key positions in the state administration, and new entrepreneurs; and growing segments of an impoverished population, along with the emergence of a »transfer class«, sometimes also called »international private civil servants«, earning their livelihoods in the institutional servicing of the transformation process. Staniszkis describes the political system corresponding to this social structure as »managerial corporatism with a weak political sphere of the state and a weak, atomised society«. Although she acknowledges the existence of »a facade of parliamentary democracy«, Staniszkis argues that »the real centres of power are situated below the level of parliamentary and party politics, within the structures of a strongly internationalised corporatism« (Staniszkis 1995: 41). Additionally, she points out that nationalism also has different functions in early modern and post-communist contexts. In the first case, nationalism contributed to the integration of nation states through the creation, standardisation, and dispersion of national identities. In the second, by supplying a terminology for the articulation of conflicts generated by the competing claims of different groups on the resources of the state in transformation, nationalism exerted a disintegrative function.

Staniszkis applies the argument outlined above to every post-communist society. However, she admits the existence of a »diversity of routes taken in abandoning totalitarianism«. She considers these specificities as path-dependent in the Braudelian sense, being determined by a series of factors like the »disparate cultural fabric«, the historical circumstances of the communist takeover, and the initial splits within the communist elites during the transition from totalitarianism to authoritarianism, as well as by of a series of accidental events (Staniszkis 1995: 23–24).

Jadwiga Staniszkis' arguments are further developed by Melanie Tatur (1998), who claims that the specific transformation paths of particular post-socialist countries result from the reconstruction of their core political and economic institutions. In her opinion, post-socialist transition implies a paradigmatic break in three central dimensions of the former order. First, the institutionally anchored political dominance of the Communist Party is replaced by a democratically constituted power and a differentiated political system. Second, private property is re-established, with state property ceasing to be the unique form of property. Third, economic autarky is abandoned, and integration into international economic networks is sought. These three paradigmatic changes are considered to be complementary: democratisation is a precondition for the institutionalisation of private property, and privatisation is a precondition for integration into the world economy. Tatur argues that the basic criterion for successful transformation is a differentiation of institutional spheres, that is, the absence of interference between politics and economy that is not institutionally mediated. Based on this assumption, she develops three ideal typical models of capitalism: criminal capitalism, political capitalism, and democratic capitalism. The model of democratic capitalism is characterised by the rule of law, the dominance of the market in the economy, and an integrated population. The model of criminal capitalism is characterised by the appropriation of the state's monopoly of power by criminal groups, who also introduce an economy of destruction against the background of social disintegration. Political capitalism is characterised by a partial differentiation between politics and the economy. Certain segments of state activity are subject to the rule of law, and certain economic domains function according to the rationality of the market. However, the dominant form of economic activity is constituted by rent-seeking and extraction facilitated by the manipulation of political decision-making. The corresponding social background is a segmentation of the population. Along with Staniszkis, Tatur conceptualises post-socialist transitions as political capitalisms and attempts to explain the different paths taken by the different post-socialist societies by reference to their civic competences. By analysing a series of particular cases, she concludes that historically developed civic competences help post-socialist societies to develop closer to the model of democratic capitalism, whereas their absence may lead to a development closer to the criminal model.

Both Staniszkis and Tatur describe political capitalism as a transitory historical state, or a mode of transition. They argue that the theoretical framework they put forward is less deterministic than it seems at first glance, claiming that their model leaves enough room for internal dynamics of change, triggered by the learning processes undergone by the actors involved in the transformation process.

Stabilisation of clientelistic regimes

In contrast to the authors quoted above, the US economist Joel S. Hellman (1998) concludes from a comparative analysis of transition economies that political capitalism has stabilised as a state of »equilibrium of partial reforms«. He further shows that, contrary to initial expectations, not the short-term losers, but the short-term winners of economic reform became the main obstacles to creating a performing market economy. Hellman explains that, »instead of forming a constituency in support of advancing reforms, the short-term winners have often sought to stall the economy in a partial reform equilibrium that generates concentrated rents for themselves, while imposing high costs on the rest of society« (Hellman 1998: 204).

But it was not only the post-socialist elites who betrayed the expectations of the scholars. Instead, transnational actors, who were expected to play a regulative role in transition economies by introducing and enforcing market behaviour, considered the adaptation of rent-seeking behavioural patterns more rewarding. Recent surveys by World Bank economists Hellman and Kaufmann (2001) show that new entrants to the market are more likely to engage in state capture than well-established domestic firms. Hellman and Kaufmann find that foreign companies with local partners and domestic headquarters are nearly twice as likely to engage in state capture as domestically owned firms (Hellman/Kaufmann 2001). This picture is completed by the results of another World Bank survey, which point to the fact that transnational firms headquartered abroad that engage in transition economies are more likely than domestic firms to bribe public officials when competing for public procurement contracts (Hellman/Jones/Kaufmann 2002).

Party clientelism represents the mode of political incorporation corresponding to a society caught in »the equilibrium of partial reform«. Comparing the emerging institutionalisation patterns of political life in different post-socialist countries, the political scientist Herbert Kitschelt (1994) comes to the conclusion that the design of new institutional arrangements is shaped by a multi-dimensional system of constraints. Rational choice represents only a partial explanation in this context. On the one hand, actors are seldom able to predict the impact of the emerging institutions on their power interests. On the other hand, the emerging institutions are in their turn likely to contribute to the reconfiguration of the actors' alliances and interests (Kitschelt 1994: 4).

For post-communist societies, Kitschelt identifies three main political groupings of actors: post-communist parties, liberal-democratic parties, and ethno-nationalistic parties. Due to their ideological reluctance towards a decentralisation of power, as well as to the hope of gaining electoral sympathies with the help of popular personalities, post-communist parties mostly prefer presidential systems. In contrast, liberal-democratic parties favour parliamentary systems, as they have a preference for party competition based on programmatic differences. Ethno-nationalistic parties aim at an exclusive definition of citizenship rights and at the protection of their constituencies from the economic consequences of integration into the world market. Consequently, they also prefer presidential arrangements (Kitschelt 1994:16–18). However, the actors are only capable of institutionalising their preferences if they have the necessary organisational resources. These may include the organisational capacity to coordinate a multiple network of actors and to define common strategies and/or the personal leadership capacity of a charismatic leader with appeal to the electorate. Kitschelt argues that, irrespective of their ideological preferences, parties are more likely to favour presidential arrangements if such a personality is available to them (Kitschelt 1994:18–21).

Kitschelt concludes that the general framework for the post-socialist institutionalisation of politics is given by the normative consensus with regard to the establishment of a liberal-democratic system. Within this framework, the actors use all the means available to them in order to maximise their power. Cognitive maps shape the way actors define their power interests and choose the means to achieve them. These are in turn influenced by cultural patterns and past experiences. Finally, the actors are constrained by their own organisational resources, which may or may not enable them to achieve their goals (Kitschelt 1994: 8–9).

Kitschelt further takes a path-dependent stance, and claimsthat presidential systems are more likely to emerge in societies where individual property rights have never been strong, pre-communist democratic traditions are weak, civic associations could not emerge during communist rule, and transition took place under the form of an elite pact.

Building alternatives from below

If Kitschelt's considerations focus on the political system in a strict sense, other authors also use the term clientelism in order to describe a mode of societal incorporation. Starting from a broad definition of clientelism as »the exchange of political rights for social benefits« (Fox 1997: 393), Jonathan Fox differentiates between authoritarian clientelism and »modernised semi-clientelism« (Fox 1997: 400). A »modernised semi-clientelistic« regime is therefore a regime that is no longer entirely authoritarian and clientelistic but which still falls short on pluralism and democracy. According to Fox, semi-clientelistic regimes are differentiated from democratic ones by the constant efforts of those in power to establish clientelistic power structures from above. However, the overall democratic framework created by the institutionalisation of political alternatives and competitive elections means that they cannot impose state patronage by force. Therefore, the degree of clientelistic incorporation of a society depends on the extent to which the actors »below« accept the clientelistic incentives from »above«.

Thus clientelistic, semi-clientelistic, and democratic patterns of action can coexist within the framework of the same formal regime. Their comparative significance is influenced by the balance of power between the old elite, technocratic reformers, and autonomous societal actors, as well as by the general social and cultural background. But even if clientelism is consistent with the internal cultural logic of the society, the degree of clientelistic incorporation can vary considerably both locally and regionally, as well as across different issues once authoritarian control is loosened.

Douglas Chalmers and his associates investigate a number of such cases in their works focussing on Latin America (Chalmers, Vilas, Hite, Martin, Piester, and Segarra 1997). Guided by the question of how local societies can overcome the lack of cultural resources that would promote development, they show that the new spaces for social action created through macro structural changes can be used for the development of alternative policy patterns and the incipient creation of new cultural resources like trust and cooperation.

Local-global interconnectedness as an object of investigation

The starting point of my analysis has been the assumption that the present development of post-socialist regions and localities is influenced by national transformation regimes, legally defined institutional structures for local and regional development, local and regional economic structures, and historically shaped structures of long duration that determine the formation of social capital and trust on local and regional levels. In choosing Timisoara and Timis County for the empirical investigations, it is further assumed that their specific historical legacy endowed them with historically accumulated social and symbolic resources that offered incentives for development distinct from those available within the national transformation regime. However, during the empirical investigations it soon became clear that this approach needed to be complemented in order to be able to grasp the local reality. Foreign investment did more than play a crucial role for changes in the local industrial structure. Almost every local initiative encountered during my fieldwork turned out to be the result of transnational cooperations initiatives, mainly in the framework of European integration. Moreover, many phenomena perceived and described as institutional innovations by my local interview partners proved to be, in spite of their specific local features, developments related to the emergence of urban governance patterns that can be encountered all over the world in contemporary cities. Hence, I also chose to take selected aspects from this body of theoretical knowledge into consideration.

As globalisation brought about an increase in the available modes of organisation in structural terms (Pieterse 1995: 50), social scientists turned their attention to the investigation of the newly emerging structures: of where, when, and how they were constituted. Political scientists analysed the emergence of transnational, international, regional, and local governance in contrast to modes of government that were formerly rigidly inserted within the regulatory framework of the nation state. Political economists studied the creation of transnational production networks as a way of linking together different production sites embedded in different local, regional, and national contexts. Border zones and metropolises also received increased attention as sites where populations, not only with different cultural backgrounds, but also acting within different legal frameworks, could interact.

In the Romanian context, the inability to overcome the paradigm of the centralist nation state came to be considered as a reason for the failure of the anti-communist reform project (Chelcea/Latea 2000: 243). Under these circumstances, the claim for political decentralisation went hand in hand with calls for an intellectual »decentralisation« of research practice (Nemoianu 1999, Antohi 2000) and for greater consideration of fieldwork-based empirical perspectives (Mihailescu 2001). The aim of these initiatives was twofold. On the one hand, they intended to contribute to the development of more complex scientific interpretations of the Romanian reality. On the other hand, they also wanted to contribute to the emergence of less hierarchic communication patterns in Romanian public space, as well as to the discursive legitimisation of various local interests other than »the« national interest (Chelcea/Latea 2000: 242–243).

Urban governance

On the local level, one of the most interesting outcomes of present-day social, political, and economic restructuring processes is urban governance. Supranational political integration within the EU, global economic pressures, and the retreat of the state from policy domains such as welfare or public service provision are reshaping the conditions for local action. Urban elites encounter these challenges by attempting »to make the city into a collective actor, a social and political actor possessing autonomy and strategies« (Bagnasco/Le Galès 2000: 25).

Regionalisation processes supported by the EU, together with the need for global competitiveness, have triggered a pro-active attitude in European cities. In the opinion of the urban sociologists Arnaldo Bagnasco and Patrick Le Galès, »emancipation from the state has led to the mobilising of localised social and political energies, thus giving rise to the notion that certain cities or regions can become political and social actors and give renewed coherence to an area of territory in promoting public action and [...] in boosting economic development« (Bagnasco/Le Galès 2000: 26). Under these circumstances, local politics transgress the traditional borders of urban government and become formulated and implemented within urban governance structures. In this context the term »governance« conceptualises something different from political decision-making within a clearly defined institutional framework. It instead designates processes that take place beyond an organisation, referring to the ability of organised actors to mobilise for collective action and to build coalitions and partnerships directed towards specific ends. Governance is thus »a process of coordinating actors, social groups and institutions in order to reach objectives which have been collectively discussed and defined in fragmented, even nebulous, environments« (Bagnasco/Le Galès 2000: 26).

Urban governance therefore represents something different from the local reproduction of the national regime. Bagnasco and Le Galès point out that «the reinforcement of social and political organisation in certain cities, which the concept of governance is an attempt to explain, is different from the political as defined in terms of legal and rational domination« (Bagnasco/Le Galès 2000: 25).

However, urban governance cannot be studied without taking into consideration the national level, as the nation state continues to define the arena for sub-national activities through legal and financial provisions. Thus, the unilateral retreat of the central state from a series of policy domains, coupled with its reluctance to provide local government bodies with sources of revenues in order to finance their new tasks, may considerably limit the options open to local actors. The lack of legislation that would enable sub-national actors to act freely in supranational arenas may also put restrictions on their options.

On the symbolic level, emancipation from the nation state can lead to the rediscovery/reinvention and re-enactment of regional and local identities, which local elites consider helpful for the creation of social cohesion and/or for the support of economic development. With regard to the latter, the creation of locational advantages for attracting investment in locally prioritised domains becomes a central issue.

The redefinition of the city

Thus far European cities have mainly understood themselves as products of long historical duration. However, confronted with global competitive pressures, they increasingly must redefine themselves as products of local organisation. In this process of redefinition, the definitory markers of historical legacy are replaced by »the risk capital« needed for the creation of strategically competitive locational advantages (Dematteis 2000: 62–65).

The city thus becomes «a node of global networks, where local identity and the urban territory, as a stratified deposit of natural and cultural assets, no longer have value for what they are but for what they become in the process of valorisation« (Dematteis 2000:63).

Local society is regarded as »a changing collective configuration with variable actors that can be thought as ›nodes‹ of local and global networks« (ibid.). Global networks are not connected to urban spaces via lasting »roots«, but by mobile »anchors« (Veltz 2000). The creation of these connections can be observed empirically at the moment when the urban space provides »grips« for these anchors and through their subsequent effects.

Local elites react in different ways to the global challenge posed by the need to redefine the city actively. Pierre Veltz (2000) has described three possible scenarios. Reactive strategies are most likely to use politics and culture as a means to recapture the local identity that the economy has tended to dissolve. On the contrary, active strategies not only show assertiveness and/or win over investors, but also re-establish the value of historical/territorial structures as competitive resources. The third strategy, regarded by the author as a specifically European response, implies the »capacity to mobilise – within the market economy itself – resources that are generally considered to be outside the economic sphere – shared cultures, social networks of multiple types, structures of cooperation – in line with methods that soften the brutal and impersonal effects of the markets« (Veltz 2000: 34).

The restructuring of urban government

In order to be able to redefine the city actively and to pursue successful economic strategies, urban government also needs to be redefined. The first step consists of redefining local welfare, as the major objective of local government, in terms of the economic success of a local area. As a result, local politics is increasingly directed towards mobilisation for support of economic development. Different policy areas become interlocked with and integrated into objectives of economic development. The sphere of local political action, as well as the degree of involvement of private actors in local policy strategies, expands, and new organisations outside the local authority come into being. These developments lead to the emergence of new administrative structures and inter-agency networks. Bargaining systems characterised by a cooperative style of policy-making emerge in order to coordinate them. Scholars have identified the non-hierarchical style of political decision-making resulting from these arrangements as a precondition for efficient policy-making under the new circumstances (Hesse 1987: 72, quoted in Mayer 2000). This implies coalition building by identifying and acting upon the intersecting areas of interest of the different actors.

However, this horizontal or pluralist style of policy-making does not necessarily mean that these local negotiation systems are widely open to democratic influence. On the contrary, the participants in the system may form an exclusive group, and only selected interests may be represented. However, they differ from the traditional local government structures in so far as bargaining and decision-making processes do not take place among elected representatives of interest groups organised in political parties. Bargaining and decision-making take place outside the local government structures, leading to the emergence of new forms of governance based around the explicit representation of functional interests (Mayer 2000: 260).

The shift in focus from the aspect of »care« to the aspect of »enabling« in the functions of local government is also mirrored in the fact that public service provision ceases to be a priority for local authorities. The local state withdraws from its collective consumption functions and is supplemented and/or replaced by a series of different private, semi-public, or voluntary agencies and initiatives. Instead of providing public services directly, local government bodies increasingly oversee and regulate other agencies that provide the actual services. In these agencies, again, hierarchical forms of management led by the public sector are scaled down and/or replaced by a diversity of private, semi-public, and voluntary agencies and initiatives. Traditional redistributive policies of the welfare state also become supplemented and/or replaced by employment and labour market policies. Social welfare measures become an arena of struggle and are implemented in a fragmented fashion via extractions from investors. Unitary welfare provision through authorities moves towards more fragmented structures with increased involvement from local business and other private and voluntary organisations. Under these circumstances, local struggles may result in more divisive or more responsive and accountable versions of the new local state.

In these new institutional environments, the local authority acts as a moderator. One of its definitory new characteristics is its »enabling« quality. The »enabling« quality refers to the role of local government bodies in enabling negotiation both between particular departments within the traditional local administration structure and with »outside« actors (Mayer 2000: 261–262). This understanding of the role of local government encompasses the breakdown of organisational barriers within the traditional local government bodies and between local government bodies and other organisations. It can lead to the reduction of bureaucracy and to an increase of grassroots democracy, but also to a preference for technocratic solutions instead of democratic negotiations and even to an increase of corruption and clientelism.

The specificity of place

Within this general framework, specific conditions and specific policy and political traditions generate particular place-specific development paths (Mayer 2000: 255). Local answers to the need for both the symbolic redefinition and the political and economic restructuring of a city are defined by a set of factors ranging from location to socio-cultural background. However, apparently exogenous factors such as location cannot be clearly separated from obviously endogenous factors such as local policy patterns, as the specificity of a locality is a result of both its natural/historical endowment and the way this endowment is locally interpreted and used. Under the conditions of intensified inter-urban competition for the production of locational advantages, the particular location of a place within the international division of labour not only sets certain constraints, but also itself becomes an asset to be exploited on the basis of locally set priorities. Similarly, the expansion of the local political system to include diverse functional groups, as well as the new »enabling« quality of the municipality, creates opportunities for influence and intervention of a new type, which can be used in different manners. Also, the incentives set by national and supranational programmes can have different outcomes in different environments.

In the analysis of place-specific development paths, economic and political constraints determined at the national level and social and cultural constraints represented by regionally specific traditions and structures should be distinguished from other constraints that are the outcomes of locally fought political conflicts and locally decided political priorities. Studies of the transformation processes of local and regional politics in Greece and Southern Italy have found specific, informal styles of coordinating local activities and linking them with central state regulations and funding possibilities that are characterised by clientelist relations, relying on the »patron« as political entrepreneur and broker. In contrast to the »Mediterranean« model, the »continental« model is characterised by binding the participants to abstract rules rather than to concrete persons (Piattoni 1992).

The variations due to locally set priorities are twofold. First, local skills in negotiating with supraregional and multinational capital, and the effectiveness with which the particular set of local production conditions are customised, have become decisive factors in shaping the profile of a city as well as in defining its place in the international urban hierarchy (Mayer 2000: 264–265). Second, there are variations in the type of local development policy, which may focus on accountability towards local social needs, or rather towards less inclusionary forms of business policy.

Efforts to adapt to localised expressions of crisis and the emergence of new organisational structures are further mediated by a series of factors that may be locally specific: class relations, political parties and other forms of interest mediation, cultural norms, etc. Additionally, the material resources of a city and its degree of wealth and modernisation should also be considered when the local conditions responsible for the implementation of local development policies are analysed.

The emergence of international production networks

In his influential analysis of contemporary global development trends, Manuel Castells has identified direct foreign investment (FDI) as the driving force of globalisation. The most important actors in this process are multinational corporations (MNCs), as they have both financial resources and technologies at their disposal. As such they also represent the cores of the international production networks (IPNs) (Castells 2001: 266).

International production networks emerged as a consequence of competition shifting away from final assembly and vertical control of markets to a struggle over setting and evolving product standards in the market and introducing information technologies into the production process. Consequently, production became increasingly separated from both product development and design and marketing (Graziani 1998). The latter usually tended to remain concentrated at the company's headquarters, while different production segments were delocalised to production sites distributed all over the world. The decision concerning the delocalisation of a certain production segment was dependent on the type of product and the company's market position (Mariotti 2003). Therefore the aim of the IPNs was not restricted to exploitation of lower wages or access to markets and natural resources. They sought and contributed to the emergence of locations »that can deliver different mixes of technology and production at different cost-performance points« (Borrus/Zysman 1998: 43).

The operation of multinational corporations thus became embedded in a complex system of interdependent networks. Internally, multinational corporations are decentrally organised in a series of production networks that are culturally and institutionally embedded in nations, regions, and localities. Under these circumstances, the strategic decisions of a multinational corporation result from the controlled interaction between the MNC's global strategy and the nationally or regionally embedded interests of its components (Castells 2001: 221–223). Consequently, the importance of the innovative and entrepreneurial capacities of the local nodes increases. Borrus and Zysman conclude that »particular producers or districts must absorb technology and skills to alter in any meaningful way their position in the value chain« (Borrus/Zysman 1998: 46).

The economists Barry Eichengreen and Richard Kohl reassess the importance of DFI for the case of Eastern Europe. They argue that Eastern European countries must rely on direct foreign investment and outward-processing trade (OPT) in order to achieve sustained economic growth and to converge with the West (Eichengreen/Kohl 1998: 2). However, the danger persists that if they are not integrated within the framework of a consistent economic policy, DFI and OPT will induce a unilateral specialisation in low-wage, low-value-added activities, creating new forms of local dependency. Research on Asian and Southern European countries has further shown that openness towards investors, tax incentives, and the privatisation of large, capital-intensive public utilities, like the telecom sector, did attract considerable amounts of FDI. However, the mere presence of foreign investment enterprises (FIEs) did not guarantee development.

The Romanian economist Daniel Daianu also powerfully argues that »it is pure naiveté to believe that the openness towards a global economic space dominated by glaring asymmetries, by effects of agglomeration and cumulative causality, by structurally volatile financial markets ensure, ipso facto, economic development«. He further stresses the importance of institutional factors and an own development strategy as factors that enable post-socialist countries to influence their mode of integration up to a certain point (Daianu 2002).

Under these circumstances two major approaches emerge, aiming at favourable integration and closing the gap in the knowledge economy. One of these, represented among others by the regional development expert Ayda Eraydin, recommends attracting leading innovative firms coupled with strengthening the learning support mechanisms of public bodies. She implies that even if close proximity to the source of knowledge may not imply innovation, it may facilitate imitation, assimilation, and creative synthesis and thus enhance local learning processes (Eraydin 2002). This argument has often been applied to the attraction of FDI into the IT sector, which was expected to bring about not only the promise of integration into the emerging knowledge-based economy, but also the hope for spillover effects and backward linkages (Ilyes 2003).

A different approach is put forward by regional geographers working in smaller countries. They believe that forcing the development of a competitive high-tech sector might not be the best policy choice after all. Scandinavian economists and economic geographers suggest that high-tech industries are associated with a series of factors like high risk, high cost, high domestic demand, science-based input, domestic technological spillovers, and open labour markets that will always favour larger countries in contrast to smaller ones (Maskell/Eskelinen/Hannibalsson/Malmberg/Vatne 1998:

84–89). Referring to examples from Scandinavian countries, they suggest that small countries can achieve and sustain economic competitiveness and prosperity by investing in localised capabilities. In a similar vein, analysts of the Northern Italian industrial districts argue that »the future of the districts may not lie in some improbable leap from today's industries to a high-technology frontier, but in incorporating new technology and services into traditional sectors« (Berger/Locke 2001).

When following this line of argumentation, however, one has to bear in mind that IPNs have also altered the global organisation of the traditional sectors. The example of the European Union's textile and clothing industries shows that, in ways similar to the case of the electronics industry, textile production has become separated from garment production and, within the garment production process, capital-intensive, pre-assembly activities have become separated from labour-intensive assembly activities (Graziani 1998: 247). Consequently, more capital-intensive and technology-intensive activities remained localised within the traditional headquarters, while more labour-intensive activities were relocated (Graziani 1998: 247–248).

This dynamic had a series of negative consequences for the relocation sites. As OPT directed towards the EU required the use of textiles produced in the EU, it prevented the development of local textile industries and made backward linkages impossible. It also induced a double-edged dependence on foreign partners with regard to both input and output. OPT can further lead to a lasting downgrading of R&D, financing, and marketing functions, resulting in a lock-in in labour-intensive activities (Graziani 1998: 250).

However, in both cases individual enterprises still had the opportunity to improve their position in the value chain of the international production network by generating or absorbing knowledge. Assuming that knowledge is path-dependent and cumulative (Saviotti 1998, quoted in Eraydin 2002). this seems to be more likely if the enterprise already has some localised capabilities. Maskell, Eskelinen, Hannibalson, Malmberg, and Vatne also assume that some forms of knowledge creation are localised and »sticky« in their nature and argue that, for a company

»the size and composition of the tacit knowledge-base [...] constitute fundamental ingredients in its ability to perceive and absorb any valuable innovation generated outside its borders« (Maskell/Eskelinen/Hannibalson/Malmberg/Vatne 1998: 39).

The social creation of meaning

Another type of investigation resulting from the structural pluralism enhanced by processes of globalisation and transnationalisation focussed on the actor's efforts to make sense of the new realities with which they were confronted. Terms such as hybridisation and creolisation entered the scientific discourse, mirroring the efforts of scholars to come to terms with the new identity constructs used by actors to redefine their position in an increasingly interconnected world.

The Swedish social anthropologist Ulf Hannerz (1992) proposes a model for the social creation of meaning derived from Wallerstein's world system theory (Wallerstein 1979). Hannerz adapts Wallerstein's argument on intellectual production and makes a distinction between intellectual production in metropolitan centres, semi-peripheries, and peripheries. He argues that intellectuals, as producers of culture, form »substantial communities of their own« in metropolitan centres. Semi-peripheries can also be considered »to some extent self-sufficient«, although the centres »draw a fair amount of attention«.

On the other hand, at the peripheries »the curious situation develops that [. . .] intellectuals [...] speak to their compatriots, but are heard mainly as weak voices at the centre [...]« (Hannerz 1992: 259–260). As concerns the peripheries, the Swedish author distinguishes between provincialisms of openness and provincialisms of closure. He identifies the former in the guise of an »audience waiting anxiously to catch the *dernier cri* of the metropolis, perhaps brought back and replayed by an enthusiastic local entrepreneur« (Hannerz 1992: 261). Hannerz sees the latter characterised by a relationship of refusal with the centre, which »involves a stagnant backwater, largely self-satisfied with a life of ideas which tend toward repetitiousness and involution« (Hannerz 1992: 260).

Under the conditions of globalisation and transnationalisation, the demarcations between centre, semi peripheries, and peripheries may be transgressed. Thus elements from the centres and peripheries can mix freely and result in cultural creolisation. Hannerz argues that »cultural processes of creolisation are not simply a matter of constant pressure from the centre toward the periphery, but much more a creative interplay« (Hannerz 1992: 265). He believes that creolisation »creates greater affinity between the cultures of the centre and periphery« and suggests that »the flow of culture may result in another diversity of culture, based more on interconnections than on autonomy« (Hannerz 1992: 265–266). However, he also concedes that »there may come a time of decreolisation, the metropolitan Standard eventually becoming dominant« (Hannerz 1992: 266).

Empirical investigations focussing on global discourses such as feminism (Thayer 2000) or the role of IT for development (Ilyes 2003) have pointed out that creative interplay remains more or less confined to the peripheries and semi peripheries. Globalisation gives actors from outside the centre access to global discourses, which they are able to receive, transform, and adapt to local conditions and needs. However, hardly any of the results of their creative appropriation of global discourses flow back to the centre.

Research methodology

Research objectives and methodological approach

Against the theoretical background outlined above, I proceed with the gradual development of my argument. I start with the description of the Romanian transformation regime, a theoretical construction that has central importance for the further analysis. By using a historical approach based on the assumption of path-dependency, I construct a »Romanian« model of development characterised by agrarianism in the economic realm and nationalism in the political.

Referring to selected aspects of Romania's modern history, I argue that Romania has never succeeded in overcoming its peripheral position in the world economic system. Ever since the 19th century, when the Romanian principalities gained access to the world cereal markets, Romania's economic exchanges continued to be characterised by an imbalance between capital-intensive and technologically sophisticated imports and labour-intensive and less-technologically-sophisticated exports. Against this background, the appeal of the ideal of economic autarky propagated by communist ideology is easier to understand, just as is the Romanian Communist leadership's resistance to the idea of an intra-COMECON division of labour. Fears of a definitive economic peripherisation can also be found in more recent discourses on privatisation.

Moreover, since the incorporation of the principalities into the world cereal trade, economic exchanges between internal and external actors continue to be controlled by Romanian political elites. The political control of an imbalanced international trade offers many opportunities for clientelism and rent-seeking. Import and export licenses are obtained on a clientelistic basis. Only lower labour costs and protectionist measures can achieve international competitiveness. In both cases, the costs are redistributed to the whole population, while the political clientele of the ruling elites prospers.

In the pre-war era this pattern of economic development coexisted with subsistence farming, the form of economic activity characterising the largest parts of the population. Communist rule significantly altered this situation by taking control not only over international exchanges, but also over the whole economy through nationalisation and collectivisation. However, the transition period seems to reproduce pre-war patterns. And although international involvement in the Romanian economy is significantly higher under the conditions of globalisation than before, the behaviour of the transnational actors involved in Romania does not function as a corrective; rather it provides proof of rent-seeking and clientelism.

Additionally, the high discrepancy between urban centres and rural hinterlands also seems to be returning. However, under the conditions of globalisation, the lack of industrial employment does not automatically result in pauperisation in the countryside and political radicalisation in the cities as in the pre-socialist period. Seasonal labour migration to Western Europe offers a solution for people willing to do lower-level jobs. More qualified urbanites are eligible for immigration to Australia, Canada, and the United States.

Nationalism represents the characteristic form of political integration in Romanian society. The central topoi of the Romanian nationalist discourses, Latinity, continuity, insularity, and unity, all refer to a nation perceived as an ethnic body. The power of nationalism lies in its ability to bring together a socially segmented population through reference to a common ethnic past. Thus contemporary society is stylised into a community of fate. The backward orientation of the nationalist discourses also makes them easy to manipulate by elites who possess the cultural skills necessary for reinterpreting the past and, what is more, the fate of the community.

Nationalism also determines the underlying cultural logic of institution building. The central point of reference of the Constitution of Romania is the »Romanian people« and not »the citizens of Romania«. This latter term is used only as a generic reference to both »the Romanian people« and »persons belonging to national minorities« (Barbu 1999: 25–33). Continuous reference to »the people« not only creates an awareness of a common destiny, but also helps to keep responsibilities vague and easy to externalise. Thus it is not the acting government that is responsible for a failed economic reform, but, either »the Romanian people«, which has never been so industrious as to achieve economic prosperity, or evil external forces, which have always blocked Romania's road to prosperity. Similarly, although corruption and rent-seeking are perceived as problematic, individual responsibility is declined by reference to generally valid »truths« such as: »The Romanian was born to steal«. A collective ethnic nationalism such as in the Romanian case thus hinders social, economic, and political conflicts from emerging and, additionally, interest groups in society from crystallising.

Romania's growing political and economic global and European integration is likely to challenge the power of nationalism. The interaction with Euro-Atlantic and European institutions may slowly alter the perceptions of the political elites. At the same time, migration may erode the population's perceptions of the common destiny of the Romanian people. However, I have not included these aspects in my analysis. I only mention them at this point in order to make clear that the picture of Romania that I present is a theoretical construct based on generalisations and not a historical account.

Following Braudel, I then focus on the micro dimension of path-dependency and describe familism and the social organisation form of the »mixed diffused household« as the social and cultural correspondents of clientelism on the level of everyday life. Like »the Romanian model of development«, »familism« and the »mixed diffuse household« structure represent theoretical constructions and not accounts of the actual reality.

The Romanian development path determined by agrarianism and nationalism has been affected by two major institutional changes: Communist rule and the 1989 revolution. In my analysis I show that although communism destroyed both the material basis of the agrarian economy and the village community as a model of social organisation, it reproduced elements of a peasant mode of thinking on the level of the socialist society's organisation. I further show how nationalism blended with socialist ideology during the intra-COMECON disputes in the Communist leadership and how national communism became the dominant ideology during the Ceausescu era.

With regard to the transformation period starting from December 1989, I show that in spite of the major institutional changes it brought about, so far it has also reproduced clientelism both as the dominant form of political incorporation and control of the economy. I refer to the impact of ethnic nationalism in shaping the constitution as well as its function in power struggles and distribution conflicts between conflicting elites. I argue that this situation results from cultural continuities both on the level of the elites and the population. Along with Putnam and Tatur, I argue that lack of civic resources makes the institutionalisation of democracy and a market economy difficult, especially if the opposite cultural models are readily available. Another explanation for the shortcomings of the democratisation process and the failure of economic recovery is offered by arguments focusing on peripherisation and economic dependency. I do not take up these arguments at this point of the analysis, but I will consider them in the empirical section. The main reason I do not take dependency into consideration as a general argument is my belief that all external influences that arrive in a society are filtered through the host society's institutions. Therefore the same global trend can have radically different impacts in different societies.

However, as I have already mentioned with reference to European integration and immigration, cultural patterns do not remain unaltered over time. Even if certain specific patterns continue to maintain their dominant position, this does not mean that there are no alternatives that may become relevant during certain circumstances. With reference to the Romanian case, I believe that the dismantling of authoritarian power structures represents a major institutional change induced by the democratisation process. Even if authoritarian structures were replaced by clientelistic structures in most cases, the latter lack the coercive character of the former, thus making possible the emergence of alternatives. I refer to the findings of Fox and Chalmers at this point and argue that within the framework of a modernised semi-clientelistic regime such as the Romanian one there are spaces for actions and alliances directed towards non-clientelistic ends. However, the availability of these spaces varies both regionally and across different issues. Additionally, the readiness to make use of them depends on the actors' perception patterns and cultural skills.

At this point in the analysis I have modelled the dominant patterns of political, economic, and social organisation in Romania as they have evolved during history. I will use this model in a twofold way in the further analysis. First, it serves as the description of the national context in which the specific case of Timisoara is embedded. Second, it also serves as a contrasting model for the case of Timisoara, whose historical evolution differs in significant dimensions from the »Romanian model«. The theoretical concept of the modernised semi-clientelistic regime makes possible the simultaneous use of the »Romanian model« both as a general context and a contrasting model. Against this background, the research objective is to find out to what extent the institutionalisation patterns in Timisoara represent a regional/local alternative to the nationally dominant clientelistic patterns.

In the empirical part of my thesis I address this question by analysing first Timisoara's strategies as compared to the strategies of other localities from Timis County and then the strategies of local actors in the city of Timisoara. The focus of this analysis is on the strategies of actors from the sub-national level and their modes of interaction with the different incentive structures incorporated into the framework of the semi-clientelistic regime. I also consider the impact of global pressures on the actors' strategies and the question to what extent global incorporation extends, or rather restricts, their room for manoeuvre.

In my analysis I start from the assumption that both legal/institutional frameworks and the economic, social, and cultural resources of a local actor influence the possibilities for local action. With regard to the legal/institutional framework, I stress the role of the European Union, which has a continuous impact both on the definition of the legal competences of local and regional actors and on their budgets. I then describe the legal framework for the operation of local and county governments and refer to the restrictions created by the lack of adequate funding and clientelism. I then look into the intra-regional and transnational cooperation structures emerging between local and county-level government bodies and the possibilities for common action thus created.

In order to evaluate Timisoara's economic resources I refer to a collection of statistical data. Based on statistical records, I show that the industrial structure of the region has changed due to foreign investment and export-oriented trade. Although I consider the growing relevance of light industries as compared to heavy industries a positive development, I also point to the fact that dependency on outside actors may induce new types of vulnerabilities into the local context.

As concerns cultural and symbolic resources, I give an account of the history of Timisoara and the Banat, which I consider the source of Timisoara's specific cultural resources: local identity and political mobilisation. I regard the reconstruction of the city based on the model of Vienna following the Habsburg reconquest as the key element of local identity. In this historical context urbanisation becomes an equivalent for modernisation, which in turn becomes an equivalent for Habsburg rule. The colonial past is therefore not contested; on the contrary, it becomes a model for the present.

Throughout this whole chapter I place Timisoara in the context of both Timis County, the higher-level administrative unit in which it is embedded, and the Banat region, whose historical centre it represents. At the same time, I stress the specificity of the city in both contexts. Timisoara is not only by far Timis County's most important settlement, it also is the social, economic, and cultural centre of the whole region. As such it has a concentration of economic, social, and cultural resources that can hardly be equalled by all the other Timis County settlements combined. The question that arises against this background is how Timisoara deals with its privileged position within Timis County.

I address this question in the following chapter, where I compare the development strategies of three localities from Timis County: Timisoara, Lugoj, and Ciacova. I conclude that local action is determined by a series of factors. First, the legal framework for local government defines the competences of local actors and their possibilities to obtain funding. Second, the social and economic situation of a locality determines the priorities for local development. Third, local identity serves as a cognitive framework in which the legal framework and the social and economic situation are reflected and interpreted. And last but not least, the socialisation and the cultural skills of the local elites also influence the strategic options that are finally adopted.

In my subsequent analysis I show that Ciacova's strategies are clearly clientelistic, Timisoara's strategies are external-oriented, and Lugoj's strategies are of a mixed type. I also point out that in spite of its privileged position Timisoara's strategies are individualistic and not oriented towards integration on the county level. Nevertheless, Timisoara also serves as a model for the other localities.

The next chapter is devoted to a more detailed analysis of the strategies of local actors in Timisoara. After having described the frameworks of action and the resources available for local actors in a previous chapter, here I focus on the local actors themselves. I begin with a short overview of the most important organisational actors from the city level: local government and the chamber of commerce. By showing that both local government and the chamber of commerce represent genuine institutional innovations resulting from the political mobilisation in December 1989, my intention is to ask if there are relevant alternative institutionalisation patterns on the local level in Timisoara.

I then describe and analyse the local elites, who occupy the key positions in the organisations dealing with local development issues. I consider Timisoara elites to constitute a homogenous social milieu integrated by a common discourse on local identity.

The following part of the analysis consists of a series of small case-studies focussing on institutional innovation within the framework of transnational cooperation. The first two cases, the creation of the development agency ADETIM and the elaboration of the Timisoara area's development strategy, present local efforts directed towards the creation of instruments that help to deal efficiently with local development issues. If the first cases consider the realm of local politics, the following two cases address economic issues by focussing on the local impact of international production networks. They are devoted to the cooperation between Timisoara and northern Italian regions and to technological innovation and localised learning. The last two cases focus on issues of urban governance. The case of drinking water provision highlights the difficulties of a local government faced with the global challenge of competitiveness. In this case, the local elites accept the challenge, led by a vision of a prosperous city populated by an affluent middle class. The case of the municipal elderly care programme addresses the more ambiguous aspects of this vision by focussing on the necessity to find solutions for the more vulnerable segments of the population as well.

Methodology of the empirical investigation

A combination of both qualitative and quantitative methods has been used in carrying out the empirical research. The quantitative data collection and analysis mainly consisted of compiling a statistical profile of Timis County. The profile was prepared by the Centre for Social Science Research, an academic NGO affiliated with the economics department of Vest University in Timisoara. The role of the profile in the analysis was twofold. By considering a range of data from 1989 to 1999, the profile should have been able to mirror the dynamics of the county's social and economic development during the transformation period. By presenting a comprehensive image of the county's economic and social situation at the time of the investigation, it could also be used as an evaluation foil for the statements made in the interviews.

Due to the fact that statistical data were in some cases either simply unavailable or prohibitively expensive or »just« unreliable (for the collection of statistical data in Romania see (*http://www.sinta.ro/RNE/cartax2.htm*), this profile is neither complete nor exhaustive. Therefore it is not possible to make clear statements by using the profile as a unique point of reference. However, by including further information from different local and regional development strategy papers and media reports, I have succeeded in outlining the general local development tendencies.

An additional difficulty arose from the interdisciplinary context of the research. In economic science, the analysis of statistical data is mainly used as a means to verify a pre-formulated hypothesis, whereas I expected my cooperation partners to provide me with »objective information« that I could then use in formulating my research hypothesis. Neither able nor willing to provide such a hypothesis, I only insisted on collecting data on issues that were of central interest for me and did not interfere much with the statistical analysis. The final result did not confirm my initially optimistic expectations, but offered a more realistic image of local realities. In a very subtle way, my cooperation partners also succeeded in raising issues like inequality and social exclusion, which then found their way into my analysis.

Apart from the issue of the profile, the main methodological approach of the study is qualitative. During the period from September 1999 to October 2002, I conducted more than sixty qualitative expert interviews based on semi-structured interview guides in Timisoara and Timis County. Most of my interview partners could be considered local elites. They represented state administration bodies, local government bodies, companies and business associations, political parties, trade unions, NGOs, education institutions, and media. I also participated in four workshops concerned with formulating the local development strategy of the Timisoara area in autumn 1999, as well as the final workshop in March 2000, when the final version of the strategy was presented to selected representatives of the local public.

The interviews were analysed on three levels. First, they represented a source of information on the local political, administrative, and economic situation. Second, the interviews were regarded as explicit self-representations of the interview partners. As such they contained important evidence on local identity discourses and their impact on behavioural standards and institutionalisation patterns. In a third approach, the interviews were treated as potential sources for information on the interview partners' implicit perception patterns and modes of behaviour, which may not correspond to the standards that they derive from the historical identity discourses. At this point, the perspectives of different interview partners were confronted with each other as well as with press material and my own empirical observations. The tension between self-representations and self-defined standards of behaviour on the one hand and actual perception patterns and modes of behaviour on the other were analysed under several dimensions. Different explanatory approaches resulted from the consideration of »hard« and »soft« constraints. The national transformation regime, the legally defined competences of different local actors, the economic situation, and the modes of incorporation into transnational entities were regarded as »hard« constraints. I considered local identity discourses and political mobilisation as »soft« constraints.

The Romanian transformation regime

In order to grasp the specificity of Timisoara, it is necessary to understand the emergence of the Romanian transformation regime and the way it functions. Understanding the logic of the central state is not only important as a term of comparison for Timisoara, but also because it is the instance that defines the framework for processes of political and economic development in Timisoara, and it mediates the city's interactions with external actors.

The description and analysis of the Romanian transformation regime is based on a series of theoretical assumptions. The first assumption refers to historical development, which is conceptualised as path-dependent in the sense of Braudel's *longue durée* (Braudel 1992). Braudel's theory assumes that present actions are shaped by a historical infrastructure that sets the constraints and selects the opportunities for political action. The influence of these structures can be analysed both on the level of social and economic macrostructures and on the level of socio-cultural microstructures like mentalities and behavioural patterns.

The following chapter is divided into two subchapters, one of which focuses on macro, the other on micro dimensions of path-dependency. The first subchapter deals with both the pre-socialist and socialist legacies on the macro level. The second subchapter deals with the patterns of thinking and action that develop along with and in interaction with these macrostructural processes.

Historical patterns of political and economic development

In this subchapter the analysis concentrates on the issues of agrarianism and nationalism, which I regard as definitory for the Romanian development path. Romania's modernisation was achieved as a top-to-bottom process, with elites controlling the central economic and cultural resources at that time: agrarian production and the nation. More so, agrarianism and nationalism not only had a major impact on inter-war Romania, but also they left their imprint on socialist Romania (Jowitt 1992). Agrarianism and collective ethnic nationalism, characteristic of peasant societies (Greenfeld 1996), further influenced the relationship between elites and the population, leading to the institutionalisation of clientelism.

Pre-socialist development

While Western and Central Europe witnessed the development of autonomous societal spheres for politics and religion, vassalage, new urban orders, and property rights in the Late Middle Ages, the Romanian path to modernity was altogether different. Before the Ottoman conquest, the Romanian principalities consisted of village communities making payments to an upper class of boyars who derived their income not from the agricultural exploitation of land, but mainly from control of international trade flows. When the Ottoman conquerors took over control of the trade flows, the boyars were not able to raise their incomes through imposing serfdom, due to low population density and opportunities for peasants to escape by fleeing to mountainous regions. The necessity to pay tribute to the Ottoman rulers, however, made the boyars eager to control the agricultural production of the village communities. Still, ownership theoretically remained with the central ruler, who invested the boyars only with the right to collect tithes and labour service from the village communities.

In the 19th century, after the integration of the principalities into the world cereal trade, labour service requirements imposed on peasants intensified. In 1864, after independence, an agrarian reform intended to relieve the peasants from their labour obligations was enacted. It fixed ownership rights for the first time in Romanian history. The boyars received one-third of the properties under their stewardship, while the peasantry kept the remaining two-thirds, for which it had to make compensation payments. In order to be able to repay their debts, the peasants had to continue working for the big landowners, so that their situation grew worse in spite of the intentions of the legislators. At the turn of the century, the landowner elite came to control huge estates divided into tiny sharecropped holdings and, additionally, a growing system of demesnes worked by a peasantry enmeshed in relations of neoserfdom (Stokes 1989: 227–229).

In Transylvania the situation was different from in the principalities, as it never came under Ottoman rule and developed closer to the Central European model (Szücs 1990). However, the situation of the Romanian peasantry was similar to the situation in the principalities. Until 1691 Transylvania was ruled by the Unio Trium Nationum, the three state-constituting nations consisting of the Hungarian nobility, the Saxon urban settlers, and the Szekler peasant-soldiers. As the Romanian peasants were not recognised as a state-constituting nation, they remained excluded from socio-political development processes like urbanisation and the development of trades.

This situation changed with the incorporation of Transylvania into the Austro-Hungarian monarchy and the increasing efforts of the Habsburg rulers to gain support among the Romanian population. The Uniate Church was created in the 18th century and became the starting point for a movement aiming at national emancipation. Romanian nationalism emerged as an expression of the upwardly mobile intelligentsia both in Transylvania and the principalities. Nationalist discourses were centred on the issues of Latin origin, continuity, unity, and insularity. The aims of the national movement, the autonomy of the principalities, the union of the principalities, the introduction of a constitutional monarchy, the independence of the Kingdom of Romania, and finally the creation of Greater Romania through uniting Transylvania, the Banat, and Bessarabia with the Kingdom, were gradually achieved.

The creation of Greater Romania after the First World War went along with the introduction of an agrarian reform and an educational reform. Both measures represented the efforts of national elites to foster modernisation as well as national integration, both among the formerly excluded peasants and the non-Romanian population, which amounted to four million people after the union. The reforms triggered social mobility but could not overcome the development barriers of the agrarian economy. Without the prospects of industrial employment, they only led to increasing pressure on the bureaucratic apparatus and the free-lance trades, which were traditionally occupied by non-Romanian urban elites. Social and economic competition increasingly became articulated in terms of a nationalistic discourse, leading to the rise of populist movements that laid the groundwork for the emergence of fascist organisations. Parliamentary democracy was undermined. Marshall Antonescu instituted a military dictatorship and joined the axis powers in the war against the Soviet Union. With the advance of the Soviet troops, an antifascist coalition constituted by the traditional parties, Social Democrats, Peasant Front, and Communists staged a successful coup against Antonescu. As a consequence, the Romanian army switched sides and continued the fight on the side of the Soviet forces.

Development under socialist rule

The communist takeover took place gradually. A pro-communist government replaced the provisional government constituted by the antifascist coalition, and the key government positions became the monopoly of the Communist Party. After the expulsion of King Michael and the proclamation of »The Popular Republic of Romania«, the Party's monopoly on political power was extended and legally reinforced.

Within the Party, the »national« wing, led by Gheorghe Gheorghiu-Dej, maintained its prominent position against the »internationals« returning from Moscow. This was made possible due to Gheorghiu-Dej's strict adherence to Stalinist principles. The blend of Stalinism and nationalism became the dominant ideology in Romania, reaching its full bloom during Nicolae Ceausescu's rule. The lack of ideological alternatives resulted from a lack of intellectual debates within the Party. The communists had eliminated the traditional intellectual elites, and, as there had been no previous industrialisation and urbanisation in Romania, the majority of the Party members had a peasant background. Being of »healthy origin« became an asset for social ascension during the 1950s.

However, it would be misleading to assume that socialist rule represented a continuation of rural traditions. The village community was destroyed through the collectivisation of agriculture, and industrialisation led to an increasing atomisation of the population. But rural mentalities found their way into socialist institutions. Jowitt (1992: 1–49, 121–158) has shown that due to its »charismatic impersonality« the Party was able to break up the basic institutions of the rural society: the household and the village community. Meanwhile, it reproduced them on an institutional level by organising the totalitarian society as a unique household and forcing the atomised individuals into the impersonal community of the work collective.

Gheorghiu-Dej's successor, Nicolae Ceausescu, gained his popularity by condemning the Soviet invasion of Czechoslovakia in 1967 and by allowing for a certain degree of political and cultural liberalisation. Through an appeal to popular anti-Russian sentiments and the reactivation of the topos of insularity, his moderate critique of the Soviet Union helped him to gain internal legitimacy. This allowed him to enact a neo-Stalinist turn in the 1970s.

However, collective ethnic nationalism alone does not represent the complete explanation for this development. Jowitt (1992: 121–158) has argued that once the heroic charisma of the Party is exhausted, the borders between the party organisation and its environment become fluid, leading to systemic corruption. Possible reactions to this challenge are represented by the technocratic reforms that were enacted in both Poland and Hungary during the same period. The Romanian Communist Party, led by Ceausescu, reactivated Stalinist strategies of development and power. Economic autarky as a supreme goal of politics, a new wave of industrialisation, and the erection of absurd prestige buildings were legitimised by a rhetoric of the heroic, of the ideal of the »socialist nation«, and of the creation of the »new man«. These policies were implemented through coercion. The secret police, whose structures paralleled the state and Party structures, became an all-encompassing organisation reporting only to Ceausescu. Together with the principle of cadre rotation, it contributed to the transfer of the monopoly of power from the Party organisation to the Party leader in the person of Nicolae Ceausescu. The »supreme leader« came to be worshipped as the source of political power and spiritual inspiration and the incorporation of the highest achievements in Romanian history. The personality cult, coupled with an ideologically primitive, egalitarian, anti-intellectual, demagogical, and slightly xenophobic rhetoric (Cornea 1993: 101–109), appealed to the peasant masses mobilised through the second wave of industrialisation. However, it could not prevent the corruption of the Party, state, and secret police apparatuses, which came to function according to the private interests of their members. The Ceausescu family itself occupied all the central positions in the state, transforming familism and nepotism into a state ideology. Nevertheless, economic progress could not be realised, and industrial production continued to decline throughout the 1980s. As a consequence, the population expressed increasing dissatisfaction, which was met by brutal repression. Under these circumstances, a democratic opposition could not develop in socialist Romania, neither within the Party nor within (a potentially civil) society.

Social and cultural background

In what follows I focus my analysis on the micro level in an effort to grasp the logic of the everyday practices of the population. I assert that everyday socio-cultural practices correspond to the macrostructural frame. On the one hand, they represent an effort to adapt to a situation in which resources necessary for social mobility, and sometimes even survival, are beyond one's reach. On the other hand, they support the dominant systemic logic by resisting the imposition of regulation in terms of generally valid principles and universal norms.

Persistence of familist patterns: »It stinks a bit, but it's warm«

As I have suggested in my short overview of Romanian history, collectivist concepts reach back to the village communities of the past and were also reinforced by communist rule. Anthropological investigations have shown that the village community, *obste devalmasa*, was not only the dominant form of social organisation, but also a legal subject until the beginning of the 20th century. Under the pressures of modernisation, village communities dissolved first into lineages of kinship and then into households, which were held together by both blood ties and common property. The members of the household jointly owned the household's means of production, which they used collectively. Therefore legally defined individual private property was in effect replaced by common property, which could not be alienated under customary law. By custom, this property was equally divided among all the heirs at the time of their marriage (Mihailescu 2000).

These traditional structures were destroyed by the communist »push, pull and chop« strategies (Kideckel 1993: 78pp.) carried out against the background of collectivisation and industrialisation. Nevertheless, complete atomisation was prevented by the pressures of an economy of shortage, which forced Romanian families to reorganise into »mixed diffuse household structures«. These structures can be understood as a series of strategies based on the construction of real or symbolic kinship networks more or less capable of ensuring the functioning of the household as a production and consumption unit. Mixed diffuse household structures transgressed social boundaries, linking together urban and rural residents as well as members of different social categories. They generally consisted of the traditional household members, but could be extended to include neighbours or colleagues through ties of reciprocity, including links of symbolic kinship or just regular invitations to family reunions (Mihailescu 2000). With regard to the performance of ritual acts, »diffuse mixed households« bore a strong resemblance to the traditional household. Nevertheless, they lacked both the common economic basis and the moral authority of the former. Therefore normative reciprocity, which had formerly been the constitutive element of the traditional village community, became increasingly selective and was finally replaced by contextually defined norms of proper behaviour. The erosion of reciprocity implied the reorganisation of the networks along the lines of cost efficiency.

As far as the question of trust is concerned, »diffuse mixed household« networks are rather ambiguous. On the one hand, they are trusted as institutions, as people believe that being part of a network is more advantageous in the long run than trying to get along by oneself. Nevertheless, the other individual members of the network are not trusted. Relations of reciprocity based on giving and receiving gifts are preserved, but meanwhile every single participant tries to amass the maximum amount of control and initiative in relation to the others in order to manipulate the whole network to his or her own advantage (Mihailescu 2000).

The evolution of trust in Romanian society can be described as a generalisation of particularistic reciprocities, rather than a development towards the type of trust described by Putnam as »generalised reciprocity« (Putnam 1993). The absence of a »civic community« built upon generalised trust, as well as the extremely low level of involvement in »public life«, are therefore not surprising. Moreover, investing trust in networks of selective reciprocity as opposed to democratic institutions undermines the formal functional logic of the latter, making it impossible for them to »structure preferences and constrain choices in ways that create new political and economic cultures« (Crawford and Lijphardt 1995: 172).

The outcome is not necessarily a syndrome of »amoral familism«, as Edward Banfield (Banfield 1956) described the situation of a Sicilian village in the 1950s, but rather a syndrome of »competitive individual familism«, a term applied by the Cypriot political scientist Caesar Mavratsas (Mavratsas 1994–1995) to modern Hellenic societies. »Competitive individual familism« is characterised by an ethics of indifference, which only recognises the particularistic imperative to further the interests of one's family. Unlike »amoral familism«, it allows for individual as well as common action, but only as long as it is legitimised by a concrete personal interest. Actions motivated by the abstract idea of a common good generally meet with suspicion or derision.

The economy of »getting along«

As stated above, diffuse mixed household networks are preferred as a form of social organisation in Romania not only because of their cultural familiarity, but also because of their economic performance. Their economic success can be best understood against the background of the social dynamics of public-private exchange, which has characterised Romanian society during and after communist rule. Economic strategies of public-private exchange initially stemmed from the socialist state's attempt to exert total political control and were reinforced by the economy of shortage.

While the socialist state attempted to gain total control over social life, defining even domains as intimate as sexuality as »public« matters, its subjects resisted with the help of private subversion strategies. Thus the attempted »nationalisation of leisure time« by means of private household consumption control (Verdery 1996) was countered by the »privatisation of work time« through absenteeism, endless coffee-breaks, and the like (Oproiu quoted in Mihailescu 2000). In a similar manner, the nationalisation of industry was countered by a »domestication of industry« on the part of the workers, who used the resources to which they gained access through their employment in industry for private ends (Creed quoted in Mihailescu 2000).

In its turn, the socialist economy of shortage led both to the devaluation of formal income and to the emergence of an informal »second economy« as a corrective mechanism. Thus individuals with less prestigious formal status were »upgraded« within the social space of the informal networks due to their access to scarce consumption goods. The result was a double social position, enabling individuals to transform formal assets into informal ones and vice versa. During the institutional implosion following the fall of communism, this knowledge was reinvested against the background of a weak state unable to fulfil its regulatory competences. The double social position merged into a single one resulting from the free interplay of different political and economic opportunities. For example, a well-known textile factory in Timisoara was taken over during the privatisation process by a former canteen employee who had successfully built upon her contacts established during the period of foodstuff shortage with both co-workers and the police headquarters located next to the factory building. Lacking both capital and know-how to run the enterprise, the new owner ruined it within a short period by using it purely as a source of personal income, partly redistributed among her patrons and clients inside and outside the enterprise (România libera, 28.2.2001).

As described in the example above, the economies of the diffuse mixed household networks function via the recombination and redistribution of the specific resources to which their single members have access due to their specific occupations. Both cooperative and redistributive types of exchange occur within these networks. They range from the simple redistribution of resources within the network to more complex, quasi-commercial exchanges. The first type of exchange is similar to the types of exchange practised in traditional households and occurs most frequently against the background of generalised poverty. The second is characteristic of households with access to scarce resources where redistribution occurs in larger networks also involving exchange partners from outside the network. Whether cooperative or quasi-commercial, exchanges occurring within the networks are never formalised, thus resisting both marketisation through the involvement of generally valid exchange standards (e.g. money) and transformation into cooperative associations through the acceptance of generally valid rules for all members. The flexibility of the networks allows them to perform informal exchanges and also ensures their economic success through the combination of both formal and informal exchanges. Their outcome is thus not a market economy, but an »opportunistic« economy where regulation is replaced by social embeddedness in mixed diffuse household structures.

The »chaotic democracy« and its consequences

After having provided a short overview of Romanian history, I continue my analysis by describing the democratic transition and the creation of basic democratic institutions, such as free competitive elections and a new constitution, followed by a description of the emergence of the party clientelist system. The focus then moves to the economic dimension of the transformation, describing how clientelism and corruption have lead to economic decline and the loss of the population's trust.

The emergence of a party clientelist system

The end of communist rule in Romania was brought about by the violent urban revolution in December 1989. However, the spontaneously constituted opposition groups only succeeded in overthrowing the Ceausescu regime without altering its underlying power structures. Power was seized by a body calling itself the Council of the Front of National Salvation (CFNS), which drew its legitimacy from the widely publicised participation of its members in the revolutionary events. Although it took over all the structures of the former Romanian Communist Party, the Front for National Salvation (FNS) publicly committed itself to democracy through an announcement that constituted the normative framework for subsequent debates on basic political institutions.

Following the pluralist principles of the announcement, alternative political parties were constituted and the FNS formally agreed to share power with them. However, it retained half of the seats in the Provisional Council of National Unity (PCNU), a body which exercised both legislative and executive functions. Thus it had the opportunity to enforce its own agenda with regard to organising the founding elections in May 1990. The FNS used its position again when it made public its decision to run in the founding elections, even though it had formerly committed itself to act as a non-political caretaker government. Romanian society could not look back upon strong pre-communist democratic traditions, nor was it able to develop forms of associational life during communist rule. Therefore the FSN not only had a widely publicised »hero of the revolution« in presidential candidate Ion Iliescu, but also it had much better organisational capacities than its competitors. According to its constitutional ideology (Kitschelt

1994: 16) and organisational resources (Kitschelt 1994: 8–9), the post-communist elite, who dominated the institutionalisation of political power, should have favoured a presidential system. However, the FNS opted instead for a historical arrangement characterised as semi-presidential. This arrangement made the establishment of political parties possible, which acted as mediators of the political process.

The founding elections in May 1990 resulted in an overwhelming victory for the FSN. Its candidate for the presidency, Iliescu, obtained 85 per cent of the votes, while the party itself obtained large majorities in both chambers of parliament. The newly elected legislative assembly issued a new constitution,[1] which anchored the basic democratic principles already present in the FNS's announcement. Although the parties belonging to the group of liberal-democratic forces disagreed with the new constitution on basic issues like the form of government (the »historical« parties) and the definition of citizen rights (DUHR), none of them contested the powers[2] it accorded to the president. The constitutional framework, the FNS' dominant position, and Iliescu's popularity favoured the emergence of a political system characterised by the personalisation of politics and the emergence of client-patron relationships. The lack of a national liberal-democratic platform and the weak organisational capacities of the liberal-democratic forces made it impossible for them to hinder these developments.

The incipient Romanian party system presented two basic cleavages at that time. The ideological dimension separated the FNS, with its clear lineage from the former Romanian Communist Party, from the so-called »historical« parties, the Christian-Democratic National Peasant Party and the National Liberal Party, which traced their roots back to the inter-war democracy. A sociological analysis conducted with a sample of 410 members of parliament and 52 additional high officials of the first Romanian post-totalitarian government revealed that the ideological differences between the two blocs corresponded to a series of further differences relating to the social and cultural characteristics of their representatives. While the majority of FNS representatives were in their forties, had a tech-

1 The new constitution was adopted through a plebiscite in November 1991.

2 These included naming the candidate for the office of prime minister and designating the members of the government after the approval of parliament (article 85), the command of the armed forces and the presidency of the Country's Supreme Defence Council (article 92), the role of mediator between the different state powers (article 80), and the power to appoint persons to public office (article 94).

nical background, and stemmed from the former party-state apparatus, the opposition politicians were approaching their seventies and looking back upon a career in law or the humanities during the interwar period and a long history of detention, humiliation, and marginalisation during communist rule (Tibil 1995, quoted in Culic 2001: 126–129).

The incipient party system was further marked by ethnic, regional, and urban-rural divides. The ethnic dimension separated the Democratic Union of the Hungarians of Romania (DUHR) from the rest of the political spectrum and made it a rival of the Party for All-Romanian Unity, created to form a regional counterweight to the DUHR in Transylvania, the DUHR's stronghold. Both the DUHR and the Party for All-Romanian Unity were »Transylvanian« parties, and both »historical« parties were urban parties, while the eastern and southern parts of the country, the *regat*, and the countryside were dominated by the post-communists. Specific regional policy patterns emerged under these circumstances. Transylvania was characterised by the liberal-democratic preferences of the urban population and the ethnic polarisation of a population with a rural background. In the Banat, where the political mobilisation in Timisoara reinforced the discourse of a common multiethnic identity, ethnic polarisation could be avoided and coalitions of liberal-democratic forces acceded to the politically dominant positions.

Before the presidential elections in 1992, the FNS split into old-style apparatchiks following President Iliescu and more reform-minded younger technocrats following Prime Minister Petre Roman. This led to a differentiation of political concepts and political milieus, but the overall clientelistic orientation of the system was not challenged. After all, it was Iliescu who stayed in power and was re-elected president in September 1992.[3] President Iliescu appointed Nicolae Vacaroiu, the former head of the Planning Bureau, as prime minister. Vacaroiu formed a minority government backed by both the extreme right (Greater Romania Party, Party for All-Romanian Unity) and the extreme left (The Socialist Party of Labour).

Given their overall low performance, the rulers tried to create popular support through a political discourse and practice oscillating between au-

3 Iliescu obtained 66.43 per cent of the votes. His party, re-named Party of Social Democracy of Romania (PSDR), obtained 117 seats in parliament, while its main opponent, the Democratic Convention, a coalition representing the democratic opposition made up of the »historical« parties, the DUHR, and civic associations, obtained 82 seats. Roman's Democratic Party-National Salvation Front came third.

thoritarianism, populism, and nationalism. Nationalism was used both in order to gain legitimacy and to counteract social tensions rising as a result of the population's declining living standards. Economic reform remained only partial, thus offering the new rulers and their followers opportunities for rent-seeking. Romanian analysts identified different »corridors of temptation« leading to a symbiotic relationship between political power and emerging economic oligarchies (Brucan 1996). According to the influential political scientist Vladimir Pasti, there was no political control over the economy; rather the economic interests controlled the political process. It was not the elected political representatives, but the state bureaucracy, controlled by both old industrial technocracy and the new economic elites, that exerted power in Romania (Pasti 1995: 140). These groups were defined as »unruly coalitions« by Katherine Verdery (Verdery 1996: 193–194) and described by the sociologist Stelian Tanase as having a consolidated clan mentality based on both common economic interests and manifold personal relationships (Tanase 1996: 39).

The growing discontent of the population and the threat of a complete economic breakdown led to a change of government in 1996, described by analysts as a »change of regime« (Shafir 1996; Tismaneanu 1996). Emil Constantinescu, the opposition candidate, won the presidential race. The Democratic Convention came first in the parliamentary elections, winning one third of the seats in both chambers. Iliescu's PSDR came second, followed by the Social Democratic Union, a coalition formed by Roman's Democratic Party and the resuscitated inter-war Social Democratic Party. The DUHR came fourth, followed by the extremist parties. In order to realise its ambitious programme focussing on priorities like the restoration of private property, the acceleration of reform, and the struggle against corruption, the Democratic Convention decided to form a coalition government including all the parties with a liberal-democratic ideological orientation. This coalition of coalitions proved to be extremely unstable. In order to overcome chronic governmental instability, it created the Coordination Committee of the Coalition and the Political Coordination Committee of the Coalition. Through the latter's activity, political decision-making moved away from the elected bodies towards the party leaders (Pîrvulescu 1999). It was the party leaders who negotiated the »algorithm«, i.e. the formula by which the coalition parties divided among themselves all the influential positions. These included positions in different branches of the economy like industry, agriculture, trade, transport, and tourism, and also positions in institutions like local administration, the police, the courts, different local branches of the ministries, and so on (Pavel 2000). Via the extension of the »algorithm« to sub-national levels, the party leaders consolidated not only their own personal authority, but also the Romanian party-clientelist system. However, the institutionalisation of patron-client relationships with regard to the assignment of public positions also added a certain degree of transparency and rationality to the political process. Even if its legitimacy remained questionable, the »algorithm« was openly negotiated and thus moved the political process away from the preferential style of »palace politics«.

Under the impact of continuous infighting, cleavages formerly separating liberal-democrats from post-communists became relevant within the liberal-democratic coalition itself. They mainly separated the representatives of the Democratic Party, whose background was much more like the background of the post-communists than that of representatives of the »historical« parties, from their coalition partners (Culic 2001: 148). This cleavage was most relevant in relation to ideologically disputed issues like property restitution, but it led to an attitude of reciprocally blocking each other's legislative initiatives on minor issues as well (Pavel 2000). Within the Democratic Convention, the major coalition party, factions with a stronger »ethos«-orientation were opposed by factions with a more pragmatic attitude willing to give up ideology in order to keep power. Here too, cleavages corresponded to different social and professional backgrounds (Culic 2001: 148). With the replacement of Prime Minister Ciorbea by Radu Vasile in 1998, the pragmatists won. Although Prime Minister Vasile succeeded in securing more decision-making power for himself than his predecessor had had, he did this through direct negotiations with the party leaders. He succeeded in gaining more personal authority, but, by acknowledging the power of the parties, he contributed to weakening both presidential and administrative authority.

However, the authority of the parties and their leaders was not unchallenged either. Of the four types of networks linking together the Romanian political elites identified by the sociologist Irina Culic, three cut across the lines of party loyalty. Analysing the voting behaviour of members of parliament, Culic found that kinship, shared personal economic interests, or belonging to a common social milieu often had a higher explanatory value than party ideologies (Culic 2001: 150–154). Her opinion is shared by the analyst Dan Pavel, who also found that the voting behaviour of the members of parliament was determined by local, personal, or group interests and not by the pre-existing agreements between the coalition partners (Pavel 2000).

With the exception of the DUHR, Romanian parties mainly used opaque and authoritarian procedures in selecting candidates for elections. Candidates did not have to stand in their place of residence, nor did they have to have been party members for a certain period of time before running for office. Instead of building stable organisational structures, parties preferred to attract at short notice personalities willing to support the election campaign either financially or through their already established media presence, promising them public positions in exchange. These personalities were then included on the party lists and were in many cases elected by constituencies they sometimes did not even visit. They did not feel accountable to those who elected them and mainly acted as representatives of their own personal interests (Culic 2001: 165–170). Under these circumstances, the institution of party discipline proved illusory – between 10 and 15 per cent of the elected members of parliament have migrated from one party to another or declared themselves independent during the period of their mandate. When making this decision, none of them has ever consulted those who elected him or her to office (Culic 2001: 168).

The media succeeded in creating wide public awareness of the trading of positions on party lists and of certain parties' involvement with certain prominent business people (România libera, 15.05.2001). Legal regulations regarding the maximum amount of money parties are allowed to accept as donations from persons or organisations have also been adopted. Even so, there has never been an official investigation of the parties' financial activities, and efficient sanction mechanisms are also lacking (Pîrvulescu 2000).

Against this background, Dorel Sandor, one of the most influential Romanian political analysts, labels Romania a »chaotic democracy« in which all political forces, although they have enjoyed full access to the power structures, have failed to profit from the opportunities democracy offered for modernisation (Sandor 2000). The democratic alternation of governments has indeed contributed to the dismantling of authoritarianism. However, former presidential advisor Sandra Pralong (1999) has noted that short-term policies implemented on the basis of the »rule by decree« also led to the weakening of the state's already low degree of institutionalisation. The new power configuration thus proved to be a mixed blessing, as it left room for both outside influences aimed at strengthening the democratic tendencies and the emergence of new clientelistic structures.

As the distribution of public functions to their clientele has remained the main source of authority for political leaders, the evolution of political life has resulted in a permanent oscillation of political influence on both office holders in public administration and the management of the state-owned enterprises. As a result, state institutions could not evolve into spaces where public authority was exercised and continued to represent mere institutional backgrounds for the exercise of authority by certain individuals. Authority was thus derived not from the bureaucratic function, but from the personal character of the bureaucrat, as well as from his or her capacity to mobilise networks of political or economic support (Barbu 1999: 191). The personalisation of authority blocked the emergence of a routine that could have created a modern bureaucracy capable of institutional efficiency and invested with an authority of its own based on procedural rationality. Under such circumstances institutional rules were replaced by personal arrangements based on ties of real or symbolic and implicit or explicit reciprocity (Vilas 1997: 19).

Ongoing economic decline and the all-encompassing perception of politics as chaos and corruption led to the dramatic electoral defeat of the coalition at the end of 2000. Iliescu's PSDR won comfortably, followed by the extremist Greater Romania Party and Roman's Democratic Party. In spite of fears of an ideological turn, the PSDR government's policies were not very different from its predecessor's. It respected the general priorities set by its predecessor and even succeeded in pushing through controversial legislation like the law on private property, which had been disputed for years in the previous parliament. It also took over and consolidated the party-clientelist system, a phenomenon the Romanian media described as »infiltration« on the part of the PSDR (in Romanian: *pedeserizare*). It is therefore not surprising that the leading daily newspaper, *Romania Libera*, headlined its report on the governing party's annual congress: »Scholarships, future jobs, apartments were arranged for... family and friends« (România libera, 10.01.2001).

Performance of the democratic institutions

As the public perception of politics as a field of corruption became a matter of major concern for the coalition government, it requested the World Bank to draw up a study on corruption in Romania. Fieldwork was conducted in spring 2000 and the final report was published in March 2001. The report was based on the opinions and experiences of more than 1700 households, enterprises, and public officials and provided information on both the patterns of corruption as perceived by households, enterprises, and public officials and actual experiences with corruption (The World Bank 2001: VI).

According to the report, about two thirds of the Romanian public believed that all or most officials were corrupt. This perception was shared by almost the half of the officials themselves. Corruption was perceived as being so widespread that it had started to become the country's normal condition. Four tenths of enterprise managers, one third of public officials, and half of the households reported that bribery was part of their everyday lives (The World Bank 2001: VI). These findings correlated with the results of a survey conducted in 2000 in Bucharest, according to which 91 per cent of the sample regarded corruption as part of their everyday lives (Baboi-Stroe/Tiganescu 2000), necessary in order to »get by« within the framework of the institutionalised uncertainty of »the eternal transition«.

When asked about the overall levels of corruption, the survey participants identified the customs authorities and the judiciary as the most corrupt. Central political and administrative bodies like parliament, the state ownership fund, the government, ministries, and the financial authorities were also identified as corrupt. Local political and administrative bodies like local elected officials, local administration, and communal services generally reached half the perceived level of corruption of the central bodies. The army, post and telecommunications, and the media were considered less corrupt (The World Bank 2001: VII).

Even though the population continued to participate in elections, it increasingly perceived the political elites as pursuing their own narrow interests instead of acting as people's representatives. Under these circumstances, 76 per cent of the population believed that their influence on political decisions on the local level was small or very small, while 83 per cent believed that they could not influence political decisions on the national level at all. Popular discontent with the political system was further expressed through readiness to embrace various forms of protest by up to 66 per cent of the population (Chiribuca/Comsa 1999: 88). However, the associative behaviour drew attention to the fact that there was not much preoccupation with alternatives for the articulation and representation of inadequately represented popular interests. Only about 10 per cent of the population were members of political parties (3.6 per cent), professional (2.1 per cent), religious (1.6 per cent), sports and arts (1.2 per cent), humanitarian (0.7 per cent), or civic associations (0.3 per cent) (Chiribuca/Comsa 1999: 87). This low level of public activity corresponded to the general feeling of helplessness about what was happening in the country, which was shared by more than three quarters of the population (CSSR Timisoara 1999).

From this perspective, instead of a constituency of citizens ruled by the elected representatives of their aggregated interests, Romanian democracy looked more like a formal institutional facade manipulated by a political class linked together by personal networks. The electoral success of the Greater Romania Party has further shown that voters dissatisfied with the fact that their political options were not reflected in policy changes increasingly lost confidence in the democratic process altogether, turning to authoritarian ethno-nationalist forces instead.

The consequences of economic transformation

Public dissatisfaction was directed not only at the poor performance of the democratic institutions but also, and just as much, at the post-Ceausescu governments' failed economic policies. At the end of the 1980s, the Romanian economic environment had not only been ruined by the bankruptcy of the state planning system but also lacked the minimal structures of profitable private competition, as small-scale agriculture and small industrial and service enterprises had been completely eradicated. Thus the downsizing of a state sector that was putting huge constraints on the budget and the creation of a new property structure were among the first priorities of economic reform.

The State Ownership Fund (SOF) was created in 1991 in accordance with the provisions of the law on privatisation (Law 169/1991) and became operational by the end of 1992. It was defined as a public institution with a commercial and financial character and was given the task of selling

70 per cent of state assets. The SOF was independent of the government and was forbidden by law to make contributions to local or central budgets. It was allowed to reorganise state-owned companies into independent economic units in order to make them more attractive for investors and had the task of developing an appropriate selling strategy for the assets it managed. However, it had to seek the approval of the Romanian Development Agency when privatisation involved foreign capital. Its competences regarding the development of an appropriate privatisation strategy were further curtailed by the presidential think tank on privatisation, the privatisation commissions of the two chambers, the Restructuring Agency, and different ministries (Negulescu 2001: 129–132).

Under these circumstances, privatisation developed slowly and it became obvious that it could not be completed within seven years, as Law 169/1991 required. Thus the Law on the Acceleration of Privatisation, Law 55/1995, was issued in June 1995. This law stated that all the privatisation processes that had taken place previously should retrospectively be regarded as legal. It further obliged the SOF to give up 30 per cent of its assets, which were supposed to be distributed by voucher privatisation (Negulescu 2001: 133). These regulations severely undermined the transparency and legitimacy of the privatisation process. Insider privatisation was legalised retroactively, ensuringthat new opportunities were created for those who had not profited so far. As a consequence, privatisation in the SME sector was accelerated. Even so, of the 151 companies generating half of the losses in the national economy, 142 were still state-owned at the end of 1996 (Negulescu 2001: 135). More recent data compiled by economist Gábor Hunya reveal that only 40 per cent of enterprise assets had been privatised in Romania by 1998. Of these, 3 per cent were sold to foreign investors, 2 per cent were sold to domestic investors, 25 per cent were privatised by voucher privatisation, and 10 per cent were privatised by insider privatisation (Hunya 2000: 9).

Three years later, almost all my interview partners described the Romanian privatisation process as a complete failure. According to the economist Oana Negulescu, this was due to institutional and strategic restrictions as well as to the lack of foreign direct investment. The institutional restrictions resulted from the efforts of the political parties to dominate the different privatisation bodies. As the main privatisation agencies were protected against direct government influence by law, the political struggle around the issue of privatisation took place on legislative territory. With its parliamentary majority up to 1996, the PSDR kept establishing new bodies entrusted with different aspects of privatisation and issuing contradictory legislation with respect to the tasks and competences of these organisations. The »bureaucratic jungle« (Ionescu 1994 quoted in Negulescu 2001: 136) thus created scared away »honest« investors, while offering many opportunities for patronage and corruption. The privatisation of the national telecommunication service provider Romtelecom can be regarded as a showcase for a situation in which investors speculating on large country-specific rents deal with officials who use their position to overvalue public companies in order to raise the level of the requested bribes. In such a situation the tendering process is distorted and »honest« business retreats when faced with the level of requested payoffs. At the end of the day the company is sold to corrupt investors and the bribed officials define conditions that restrict competitive pressures on the newly privatised firm. Enjoying government backing and a quasi-monopolist situation, the private investor is then free to redistribute his initial costs to the whole of society and to gain additional rents by means of an uncontrolled price policy (Rose-Ackerman 1996).

During similar processes, access to economic opportunity was simply transferred from the monopolistic state to the emerging oligarchies, remaining the privilege of certain groups directly linked to the political process (Sandor 2000: 6). These phenomena were identified as state capture by the World Bank surveys.[4] If bribery and administrative corruption most strongly affect businesses engaged in bribery, state capture by private economic interests alters the business environment in which all firms must operate. Thus almost half of the surveyed company managers reported that their businesses had been significantly affected by parliamentary votes biased in favour of certain private interests. A quarter of them further reported being affected by the high level of political patronage and by the contributions of private interests to political parties and election campaigns (The World Bank 2001: X).

In the case of Romania, liberalisation and privatisation policies resulted in a cumulative inflation of 102,285 per cent for the period January 1991 – April 2000. Foreign trade has shown a continuous deficit, while both external debt and the budget deficit have continued to increase from year to

4 The term state capture refers to corruption that affects the formation of laws and regulations, while the term administrative corruption refers to corruption surrounding the implementation of rules, laws, and regulations (The World Bank 2001: IX).

year. Additionally, GDP has declined in real terms by a yearly average of 3 per cent, while real average salary earnings have continuously dropped by 5 per cent on a yearly average. The population's severely declining living standards have been further affected by the increasing unemployment rate (CSSR 2000).

As compensation for processes of impoverishment and exclusion from public life, ancient attachments were strengthened and traditionally dominant household, kinship, and ethnic ties were reinforced. Thus culturally embedded institutions whose internal logic runs contrary to the requirements of Western modernity were strengthened.

»In the land of the blind, the one-eyed man is king«: Resources and frameworks determining local action in Timisoara

Material resources: the social and economic profile of Timis County[5]

General overview

Timis County is located in the westernmost part of Romania. Timis borders Yugoslavia to the south-west and Hungary to the west. Belgrade, the capital of Yugoslavia, lies at a distance of 170 km. and the Hungarian capital Budapest is 300 km from it. The Romanian capital Bucharest is 550 km away, the same distance as Vienna, the capital of Austria (ADAR, ADECS, ADETIM 1996: 2–3).

Together with the neighbouring counties of Arad and Caras-Severin, Timis County forms the core of the historical region of the Banat. The Banat emerged as a historical region during the Middle Ages and was administratively strengthened during Habsburg rule. After the First World War it was divided between Romania, Yugoslavia, and Hungary. It re-emerged after the fall of communism as the basis of both the Romanian development region West and the transborder cooperation region DKMT (Danube-Kris-Mures-Tisza).

Timis County is Romania's largest county, its 8,697 square kilometres make up 3.6 per cent of the country's overall area. Located in the Great Western Plain, 82.2 per cent of the county's area is fertile agricultural land (ADETIM 1999: 2). Its climate is moderately continental with sub-Mediterranean influences, which makes the region even more attractive for

5 The following chapters are based on the statistical profile of Timis County prepared by the CSSR Timisoara. Due to the fact that in some cases statistical data were either simply unavailable or prohibitively expensive or »just« unreliable (for the collection of statistical data in Romania see http://www.sinta.ro/RNE/cartax2.htm), the profile is neither complete nor exhaustive. Further information from different local and regional development strategy papers and media reports has been included in the analysis.

agriculture. Food processing is the most important industrial branch, followed by machine-building, the electronics and IT industry, and textiles. Since 1990 the importance of the service sector as compared to both agriculture and industry has been increasing.

The county's 682,409 inhabitants make up 3 per cent of Romania's total population. 63.1 per cent of them live in the county's two cities and five towns. The others are dispersed among 75 communes and 318 villages. The county's settlements are connected by Romania's densest network of public roads and railways. The ethnic structure of the population is mixed. It consists of 80.1 per cent Romanians, 9 per cent Hungarians, 3.8 per cent Germans, 2.4 per cent Serbs and 4.7 per cent others. Due to the fact that different ethnic groups live together in the same settlements, one frequently encounters bi- and trilingualism.

Timisoara, the county seat dating back to 1266, lies on the banks of the Bega River. With a population of 334,115 inhabitants, it is not only the county's main city but also the most important city of the whole region and one of Romania's leading industrial, social, scientific, and cultural centres.

On the basis of comparative research conducted on the national level one can conclude that after the capital and its surroundings, the West development region, especially Timis County, is Romania's most prosperous and developed area in terms of GDP per capita (CSSR 2000: 1). Even if it seemed to be in a more favourable position than other Romanian counties at the beginning of the transition period, in the words of a project manager of a US Aid-sponsored programme, Timis was »rolled over by the wave«. Thus the percentage of total state budget revenues collected from Timis County decreased from 3.12 per cent in 1995 to 2.93 per cent in 1997. However, the contribution of Timis County to total state budget revenues collected from the personal income tax increased from 2.24 per cent in 1995 to 2.95 per cent in 1997. The county's contribution to total budget revenues generated from corporate income tax also increased from 1.87 per cent in 1995 to 2.01 per cent in 1997 (Mocan 1998: 82–86).

The less dramatic economic decline in Timis County was influenced by many factors. Both its strategic location on Romania's western borders and the open-mindedness of the regional elites made it attractive for foreign investors. The county's relatively good infrastructure and its human capital endowment further contributed to its attractiveness for investment by MNCs in the higher and high technologies sectors. Additionally, low wages and certain cultural affinities attracted investment from Italy and Germany in the SME sector. The high level of foreign investment supported the development of the business environment and created new business opportunities for local companies.

Privatisation and property structure

As far as privatisation is concerned, Timis County had a pioneering role in the Romanian context. The head of the Timis regional privatisation agency turned out to be Romania's most successful *»privatiser«*, with a record of 200 privatised SOEs from his appointment in autumn 1996 until the time of our interview in September 1999. As illustrated in the graph below, the number of companies registered at the Timisoara Commercial Registry Office increased from 4,035 in 1991 to 24,812 in July 1999 (CSSR 2000: 3). However, due to the general economic recession, the dynamics of enterprise creation have weakened since 1995.

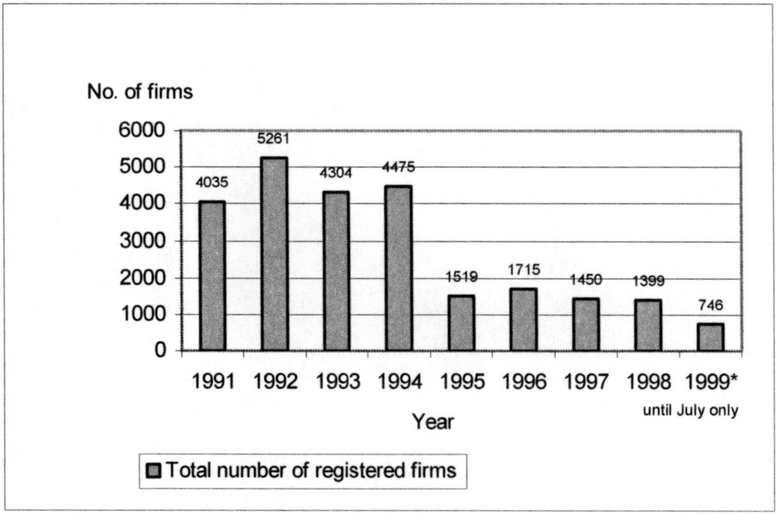

Figure 1: Number of firms registered at the Commercial Registry Office Timisoara (on 31 December for each year)

Source: Commercial Registry Office, Timisoara, taken from CSSR 2000

With regard to the property structure, private property turns out to be the most important form of property. Private companies made up over 90 per cent of the total number of companies registered each year until July 1999 (CSSR 2000: 4).

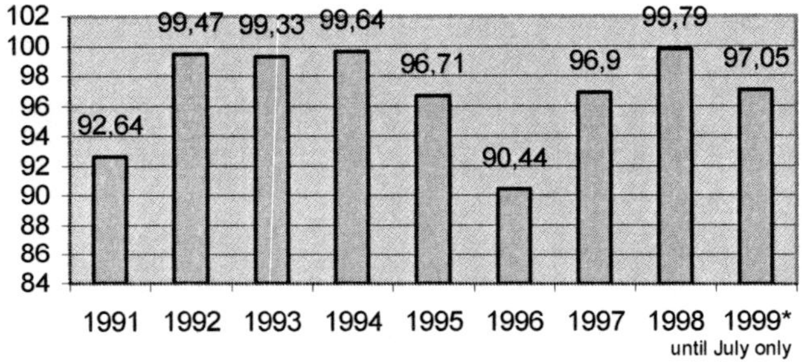

Figure 2: Registered firms in the private sector as a percentage of the total number of registered firms

Source data: Commercial Registry Office, Timisoara, taken from CSSR 2000

Given the scarcity of domestic capital, foreign investment played an important role in the process of property restructuring. Therefore it is not surprising that the number of companies financed partially or completely by foreign capital increased along with the number of private companies.

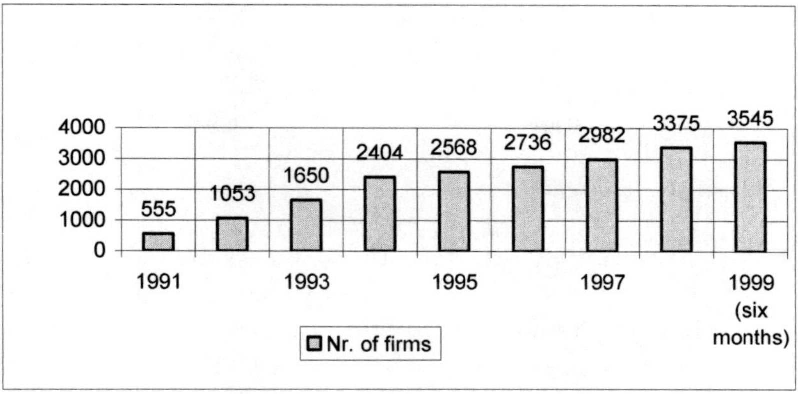

Figure 3: Commercial companies financed partially or completely by foreign capital in Timis County

Source data: Commercial Registry Office, Timisoara, taken from CSSR 2000

Of the companies with foreign capital participation registered in Romania until 1998, 6 per cent were located in Timis County. At the same time, of all the companies registered in Timis County, 15 per cent were companies with foreign capital participation (CSSR 2000: 7). This trend has been further confirmed by more recent surveys: of approximately 10,000 Italian companies registered in Romania, over 1,000 – accounting for a total of 15,000 employees – are located in Timis County, which Italian industrialists have started to consider an extension of the province of Veneto (Adesso 7/2001, La Repubblica 5 March 2001). Italian companies operate alongside 1,200 German, 203 Austrian, and 140 US-based companies registered in the county *(http://www.romanialibera.com/3ECO/07s3erom.htm).*

Given the overall dominance of private companies in Timis County's economy, their involvement in productive activities is surprisingly low. Most of the limited liability companies, the dominant form of domestic entrepreneurship here, have trade and/or service provision as their main activity. The situation is slightly different regarding the joint-stock companies, although trade remains the dominant type of activity for this type of company as well.

What at first sight looks like a record of successful privatisation turns out to be a record of production collapse. Former state-owned production units can be re-discovered under the guise of newly-created joint-stock companies, but even these have started to focus on trade instead of production. Local start-ups registered as limited liability companies focussing on trade and service provision generally consist of improvised pubs or neighbourhood stores operating in the staircases of blocks of flats.

Economic structure and performance

Although best suited for agriculture, Timis County also ranks among Romania's first ten counties in terms of contribution to national industrial production. Together with the counties of Arad, Caras-Severin, and Hunedoara, Timis County accounts for more than one-third of Romania's industrial production. Most of the county's industrial production is located in the city of Timisoara, which alone accounts for a 3 per cent share of Romania's total industrial production (CSSR 2000).

In the 1980s, the county's industrial profile was dominated by the machine-building and chemical industries, which accounted for more than 55 per cent of the county's global production structure. As a consequence of liberalisation and privatisation, the county's industrial profile underwent major changes, shifting its focus from heavy to light industry. At present, food processing industries dominate the global production structure with a share of 42.3 per cent, followed by the machine-building, electronics, and communication industries with a share of 16.5 per cent, the chemical industry and synthetic fibre production with a share of 7.4 per cent, and textiles with a share of 6 per cent (ADETIM 1999: 15).

In terms of employment figures, the food, beverage, and tobacco industries play the leading role. They are followed by the textile, leather, and clothing industries and the electric and electronic equipment industry (CSSR 2000). While the electronics and communication industries are mainly located in the city of Timisoara, the food-processing, textile, and wood processing industries are located all over the county. Performing industries like food processing, textiles, and electronics are characterised by a high rate of private participation. The share of private investment in these sectors ranged from 93 per cent in electronics to 81.5 per cent in food processing in 1995. The contribution of these sectors' shares to the county's exports has been increasing along with the investment rate (ADETIM 1999: 17).

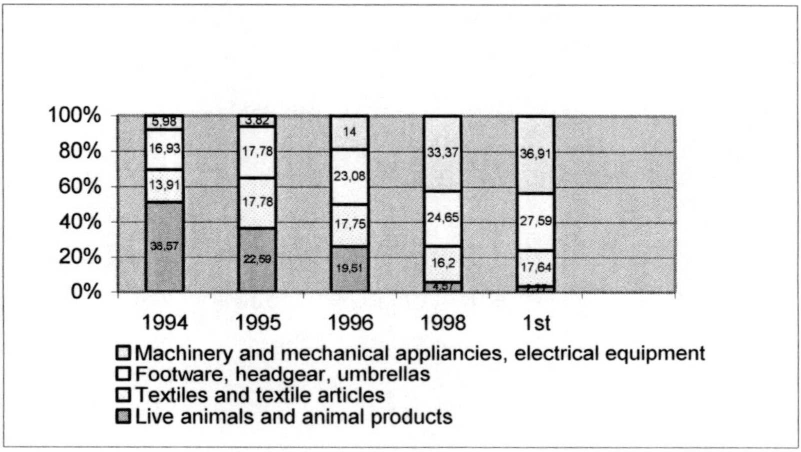

Figure 4: Structure of exports from Timis County by main categories of goods

Sources: Statistical Breviary of Timis County 1996, 1998
County Statistical Office: »The economy of Timis County in May 1999«, taken from CSSR 2000

Nevertheless, it would be wrong to conclude that one can witness the beneficial results of successful privatisation policies in Timis County. Overall industrial production has been declining since 1985 (ADETIM 1999: 16). According to local newspaper reports, industrial production shrank by almost 20 per cent in 1999 as compared with the previous year. Of the 314 products under observation, growth was registered in only 124 cases. It is therefore not surprising that of the 1,677 audited companies, 40 per cent registered losses during the 1998–1999 period (Renasterea Banateana, 3 October 2000).

Thus the relative performance of light industries cannot be regarded only in terms of internal growth dynamics. It also reflects the dramatic decline of heavy industries. The high private (under Romanian conditions mainly meaning foreign) investment rate in textiles and electronics and the high share of these branches in exports are not necessarily the consequence of re-technologisation and growing competitiveness. From the interviews conducted with company managers from Timisoara, it became obvious that almost all the export-oriented companies work according to the *lohn* system. They import their raw materials and only perform processing operations, implying high manufacturing costs. This finding is confirmed by the statistical data on the structure of the county's imports, which corresponds to the structure of the county's exports.

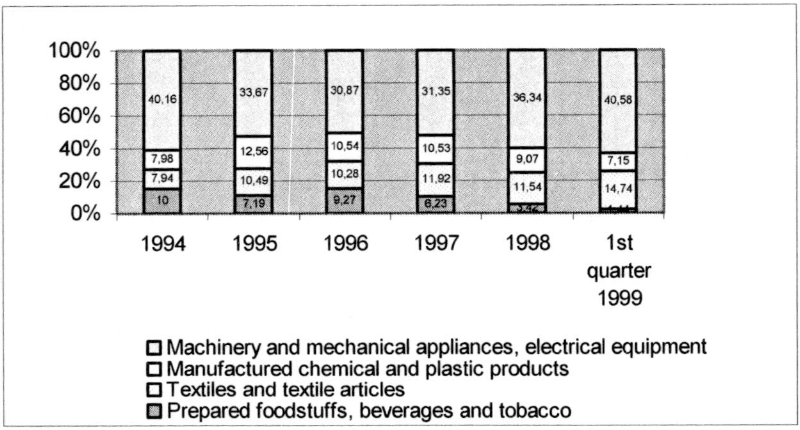

Figure 5: Structure of imports to Timis County by main categories of goods

Sources: Statistical Breviary of Timis County 1996, 1998
County Statistical Office: »The economy of Timis County in May 1999«, taken from CSSR 2000

Italy and Germany, already prominent as the county's most important foreign investors, prove to be the most important trade partners (Mocan 1998: 49).

What Romanian companies »sell« is therefore not products but a trained labour force and tax reductions for export activities. From this perspective, Timis County does indeed have certain competitive advantages, like an educated labour force with a basic knowledge of German and a comparatively good transport and telecommunications infrastructure.

Agriculture

As far as land the ownership structure is concerned, Timis County lags far behind the Romanian average. If privately owned agricultural land accounts for over 70 per cent of the total agricultural land on the national level, in Timis County the share of privately owned agricultural land is as low as 59 per cent (CSSR 2000). This looks quite surprising, bearing in mind that the members of agricultural cooperatives from Timis were among the first to divide cooperative lands among themselves, even before the relevant specific legislation was adopted (Verdery 1996; Sandu 1996). Indeed, the non-private agricultural lands are not cooperative property but the property of the yet-to-be-privatised state farms, which, for historical reasons – described in Chapter 5.2. – are more prominent in Timis than elsewhere. Despite its poor privatisation record, Timis County's contribution to Romanian agricultural production remains significant, accounting for an average level of 4.85 per cent of the country's total agricultural production between 1991 and 1998 (CSSR 2000).

As in the case of industry, the performance of the private sector increased against the background of an overall dramatic production decline. Thus, for example, the share of privately produced sugar beets accounted for 95 per cent of the county's total sugar beet production in 1998. Yet, before regarding this high percentage as a promising sign of a strong private agricultural sector, one has to remember that overall sugar beet production decreased by more than two-thirds in the period 1989–1998. Another sign of declining agricultural production is the decrease in the total area under cultivation. In the case of Timis County the total area under cultivation decreased by 15 per cent during the 1989–1998 period (CSSR 2000).

As the state is still heavily involved in agriculture, the role of the Ministry of Agriculture for the development of this sector is crucial. Many expectations were raised by the appointment of former Timis county council president Ilie Sârbu to Minister for Agriculture in autumn 2000. According to newspaper reports, government subsidies reached the agricultural producers in Timis faster than elsewhere (*http://www.romanialibera.com/3ECO/28s3emil.htm*), while the institutional framework of rural agricultural centres was maintained despite the requirements of an austerity budget (*http://www.romanialibera.com/3ECO/24s3eagr.htm*). Farmers in Timis actually seemed to enjoy a certain degree of ministerial protection as compared to their peers elsewhere in the country, but it was unclear if the preferential treatment was directed at the producers themselves or rather at the agro-bureaucracy. Accusations that over 300 land titles that should have been issued months ago were deliberately withheld by the representatives of the new authorities seemed to speak for the latter scenario (*http://www.romania.libera.com/1POL/26s1ptim.htm*).

Human capital endowment

Timisoara turns out to be the county's polarising centre not only in relation to industrial production but also in relation to the population. Almost half of the county's population lives in Timisoara, while Lugoj, the county's second largest settlement, only accounts for a 7.17 per cent share of the county's population. The demographic trends in Timisoara as compared to the rural hinterland reinforce this situation. While the county seat registers an average demographic vitality index[6] of 1.6242, over 60 per cent of the population in rural settlements is overaged, having a demographic index of under 1.00 (ADETIM 2000: 33–34).

This concentration of the active population in the cities, and especially in the regional centre, has to be seen against the general background of a declining population. This general trend is a consequence of a negative natural increase and out-migration. In-migration from other regions of the country only partly compensates for the population loss. Despite comparatively good health care provision, mortality rates are higher than birth rates, while both abortion and infant mortality rates are decreasing but still high. The prominence of heart disease and cancer as main causes of death points to the population's high level of stress. The re-emergence of tuberculosis as a cause of death can be interpreted as a sign of the ongoing impoverishment of segments of the population.

As far as education is concerned, 80.6 per cent of the school-age population was enrolled in educational institutions in the years 1994–1995 (ADETIM 2000: 40). Almost all the settlements had kindergartens and primary and secondary schools, but most higher-education was concentrated in Timisoara. 74 per cent of the county's school population attended educational institutions located in Timisoara. In 1995 these consisted of 64 public kindergartens, 47 public primary and secondary schools, 32 public high schools, 11 public institutions for medium-level vocational training, 18 vocational schools, and 6 medium-level vocational schools. Primary, secondary, and medium-level education is provided in Romanian, German, Hungarian, Serbian, English, and French.

With the exception of the »Iosif Constantin Dragan« private university in Lugoj, all the institutions of higher education in Timis County are concentrated in Timisoara. In 1999 the city had four public and three private

6 The demographic vitality index is obtained by comparing the population under 15 with the population over 60.

universities with a total number of 44 academic departments. All the public universities, Technical University, West University, and University for Medicine and Pharmacy, as well as Banat University of Agricultural Sciences and Veterinary Medicine are among Romania's most prestigious institutions of higher education. They accounted for 9 per cent of the academic departments in operation in Romania, and they were attended by 9 per cent of the country's total student population in 1999. The 23 scientific research units in Timis County are also located in Timisoara. Their profiles include medical research, agricultural research, research in chemistry, applied sciences, and other fields (Primaria Timisoara 2000: 80–82).

Accordingly, the population's general level of education is relatively high. However, there are significant discrepancies between Timisoara and the rest of the county.

	Illiteracy	Secondary Education	Medium-Level Education	University Graduation
Timisoara	1.7	55	32.1	11.2
Timis	3.6	67	22.6	6.7
Romanian average	4.7	28.8	21.7	5.1

Figure 6: Education in Timisoara and Timis County

Source: Primaria Timisoara 2000: 41

The employment situation in Timis County is relatively good when compared to the national average. In terms of unemployment, Timis was among the counties with the lowest unemployment rate – 8.2 per cent as compared to the national average of 12 per cent in 1999. Consequently, the number of unemployed persons represented only 2.4 per cent of total unemployment. Of the people who were hired as a result of the programmes for vocational integration and re-qualification, 80 per cent were workers in 1997, but their absorption had declined by 1999. They were replaced by people with a medium-level education, whose share amounted to 58 per cent of the total of newly hired unemployed people in 1999. The share of the unemployed with higher education re-entering the labour market stayed constant at a level of 9 per cent during the 1997–1999 period. Correspondingly, wages remained more or less at the level of the national average.

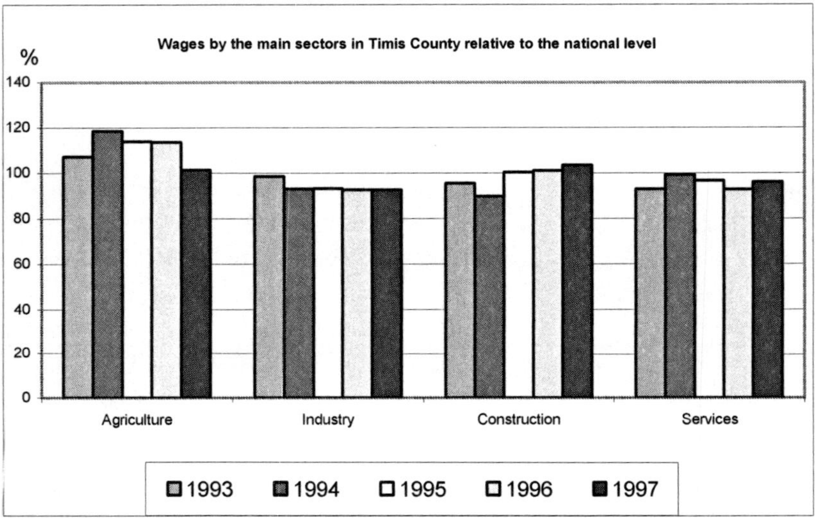

Figure 6: Wages by the main sectors in Timis County relative to the national level

Source: NCS Romanian Statistical Yearbook 1994–1998 taken from CSSR 2000

As illustrated in the graph below, employment numbers declined over the 1993–1997 period, with a slight improvement in 1998.

	1993	1994	1995	1996	1997	1998
Total number of employees	3299000	3294000	3205000	3007000	2916000	2956000
Agriculture (percentage)	32.6	33.4	31.4	34.6	35	35.4
Industry (percentage)	28.4	26	26.2	27.2	26.3	25.1
Construction (percentage)	4.2	4.3	4.2	4.4	3.9	4
Service (percentage)	32.7	34.5	32.7	29.5	32	32.2

Figure 7: Employment by branches of the national economy in Timis County

Source: NCS Romanian Statistical Yearbooks 1991–1999 taken from CSSR 2000

In spite of the slight decline in industrial employment, there was no significant change within the overall employment structure. The growing percentage of the population employed in agriculture is an indication of agriculture's function as a buffer for unemployment. The existence of a significant percentage of hidden unemployment was further indicated by the low activity rates of the population, about 32 per cent for Timis County and 42 per cent for Timisoara in 1999 (Primaria Timisoara 2000: 42).

The shadow economy and border trade

Against the background of the dramatic decline in industrial output, Timis County's unemployment rates were surprisingly low. One explanation for the discrepancy could be the fact that Romanian statistics register as unemployed only individuals who receive unemployment benefits . People experiencing long-term unemployment, who no longer receive benefits, as well as people reluctant to register, are not covered by the statistics. On the other hand, in a country with a surplus active population and weak state regulatory capacities, informal economies are likely to emerge

(Portes/Schauffler 1992). The high employment rates in the service sector also hint at a phenomenon of »hyper-tertiarisation«, whereby people excluded from regular employment invent their own employment in commercial and service activities of minimal productivity (Moser 1978, quoted in Portes/Schauffler 1992: 3). Timis County's geographic location and local traditions of border trade (Chelcea/Latea 2000) further speak in favour of this scenario.

Still, the explanation is not complete. If we are to believe a study conducted by the US State Treasury quoted in Romanian media (Agenda Zilei, 18 September 1999), the GDP realised in the shadow economy accounted for over one-third of the GDP realised in the total, formal and informal, Romanian economy in 1998. In the same vein, my interview partners' estimations of the proportion of the shadow economy in Timis County's total economy ranged from 30 to 40 per cent. It is therefore hard to imagine that it is only marketplace vendors, barmaids, and cross-border traders who account for this high percentage of GDP.

We can get closer to Romanian reality by following the argument presented by Portes and Schauffler, who define the informal sector not as a set of marginal activities, but as »all income-earning activities that are not regulated by the state in social environments where similar activities are regulated« (Castells and Portes 1989 quoted in Portes/Schauffler 1992: 4). Complaints ranging from »unserious« employers, who are reluctant to sign written contracts or refuse to pay benefits agreed on contractually, to foremen who regularly steal their co-workers' bonuses as well as company equipment or products were voiced throughout the interviews. Formal and informal activities can therefore be regarded as »alternative facets of the same economy«. Their structural articulation adopts a »variable geometry«, depending on the state's regulatory capacities, market requirements, and the size and characteristics of the labour force (Portes/Schauffler 1992: 13).

A special aspect of border trade must be seen in the criminal economy that developed during the wars in former Yugoslavia. According to newspaper reports, the oil embargo imposed on the neighbouring country gave smugglers the chance to earn up to 10,000 DM within 48 hours (România libera, 2 February 2001), at a time when the average monthly wage was less than 150 DM. Under these circumstances large segments of the local population became involved in smuggling. If, initially, people took their own chances, smuggling activities were taken over by »bosses« backed by the intelligence services (România libera, 20 November 2000) as soon as the business became profitable. Regulation of the black market was inevitable, given the involvement of central government in smuggling (Synovitz 1998; România libera, 2 February 2000). Beginning in 1996, the oil smuggling business declined and the petrol stations along the border were demolished. The social and economic capital created was invested in different ways by different actors. The »big bosses« re-invested their earnings in big business and politics. Entrepreneurial spirits who joined the smuggling business in order to earn the money necessary to start a »clean« business went on establishing their businesses. Others remained in the criminal sector, turning to other lucrative activities like looting deserted homes in war-torn former Yugoslavia or smuggling stolen luxury cars or trafficking in women[7] (România libera, 2 February 2000).

Conclusions

The findings of the profile suggest that we should classify Timis County as an agro-industrial area. Employment figures are highest in agriculture and industries processing agricultural products, but these two branches lagged behind in relation to privatisation.[8] Although these branches are still dominated by state enterprises, a large number of private companies are also active in agriculture, food processing, and the textile- and wood-processing industries. These are either local start-ups or SMEs with foreign capital participation. These branches also have a relatively balanced spatial structure, raising hopes that they might contribute to a more integrated economic development within the county as soon as the privatisation process is complete.

Industrial production is mainly concentrated in Timisoara, as is foreign investment. Consequently, industrial restructuring is more advanced in Timisoara, as direct foreign investment (DFI) and outward-processing trade (OPT) have helped to bring about a reorientation of industrial production from the heavy to the light industrial sector. As DFI favours de-

7 A report by the European Commission's Comittee on Equal Opportunities for Women and Men issued in April 2003 quotes the IOM, which states that Timisoara is »the largest centre for the sale and purchase of women« in South-Eastern Europe.

8 The privatisation of the meat-processing conglomerate Comtim, the region's biggest employer, might now have changed the situation.

veloped areas and borders with advanced countries (Eichengreen/Kohl 1998: 9), Timis County could further profit from its strategic location. In addition, one could observe that higher-tech DFI and OPT, once started, have indeed attracted additional DFI and OPT and have also become involved in the dissemination of technological knowledge (Chapter 6.2.2). Local skills improved as a result of exposing local staff to new products and procedures as well as to international standards of quality, packaging, product design, and distribution. Still, significant spillover effects have not become noticeable so far. Both the employment structure and the wage structure of the county show that DFI and OPT have not yet created highly qualified professional jobs. Even if Western economists have stated that eastern European countries have to rely on direct foreign investment and outward-processing trade in order to achieve sustained economic growth and converge with the West (Eichengreen/Kohl 1998: 2), the danger persists that, if they are not integrated within the framework of a consistent economic policy, DFI and OPT will induce a unilateral specialisation in low-wage, low-value-added activities, creating new forms of local dependency.

History and identity: The distinctiveness of the Banat

The historical development of private property, democratic traditions, and regional identity

The Banat was part of the medieval Kingdom of Hungary from the 11th century onwards. As such it was affected both by the Central European development process of the Middle Ages (Szücs 1990) and by the Ottoman conquest of 1552. In 1716 it was re-conquered by the Habsburgs and subjected to direct administration by the *Hofkammer* in Vienna. Thus the Banat became the place where the Habsburg rulers conducted their first experiments with mercantilism. The Habsburg development project for the Banat was based on four factors whose influence proved definitive for the further evolution of the region.

As a first step towards exerting control over the newly acquired territories, the Habsburg rulers built up an administrative system covering the whole of the region. Property rights were enforced, infrastructure was developed, and protectionist investment and taxation policies led to economic growth. The overall progress considerably influenced the general acceptance of the newly established institutions. Against this background, direct dependency on Vienna made it possible for the Banat to free itself from Hungary's influence and, due to the previous processes of social homogenisation, to overcome the feudal system.

The settlement policy, which selected future settlers not on the basis of their ethnicity but according to their qualifications for certain trades, also contributed to economic development. Meanwhile, it created a cultural climate where individuals were formally regarded as equals and performance was valued higher than membership in a certain ethnic group (Leber 1996).

The success of these mercantilist development policies was somewhat diminished by the incorporation of the Banat into Hungary in 1791. Nevertheless, an already established, growth-stimulating institutional pattern and an extensive network of civic associations were able to lessen the effects of economic peripherisation and the Hungarian state's pressure for national homogenisation. This was especially true of the regional centre Temesvar (Sármány-Parsons 1996). The rural hinterland was in large measure excluded from social and economic progress, although serfdom was abolished in 1867. Against the background of growing tensions between the city and the countryside, the Romanian and Serbian peasant population turned to the emerging national movements. This led to the partition of the historical Banat between Romania and Serbia after the First World War. Romania obtained two-thirds of the territory, including its centre, Timisoara/Temesvar.

Like the other newly acquired provinces, the Banat was incorporated into the Romanian nation state through institutional unification, land reform, and education system reform (Sundhaussen 1994). Unlike other regions, where the lobby of the landowners blocked the implementation of the law on land reform, the Banat saw full implementation of this measure, which mainly put non-Romanians at a disadvantage (Hitchins 1996: 373–375). The implementation of land reform led not only to the emergence of a series of viable small agrarian enterprises but also to the full institutionalisation of property rights in the Banat. Banatian peasants came to define themselves in terms of land ownership. In order to conserve and enlarge their holdings, they took over a series of practices from the German settlers, whom they regarded as technologically more advanced and culturally superior. The introduction of cash crops and agricultural machinery led to the emergence of an intensive form of agricultural production. These - usually costly - innovations were financed by wage labour in the cities of the region or even as far away as in the industrial regions of the USA. Growing competitiveness and rationalisation were accompanied by another major change: the overall dominance of the one-child family, used as a way of avoiding the dispersal of property through successive divisions among heirs (Hitchins 1996: 373–374). Its pre-eminence in the Banat shows that here property replaced the family as a central locus of personal identity.

If incorporation into Romania brought about a number of advantages for the mainly Romanian rural population, it proved to be more ambiguous for the upcoming Romanian elites. The local and regional Romanian elites came to face double competition with both the mainly non-Romanian established urban elites and the politically dominant migrants from the Old Kingdom (Chelcea 1997: 26–27). Even if they subscribed to the dominant, broadly nationalist consensus, the Banatian Romanian elites were reluctant to embrace an overall Romanian identity. As their situation of competition on two fronts did not allow for the expression of a Banatian economic and cultural superiority rooted in Austro-Hungarian modernisation policies and the intercultural learning processes induced by them, the Banatian elites fell back upon a discourse of »regional nationalism«. They claimed a »pure« Romanian identity for themselves, which they considered superior to the corrupted »Balkan« identity of the Old Kingdom (Chelcea 1998: 39–40).

Nevertheless, nationalism in the Banat never succeeded in playing the central role it played elsewhere in Romania, as wealth and achievement were still more important than ethnicity or political affiliation. This also held true for the period of communist rule. Even if socialist homogenisation policies turned out to be a failure, as they unintentionally led to the rediscovery of the democratic traditions of the region and the emergence of a multiethnic regional identity, the communist rulers were much more successful with regard to the eradication of private property. Local industries and larger and medium-sized land holdings were expropriated, and the communist regime also attempted to physically eliminate the peasant middle class, the social group which identified most strongly with its property. Banatian peasants were therefore subject to several waves of deportation, culminating in the forced resettlement of the rural elites in the 1950s (Vultur 1997).

As a consequence of large-scale expropriations and deportations, the rural society of the Banat differed considerably from the Romanian average. While the peasant household combining cooperative agricultural labour with industrial wage labour continued to be the core social and economic unit of Romanian society (Kideckel 1993: 138–140), the situation was more differentiated in the Banat, where agricultural cooperatives were outnumbered by state farms. The rural population was forced early into industrial wage labour, and it increasingly profited from the new educational and career opportunities (Sterbling 1997: 41). Experiencing the inefficiency of state and cooperative farming, Banatian peasants turned away from agriculture (Cernea 1977), and thus farms had to employ increasing numbers of migrant workers. Migrants with a peasant background arrived in great numbers from the most backward regions of the country. They were perceived as culturally inferior by the locals, and everyday dealings with them gave the dichotomy between »us« and »them« a new relevance.

The distinction between the Banat, described in terms of »progress«, »civilization«, and »Europe«, and the Old Kingdom, described in terms of »backwardness«, »barbarism«, and »Balkan«, reinforced the typical gap between society and the socialist state. The discourse of one's own »European« identity was used, on the one hand, as a means of dissociation from a regime perceived as »half Asian«. On the other hand, it was used to connect local discourses to the myth of *Mitteleuropa* created by the intellectuals of Central Europe (Chelcea 1998: 43–45). Against this background, the Communist regime's integral nationalism was outweighed by a positive valuation of multiethnicity and a positive image of the outside world, based on the reception of foreign media and everyday experiences with small-scale border trade. The gap between »us« and »them« grew deeper and finally led to the uprising against the Ceausescu regime.

The uprising started from a spontaneous gathering of parishioners of the Hungarian reformed church, who tried to protect the priest of their congregation from deportation by the state security forces on December 15, 1989. The parishioners were joined by friends, neighbours, and passers-by, and the multiethnic crowd evolved into an anti-regime demonstration, which was brutally dispersed by the secret police. Despite the efforts of local officials, the demonstrations grew in the following days. The army and secret police intervened by using live ammunition against the population. The victims were seized by the secret police in order to be cremated in unknown places, and 832 people were arrested. A state of emergency was proclaimed and the city was isolated from the rest of the country.

While the citizens continued the demonstrations and claimed their dead, the staff of local factories went on strike and the soldiers refused to obey the order to fire. »Patriotic guards« of industrial workers from the southern part of the country arrived in order to fight the »spies«, »traitors«, »hooligans«, and »agents of imperialism«. Against the background of demonstrations in other urban centres, the acclamation meeting for Ceausescu in Bucharest turned into a public protest meeting on December 21st, and the workers declared their solidarity with the people of Timisoara. The following day the Ceausescus fled and the self-proclaimed Front of National Salvation seized power in the name of the »revolution«.

Ever since, the symbol of the revolution has remained a disputed issue. Sandor states that »similar to the 'whole people's property' in socialism, the revolution belonged to everybody and nobody at the same time« (Sandor 2000: 21). However, there was general agreement in Timisoara that the revolution did belong to the population of the city and to its political representatives, the liberal-democratic urban elite. This posed a continuous challenge to the legitimacy of the central government, which had declared itself »the legal heir of the revolution« in the early nineties. In order to defend itself, it tried to isolate Timisoara by levelling accusations of separatism and crime against it. Even if the conflict was a political one, as it opposed the post-communist central government to the liberal-democratic urban elite in Timisoara, it was not disputed in political terms but articulated in a symbolic language very similar to the one used by the communist government against the former demonstrators. The bitterness over »the stolen revolution« and the absence of solidarity on the part of the rest of the Romanian population finally led to political demobilisation in Timisoara.

The legal and institutional frameworks for local action

The general institutional framework of local public administration

The establishment of an institutional framework for local public administration in Romania began with the administrative reform of 1991. This consisted of the law on local public administration, Law 69/1991, and the law on local elections, Law 70/1991. The first local elections were held in 1992. As a result, a two-tier, non-hierarchical administrative system emerged consisting of 2,948 municipalities and 41 counties. Both municipalities and counties were considered juridical persons and given the right to establish local government bodies. Directly elected local and county councils held legislative power. Directly elected mayors held executive power on the local level, and county council presidents elected from the ranks of the county council held the executive powers on the county level. The county further served as a basic unit for the decentralised public administration. Therefore the prefect, the central government's local representative, was established on this level. He oversaw the implementation of government policy on the local level and acted as the head of the decentralised public service units of the ministries and other central organs of public administration.

According to the law there were no subordinate relations either between the two tiers of local government or between the prefect and the local authorities. However, this regulation was initially undermined by the dependency of local governments on central funding.

Locally collected taxes were transferred to the central budget, where they were redistributed between local budgets and ministries. Central transfers to local budgets consisted of shares of personal income tax and money earmarked for social protection and local investment. The share a particular county received from personal income tax depended on its population, the length of its road network, its number of dwellings, the length of its water supply and sewage systems, the percentage of the population of school age, the number of hospital beds, the number of its medical dispensaries, and the number of its administrative units. This system mainly favoured the city of Bucharest, which received 20 per cent of local budget expenditures, even though only 10 per cent of the country's population lived in the capital. In 1996, Timis County received less than a third of the sum allocated to the capital.

The transfers aimed at social protection and local investment totalled the same amount as the shares from personal income tax in 1996. The transfers aimed at social protection mainly consisted of subsidies for local public transport and heating. By contrast, more than one-quarter of the total budget expenditure for local government was approved by the central government on a case-by-case basis, thus creating good opportunities for clientelistic interventions. The ministries also had a significant impact on local policies through the direct sectoral investments they carried out. Unfortunately, no data are available on the amounts of money involved.

To rectify this situation, the Law on Local Public Finance was adopted in 1998. It stated that local authorities should receive 50 per cent of the personal income taxes paid by the population. A share of 10 per cent remained at the county council's disposal, while a share of 40 per cent was put at the local councils' disposal. Though a group of mayors tried to pressure the government to allocate additional shares of corporate income tax and value-added tax to the municipalities, both proposals were rejected in parliament. However, the pressure group succeeded in pushing through a regulation stating that personal income taxes would be levied not at the taxpayer's place of residence but at the place where the company that employs the taxpayer is registered. This regulation mainly favoured the capital, where most of the MNCs and the state companies operating on a national level – and paying the highest salaries – were registered, but it was also to the advantage of other big cities. Although it allowed municipalities to capitalise on their better economic, social, or demographic situations, the law contributed to a general increase in the share of the local revenues. These grew from 28 per cent of total municipal revenues in 1995 to 44.58 per cent in 1999 and 36.28 per cent in 2000 (IPP 2001: 34).

Local government received additional revenues from other taxes that were collected locally, e.g. property tax, different taxes that were collected from the population, and other types of revenue resulting from their own economic activity. According to media reports, the most significant shares of local government's own revenues were generated by the property tax on land and buildings, the renting or selling of buildings belonging to the municipalities, and cooperation with commercial enterprises operating in the field of local public services (*http//brasov.monitorul.ro/arhiva/04_May _00/html./art/articol.php3?art=400*).

In a nation-wide study conducted in 2001, the Institute for Public Policies and the Pro Democracy Association found that the inequalities between revenue and expenditure levels among municipalities and contradictory and incomplete decentralisation represented the main problems in the realm of local budgeting. From the moment at which the Law on Local Public Finance was adopted, the president of the parliamentary commission on budgeting and finance had stated that the law had experimental character and that local authorities would receive additional shares of value-added tax from 1999 onwards. This promise was made against the background of a general economic decline, which led to an increase in the share of value-added tax as compared with the share of income tax in the total budget revenues (Mocan 1998:82–86). However, in 2000 it was still the personal income tax that accounted for the largest shares of both local and central budgets (România libera, 18 December 2000), due to widespread tax evasion among economic actors (România libera, 22 November 2001).

In conclusion, the revenues of the local authorities were supposed to be supplemented by a share of personal income tax. Additionally, a new version of the Law on Local Public Finance introduced the idea of regional redistribution, stating that the local authorities would receive a share of 35 per cent of the personal income tax, while the county authorities would receive a share of 25 per cent. As initially agreed, the county authorities would keep a share of 10 per cent of the tax for themselves and would redistribute the remaining 15 per cent among all the municipalities of the county (*http://brasov.monitorul.ro/arhiva/04_May_00/html./art/articol.php3?art=400*). This regulation was meant to remove the politically motivated bias of the former version of the law, which favoured the big cities where the coalition's traditional electoral base was located (Monitorul de Brasov, 2 March 1999). It was further intended to strengthen the position of the county authorities *vis-à-vis* the big cities and was meant to contribute to a more balanced development on the sub-national level.

This idea was put into practice in 2000. In 2001, local councils received a directshare of 36.5 per cent of the personal income tax, and the county councils were given a share of 10 per cent in order to cover their own needs. The remaining share of 15 per cent was put at the county council's disposal, which had to redistribute it among all the municipalities of the county. For the year 2002 the annual budget of the local government bodies was supplemented with a 1 per cent share of the personal income tax. Consequently, the share of the redistribution fund increased from 15 to 16 per cent (IPP 2001: 42). According to the representatives of the Ministry of Finance, who devised this formula, redistribution must take place according to precise statistical criteria. However, empirical investigations showed that actual redistribution processes were subject to bargaining processes and political influence on both the central and county levels. Net contributors, like the counties of Constanta, Prahova, Bihor, Cluj, and Timis, generally tended to oppose the idea of redistribution. On a lower level, mayors generally tended to complain that local concerns were ignored on the county level. At the same time, county council presidents admitted that intra-county redistribution was indeed based on subjective decisions and arbitrariness (IPP 2001: 50–53).

The second major budgetary concern of the Romanian municipalities was decentralisation. Although the law states that local authorities should not be charged with tasks unless they have been granted the means to fulfil them, the central state withdrew from many costly policy fields like social services, education, and culture without granting the local authorities additional resources from state revenues. Municipalities were responsible for the functioning and maintenance of local government, nurseries, kindergartens, schools, student dormitories, public libraries, museums, community centres, old people's homes, canteens for the needy, military facilities, as well as streets, parks, playing fields, public places, and housing facilities belonging to the local community (*http//brasov.monitorul.ro/arhiva/04_May_00/html./art/articol.php3?art=400*).

County councils were in charge of child protection, protection of the elderly and the disabled, maintenance of county roads, and the functioning and maintenance of cultural establishments of supra-local importance. They also had to cover the basic infrastructure costs of the local government bodies, whose budgets hardly covered their own operating costs. Many problems arose from the fact that the managements of the newly decentralised educational and cultural institutions were not legally obliged, or even competent, to draft their own budgets (IPP 2001: 59).

A different set of problems was created by the decentralisation of public service units. After the administrative reform of 1991, public service provision at the local level was included among the competences of local self-government. The law on local public administration, Law 69/1991, stated that »the public services of the commune or town shall be organized by the local council, in the principal domains of activity, according to the local character and needs, with observance of the legal provisions, and within the limits of the financial means available to the council« (art. 54, sect. 2). However, the building, maintenance, and repair of roads; the water supply and sewage systems; the heating systems; and public transport facilities continued to be financed by earmarked transfers from the central budget until 1998 (*http://www.sinta.ro/RNE/cartax2.htm*).

The situation changed after the second wave of decentralisation in 1998, triggered by the law on local public finance, Law 189/1998. According to this regulation, the local councils were responsible for the funding, establishment, and monitoring of public service provision on the local level. They had the option to concede local public service provision to specialised commercial operators, if the concession contributed to increased efficiency and benefited the citizens in the end. Still, many public services, including heating and drinking water provision, continued to receive subsidies from the central government.

In order to complete these regulations, the law on local public services, Law 326/2001, was adopted in 2001. This law clearly specifies which services are considered local public services (art. 2) and states that all the citizens have equal access to them (art. 6, point a). It further states that the operating costs of local public services have to be jointly covered by the bills paid by end-users and the levying of special taxes, which, however, are not further specified. These revenues may be supplemented by subsidies from the central and/or the local budgets (art. 8, line 2). The law also states that local public services may be provided either by a specialised branch of local public administration or by a commercial operator selected by the local council. Local authorities have the exclusive competence to establish, organise, coordinate, monitor, and control local public service provision (art. 12, line 1). All public service operators, be they private or public, are in need of certification by a national authority, which can withdraw their operating licenses if their activity does not meet the standards (art. 23, line 4, point h).

The functioning of local government

Operating within the institutional constraints set by the national transformation regime and the budgetary constraints defined by the law on local public finance, county governments as well as local government in general were vulnerable to clientelistic incentives from above. In the meantime, they themselves were in a position to exert clientelistic pressures on lower-level self-government bodies, local enterprises, and the population. On the other hand, the institutional framework also enabled them to build up local or even international support in order to act against clientelistic pressures.

Under these circumstances it is hard to describe the functioning of sub-national government in general terms. Instead, I will point out some of the systemic vulnerabilities of sub-national government, showing how different levels of sub-national government and different types of settlements on the local level deal with them.

Opportunities for clientelistic interventions

The asymmetric relationship between the tasks and revenues of local government gave rise to many opportunities for clientelistic interventions. My interview partners complained that even if a municipality succeeded in generating its own revenues, it was unable to channel them into development projects because the funds were eaten up by other tasks. Nor did the law on local public finance reduce either the strong sectoral influence on local politics or the government's discretionary decision-making powers relating to major investments. Several interview partners stressed that one had to apply to a minister with strong links to the region in order to obtain financial support from the central government for a specific investment project of regional relevance. This minister would then use his or her power to influence the decision in favour of the region. However, these persons complained that the interests of Timis County had not been represented by a minister in a strong position for a long time. This situation seems to have changed since the appointment of former county council president Ilie Sârbu as Minister for Agriculture; according to media reports, Sârbu's decision-making is strongly biased in favour of Timis County. For example, his intervention in favour of halting direct flights to Italy and Germany from Arad international airport succeeded in diverting German and Italian investment from Arad to Timis (România libera, 20 October 2001).

Another problem connected to the law on local public finance was its bias towards the big cities. As well-educated urban employees were more likely to pay higher personal income taxes than subsistence farmers, resources were increasingly concentrated in the big cities, leading to a complete breakdown of the rural infrastructure. As a result, big cities indeed gained a certain independence from central redistribution policies. Small settlements were more than ever deprived of resources and had to seek assistance on the county level. But the county councils were not favoured by the law either and had difficulties in coping with their own tasks. As the director of Timis county council's economic department bitterly complained: »We are the county of those with special needs«. He was referring to the fact that the main part of the county's budget was dedicated to tasks like the maintenance of the homes for persons with special needs like orphans, the elderly, or the disabled.

The difficulties for small settlements were further aggravated by their lack of representation in the county council. Of the 45 representatives sitting on Timis county council in 1999, only one was resident in a commune. County councils were elected in accordance with paragraph 2 of article 1 of the law on local elections, Law 70/1991, stating that »county councils shall be elected in constituencies by suffrage expressed on the basis of list ballot«. As the activity of the parties hardly penetrated the countryside, villagers could only rarely be found on the party lists and even more rarely in the councillors' seats. According to the director of the economic department of Timis county council, the best option for a village was therefore to elect an independent mayor, who then joined the political grouping that turned out to be the most influential within the council. This approach was further favoured by the election schedule. Local elections were held first, then county council elections, and finally general elections. An independent mayor willing to join a political grouping thus had the opportunity to prove the seriousness of his intentions during the general elections.

But siding with the most powerful local forces was not necessarily the best choice either. At least not in Timis, where local election patterns generally tended to be different from national ones. Once a new national government came to power a new algorithm was established, which had to be applied on the local level. Therefore arrangements that could have worked well on the local level but did not correspond to the algorithm were brought in line with the central decisions. Even so, there were variations in the degree of clientelistic incorporation, and, according to media reports, Timis County – together with the other counties on the western border – was among those less affected by political clientelism (*http://www.romanialibera.com/1POL/24s1pape.htm)*. However, when asked about cooperation on the county level, the director of the economic department of the county council stated that cooperation had functioned well during the period of the coalition government, because the general policy at the centre was oriented towards cooperation. He further described the period when the interview took place as ideal, because the parties were focussing on the general election campaign and not interfering with local issues, so that local authorities could concentrate on their own priorities. For the period following the general elections, my interview partner expected a redistribution of political power on the central level, followed by a reorientation within the county council.

Within the county itself, the local authorities of big cities were less vulnerable to the disruptive effects of party clientelism than county authorities or local authorities of small settlements. Mayors of big cities had both local resources and their own local power base that they could invoke in case of conflicts with the central authorities. According to the budget execution sheet of Timisoara city council of 1 September 2000, the budget of the city of Timisoara was more than twice the size of the county's budget. The city's own revenues already exceeded the total revenues of the county. Furthermore, an opinion poll conducted in the wake of the local elections in 2000 revealed that more than 50 per cent of Timisoara's citizens were satisfied with the activity of the local authorities. Meanwhile, less than one quarter of the same sample expressed satisfaction with the activity of central institutions like parliament, the president, or the courts of justice. Moreover, the activity of the mayor of Timisoara was considered good or very good by more than 70 per cent of the sample. He himself was characterised as an experienced, serious, and intelligent person, with good communication and administration skills. An impressive majority of about 80 per cent of the persons interviewed highlighted their involvement in local affairs, with respondents stating their intention to participate in the local elections (*http://domino.kappa.ro/imas/home.nsf/All*). Not surprisingly, the mayor of Timisoara was the only Christian Democratic National Peasant Party mayor in the country to be re-elected (Bucharest Business Week, 12 February 2001).

Administrative corruption and bureaucratic inefficiency

Two additional factors that hindered the emergence of transparent and efficient local politics are administrative corruption and bureaucratic inefficiency. Administrative corruption was favoured by an accumulation of functions by locally elected representatives. This situation was addressed by Law 215/2001. This law states that the status of councillor is incompatible with a position as a government representative on a sub-national level, mayor, MP, government official, civil servant or employee in public administration, or manager or supervisory board member in a public service company or commercial company set up by the local authorities. However, this regulation was adopted about a year after the last local elections; and in order not to disrupt the functioning of local government, the implementation of this law was postponed by governmental decree until the next elections.

As far as Timis county council is concerned, a former representative of the Christian Democratic National Alliance turned independent accused the council of turning a blind eye to irregularities connected with the operations of the road maintenance company, in which the council held shares. The supervisory board of the company included two councillors who were owners of private construction companies. Another conflict of interest was unveiled in the case of an employee of the council administration. It turned out that a company privately owned by the head of the tendering department received preferential treatment during the tenders (Timisoara, 27 July 2001).

As far as other causes of bureaucratic inefficiency and administrative corruption are concerned, it is an issue of local policy to identify and try to eradicate them. Examples from Timisoara show that the local authorities had the capacity for intervention – especially when they cooperated with other local actors and received additional international support. The first example concerns the reorganisation of the department for communication and information at Timisoara city hall in 1997. In order to promote a more efficient, transparent, and citizen-oriented local administration, the mayor of Timisoara proposed replacing the old registry office with a modern communications department. It was hoped that the confusion, loss of documents, and delays caused by the inefficient structure of the office, as well as the suspicions arising from the direct relationship between the citizen and the town hall clerk dealing with his or her request, would be eliminated in this way. The city council approved this modification and a new, computer-assisted communication office with public access was created. It consisted of an information counter and several specialized counters dealing with different issues like housing, social problems, legal documents etc. All the employees of the new office were university graduates who had to prove that they had the skills needed to deal with the public (*www.infotim.ro/primarie/strdep1.htm*).

The second example concerns Timisoara's successful participation in the deregulation competition among Romanian cities initiated by the US embassy in July 2000. After having drawn up a study on how excessive bureaucracy stifled small businesses, the embassy launched the »Simple and Fast – Five Steps to Simplified Business« programme. The good cooperation between the city hall and the Timisoara Chamber of Commerce, Industry and Agriculture contributed to the fact that of among the eighty participants, Timisoara was one of the first two cities to complete the five deregulation steps well ahead of the deadline. Its fame as a non-bureaucratic city then contributed to its ability to attract substantial foreign investment (Chapter 6.2.1).

Actors and strategies on the county level

The influence of the central authorities

Romanian counties have two different functions. On the one hand, they are considered juridical persons and thus subjects of local self-government. On the other hand, counties also serve as basic units of decentralised public administration. This is why the prefect and the quasi-autonomous public service enterprises (*regii autonome*) subordinated to the ministries are established on this level. According to the provisions of the law on public administration, Law 215/2001, the prefect is appointed by the government and acts as a central government representative on the local level. As such he oversees the implementation of government policy on the local level and acts as the head of the decentralised public service units of the ministries and other central organs of public administration. However, the prefect does not have decision-making powers with regard to the decentralised units of the ministries – the law grants him only advisory functions.

Before the law on local public finance was adopted the prefect was the most powerful actor in local public administration, as he could provide local communities with direct access to relevant, central decision-making relating to issues like local budgets and investment. He was also in charge of about 80 per cent of the locally relevant public services (Suciu 1997: 19). Thus it was him, and not the county council bodies, whom local self-government representatives preferred to address. After the legal regulation on local budgeting and privatisation of the relevant public service units, the formal importance of the prefect diminished. However, party clientelism helped the prefects to regain their power informally. But in an insecure environment characterised by varying degrees of clientelistic incorporation, the power of a prefect mainly rests upon his personal relationships with his superiors. The high turnover rate of prefects during the period of my research in Timis proves the political vulnerability of this position. Under these circumstances the other actors appreciated a cooperative attitude on the part of the prefect, but support from the prefect could not be equated with long-term commitment.

If the prefect could be regarded as the local representative of the government in the political sphere, the head of the county branch of the State Ownership Fund (SOF) was his economic counterpart. Like the prefect, the head of the SOF was appointed according to political criteria by the central government. He was in charge of the privatisation of a portfolio assigned to him by the ministry that controlled the SOF. The establishment of the portfolio was arbitrary. Thus the head of the Banat regional branch of the SOF mentioned the case of the Lugoj button factory, which his superiors had tried to privatise in Bucharest and then assigned to him after a series of failures. The role of the SOF was defined by the head of the Banat regional branch as trying to get rid of state assets as soon as possible. A privatisation process was regarded as successful if it succeeded in overcoming all the bureaucratic stumbling blocks and reached the auction stage. The creation of viable enterprises was regarded as being the task of – mainly foreign – investors. This limited understanding of privatisation implies a strictly executive function for the sub-national privatisation units. As in the case of the prefect, the head of a sub-national privatisation unit could only exert influence on the central level through his personal political connections. Under these circumstances my interview partner expressed disgust with his task, describing his position as one which forced him to put up with »human fauna« hardly imaginable for the researcher.

Although members of local elites acting as representatives of central institutions, neither the prefect of Timis County nor the head of the regional branch of the SOF were really in a position to mediate between the local/regional and the central level. Their formal competences were limited by the internal hierarchies of their organisations as well as by the pervasive influence of the ministries, which acted directly upon the local level through their local branches. The local support they enjoyed did not help them much and they lacked a reliable intra-party network reaching up to the central level to provide them with high-level political backing.

The role of the county council

In accordance with the provisions on the law of local public administration, Law 215/2001, county governments have the right and the effective capacity to settle and manage public affairs in the name and interest of the local communities they represent. This right is exercised by the county council, which holds legislative power on the county level. Executive power is held by the executive board made up of the county council president, the vice-presidents, and the secretary.

Timis county council is made up of 37 councillors. As already mentioned, county councillors are directly elected by the citizens on the basis of party lists. As a consequence, neither the rural areas nor the eastern or western sub-regions are represented in the council. In addition to the problematic question of representation, the small budget has hindered the establishment of the county council as a powerful local and regional actor. As already mentioned in Chapter 5.3.2, the budget of Timis County is barely able to cover its main tasks. Of a budget of 160 billion ROL in 2000, 64 billion ROL was dedicated to child welfare alone. The rest went to cover the maintenance costs of county public roads and the basic infrastructure costs of small settlements' local government bodies.

If formerly their complete dependence on central redistribution made the county councils weak and poor in terms of legitimacy, resources, and competences (Suciu 1997), at present they are becoming increasingly marginal for both sectoral policies and the local policies of big cities. However, they have maintained their role as transmission belts of the central authorities *vis-à-vis* the smallest and most powerless settlements. These perceived the county council both as part of the communist legacy and as a mere executor of centrally defined policies. The mayor of Giroc, a suburban commune adjoining Timisoara, mentioned in a personal interview that many of his fellow mayors spoke about »going to the county« (Romanian: »la judet«) the same way they used to speak about the county council of the Romanian Communist Party. The attitude of the economic director of the county council, who mentioned blackmail as a way of forcing small settlements to reorganise their local administrations to make them more cost-effective, fully confirms this perception.

Lack of funding and legitimacy have made the county council a good target for clientelistic interventions. The additional funding needed for infrastructure development was attracted through good personal contacts to the minister of public works, as stated by the vice-president of the county council in a personal interview. Thus Timis County received most of the investments made by the ministry during the 1997–2000 period. This strategy turned out to be successful, as the infrastructure improvements continued to attract investors, and the activities of the investors continued to generate additional revenues for the county council.

As far as cooperation within the council was concerned, the council's vice-president described it as being neither bad nor good. He stated that although he personally urged his colleagues to put county interests first and to use party clientelism to promote local priorities, this was hard to achieve. It was difficult to keep a balance between the interests of the parties and the general interest of the county. Asked for the reasons, my interview partner named personal vanities and systemic constraints rather than ideological differences. He further pointed to the less-than-optimal cooperation with Timisoara city hall, in spite of an ideological consensus. However, cooperation with city hall was expected to be more intensive in the future, especially if the three big common projects, the creation of a regional postal centre, an industrial park, and a leisure park in Timisoara, succeeded in attracting European funding.

The county council's position with regard to local and regional development is set out in the county development strategy, elaborated by ADETIM. The strategy identifies several polarising centres and zones of influence within the county, as presented in the image below.

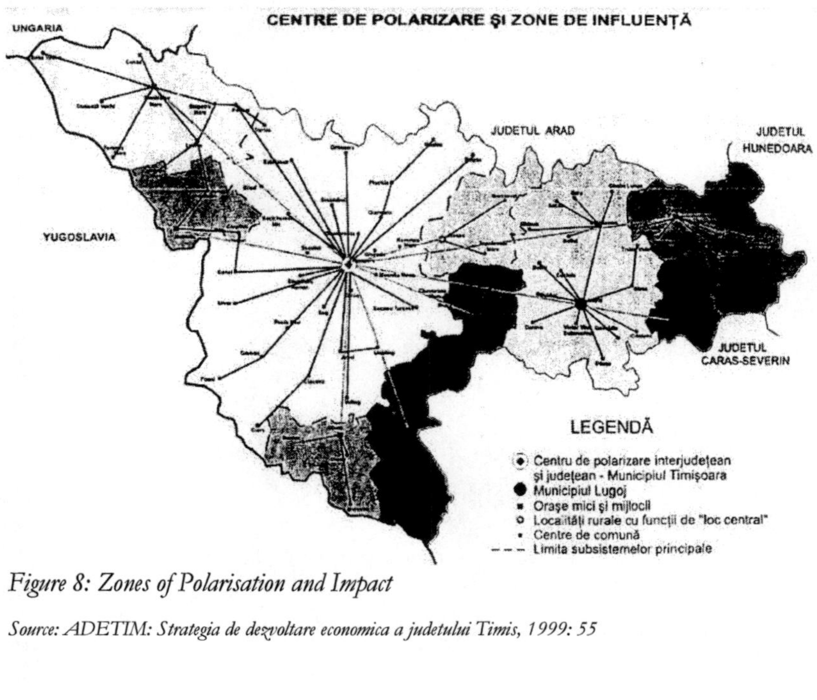

Figure 8: Zones of Polarisation and Impact

Source: ADETIM: Strategia de dezvoltare economica a judetului Timis, 1999: 55

One immediately notices the dominant position of Timisoara for the whole region. A cleavage between the eastern and western parts of the county also emerges. Prosperous sub-regions around the bustling small cities of Sînnicolau Mare (Prima Ora, 4 October 2000) and Jimbolia (România libera, 25 May 2001) can be contrasted with the depressed areas of Faget-Margina and Nadrag, which qualify as deprived zones (ADETIM 1999: 78–81).

The goal of the county development strategy was defined as follows: »Timis county – a stable and diversified economic space, able to ensure the population's general prosperity« (ADETIM 1999: 102). This goal was to be pursued through specific sectoral strategies like industrial development, development of the SME sector, development of rural areas, development of tourism, and development of service industries (ADETIM 1999: 103). The whole strategy was based on the assumption that development of the more advanced centres would generate spillover effects in their zones of influence. Accordingly, efforts should be concentrated on the centres and potential sub-centres identified above. Given the specific legislation relating to deprived zones, the county development strategy also contained a specific strategy for depressed areas. Due to its liberal approach favouring the development of potential »locomotives of growth«, the strategy did not develop a differentiated image of the problems of the countryside.

The survey of the rural areas in Timis County conducted by two local NGOs, the CSSR and the Centre for Rural Assistance,[9] took a different approach. Aiming at identifying the rural areas' indigenous development resources, the survey used location and administrative status as basic explanatory variables for the degree of development of a rural settlement. As far as location was concerned, settlements located in the border area or close to Timisoara turned out to have more positive development dynamics than settlements far from both. Communes that acted as seats of the communal administration had considerably better infrastructure and human capital endowments than villages without administrative functions (CSSR 2000a). However, due to its exclusive focus on rural areas, this survey did not put forward an integrated approach either.

The lack of an integrated approach points to the absence of an integrated vision of Timis County. Local elites perceive Timisoara and the Banat as two different entities. When asked to describe his region, the

9 The Centre for Rural Assistance is affiliated with the Open Society Network.

leader of the »Young Wing« of the Liberal Party's county organisation and former spokesman of the county council considered Timisoara and the Banat as »a clearly delimited space with specific social, economic, and mentality characteristics, and Timisoara is completely distinct from the Banat«. He described the Banat, and implicitly Timis County, as having a rather rural structure, whereas Timisoara was urban in both appearance and spirit. While agreeing that the whole region had »a special tint originating in tradition and culture«, the director of the local development agency ADETIM pointed to further distinctions between Timisoara and the rest of the county, which he described as »highly unbalanced from the economic and demographic point of view«. In his opinion this situation had been created to a great extent by »the very bad countryside re-population policies of the government«, which led to the destruction of the infrastructure in former German villages. Thus not only the bearers of local traditions but also the physical markers of a historical regional identity have disappeared. However, not all the German villages shared the same fate. The German rural population that emigrated after 1989 had the possibility to sell their houses on the free market or even to keep them as holiday residences. A famous example of such a village is Garîna/Wolfsberg, where most of the houses for sale were purchased by members of the Timisoara elites, who then contributed to the development of the village into a cultural and sports centre (România libera, 25 February 2000).

Timisoara elites focus their identity discourses on the Habsburg past and tend to ignore the period of communist rule. As both the depressed countryside and the old industrial areas fell into the latter category, they were of no major concern for the Timisoara elites. This attitude was further reinforced by a liberal policy approach according to which each community was responsible for its own fate. Their status as a government priority in relation to regional development and the availability of both government and international funding for their rehabilitation succeeded in placing the old industrial areas of the county on the agenda of the local elites. This was not the case with the rural areas, at least as long as no SAPARD[10] funding was made available for their development.

10 Special Accession Programme for Agriculture and Rural Development

Regional development policy under the impact of Europeanization

European Union accession as a general framework for regional development policy

Europeanization made a double impact on local and regional development policy in Romania and, implicitly, in Timis County. First, reforms of local and regional governance can be regarded as a particular dimension of catch-up modernisation and adoption of Western standards. Second, the financial assistance provided within the framework of the pre-accession process represented a major incentive for the creation of absorption capacities and thus enhanced cooperation on the local and regional levels.

At the beginning of the accession process, the political and economic conditions for EU membership were expressed in normative terms. The Copenhagen Criteria issued in 1993 required from the accession candidates a stable democracy, a functioning market economy, and the capacity to integrate. The resulting pre-accession strategy was built around bilateral arrangements with the national governments of the candidate states. These focused on agreements on trade liberalisation, the pre-accession sequence for enlargement, ministerial meetings aiming to acculturate national elites to EU norms and procedures, and the Phare programme of aid and technical assistance.

Starting with the Agenda 2000 published in 1997, a strategy was adopted that focused on bilateral accession negotiations and the country-specific needs of the candidate states. At this point the adoption of the *acquis communautaire* became the cornerstone of the enlargement process. The assessment of a candidate country's ability to assume the obligations of membership was structured to follow the list of twenty-nine negotiating chapters covering the acquis (European Commission 2000). With the exception of Poland, it was the requirement to adopt the regional policy and coordination of the structural instruments chapter of the acquis that gave regionalisation a priority position on the agendas of most candidate countries. In contrast to the existing NUTS II regions in Europe, which were drawn up by the individual member states and only approved by Brussels pro forma, in the case of the Central and Eastern European candidate states the EU has become deeply involved in the designation process (Hughes/Sasse/Gordon 2001: 23).

Following closer scrutiny of the EU's involvement with regionalisation in the candidate countries, Hughes, Sasse, and Gordon describe this process in terms of an ongoing tension between two hardly compatible goals. On the one hand, the EU favours decentralisation, both as a means for administering structural funds and as a means of facilitating democratisation. On the other hand, there is a technocratic emphasis on strengthening the administrative capacity at the centre in order to ensure better cooperation with the EU bodies and to enable them to better evaluate the implementation of the acquis and the dispersion of the structural funds. They conclude that:

»From 1997 a Brussels model of regionalization steadily promoted an administrative, as opposed to democratic, solution for achieving a consistent regional policy and the institutional incentives necessary to enhance administrative capacity at the local and meso level« (Hughes/Sasse/Gordon 2001: 42).

The criticism is mainly directed at the case of Romania, where the three authors note that the Commission finally accepted the recentralisation of regional policy management after a failed attempt to establish a network of regional development agencies (Hughes/Sasse/Gordon 2001: 26).

In addition to the requirements of the acquis, the availability of community assistance has further acted as an incentive for the elaboration and implementation of local and regional development policies. Three pre-accession instruments have been financed by the European Community to assist the candidate countries during the pre-accession process: the Phare programme, the SAPARD programme, and the ISPA programme. The Phare programme provides the candidate countries with support for institution building, investment to strengthen the regulatory infrastructure needed to ensure compliance with the acquis, and investment in economic and social cohesion. SAPARD provides aid for agricultural and rural development and ISPA finances infrastructure projects in the fields of environment and transport (European Commission 2002).

During the 1992–1999 period approximately 1,200 billion euros were allocated to Romania within the framework of the Phare programmes. The allocations amounted to 260 million euros and 287 million euros in 2000 and 2001, respectively. The 2002 Phare National Programme for Romania consists of 229 million euros supplemented by 36.5 million euros earmarked to support institution building. The largest share of these funds remains at the level of the central administration, targeted on »strengthening administrative capacity« and »meeting the obligations of the acquis«. However, a substantial amount of 107 million euros is targeted on »areas facing particular problems«.

The Romanian SAPARD programme was approved in November 2000. However, it was still not fully operational by mid–2002. The indicative allocation for SAPARD in Romania amounted to 157.9 million euros in 2002. The ISPA programmes were implemented within the framework of the national strategy papers for transport and environment issued by the Romanian government in 2000. The funds allocated ranged from an amount of 239.2 million euros in 2000 to an estimated 283.2 million euros in 2002. From the nine environmental projects approved in 2001, the project focusing on waste-water collection and treatment in Timisoara received a considerable share of funding, 34.1 million euros.

The instruments for pre-accession support mentioned above were complemented by twinning projects. Twinning consists of the long-term secondment of civil servants and accompanying short-term expert missions from member states to the candidate countries. Its aim is to strengthen the administrative capacity needed to implement and enforce the acquis. Romania benefited from nine twinning projects in 1999 and sixteen in 2000. In 2001 twelve twinning projects were implemented and a further 29 have been designed for 2002. However, most of the twinning projects were located with central authorities like the National Commission of Statistics, the National Bank of Romania, and the border police.

The interaction between the EU's approach to regionalisation in the candidate countries and the Romanian transformation regime gave rise to a series of specific problems. The Commission's 2002 report noted that »the level of financial support available [...] creates a substantial challenge for the Romanian administration« (European Commission 2002: 12). More clearly, the Commission's 2000 Report expressed »a general concern« about »a tendency for political considerations, as opposed to purely technical considerations [...] in the management and allocation of funding« (European Commission 2000). These vague formulations hint at the fact that EU funding is perceived as representing a welcome resource for political patronage by the Romanian elites. Although development regions were created in 1998 and a network of regional development agencies was consequently set up, the management of the pre-accession funds remained at the central level, where it represented a major incentive for infighting between different political interests grouped in ministries.[11]

Hughes, Sasse, and Gordon regard this outcome as a result of a type of regionalization induced »from without« and »from above«, through EU conditionalities and national governments' attempts to meet them. Against this background, they criticise the EU's exclusive interaction with the national governments and its lack of communication and interaction with local and regional elites (Hughes/Sasse/Gordon 2001: 42).

In spite of its shortcomings, the EU's insistence on designing regional development policies and institutions able to handle the community assistance helped to break through the nationalist and centralist blockade that had hindered the expression of any kind of regional concerns up to that point. The analysis of the cases of Timisoara and Timis County will further show that the regionalisation process supported by the EU opened up new national and transnational arenas for local action.

The Development Region West

Attempts to institutionalise economic cooperation between the three Banatian counties Arad, Timis, and Caras-Severin started in 1993, when a visiting German official launched the idea of establishing a jointly supported regional development agency. First steps to organise cooperation between the three Banatian counties and the German state of North Rhine-Westphalia and to set up a common economic promotion unit were blocked by representatives of the central government in 1994.

Three independent economic development agencies on the county level, ADAR, ADECS, and ADETIM, were established in 1995, and ADETIM, the economic development agency of Timis County, became the coordination office for cooperation between them.

At the beginning, it was managed by an international expert and financially supported by the German state of North Rhine-Westphalia. Then

11 As an example, the European Commission's 2002 Regular Report on Romania's Progress Towards Accession names the following structures as being responsible for the implementation of the SAPARD programme: the National Fund, located within the Ministry of Finance, which administers SAPARD funds under the responsibility of the National Authorising Officer and is responsible for the national accreditation of the SAPARD agency; the Managing Authority, located within the Ministry for European Integration; and the SAPARD Agency, located within the ministry of agriculture.

local staff were hired and trained. The management was taken over by an executive board made up of representatives of Timis county council, the city of Timisoara, and the Timisoara chamber of commerce.

This situation changed after Law 151/1998 on regional development was adopted and an appropriate institutional framework was established. The law on regional development was adopted and implemented on the basis of a strategic agreement between the Romanian government and the European Commission in 1996. This agreement further defined the institutional framework and the goals of regional development. Both created conditions for the emergence of centralised and redistributive regional policies. These developments were criticised as re-centralisation by an international expert who actively promoted the idea of regional development in Romania. In his opinion, the law on regional development was adopted under massive outside pressure, and »the Romanians pretend to dance to the EU's tune, but actually everything stays concentrated in Bucharest«.

According to this document, eight development regions were defined for the whole of Romania. The West development region comprises the counties of Timis, Arad, Caras-Severin, and Hunedoara. It is headed by a regional council, which decides on the regional development strategy within the context of the national regional development strategy. The regional council includes the presidents of the county councils as well as representatives of the county capital and the towns and communes of each member county. The executive body of the council is the regional development agency (Baga/Balasa 1999: 63).

After Law 151/1998 on regional development was adopted and an appropriate institutional framework was established, ADETIM became part of the national network of development agencies. As an agency established on the county level, ADETIM was entrusted with the implementation of local and microregional projects. The projects were allocated to ADETIM by the Regional Development Agency, which prepared and implemented the regional programmes in cooperation with the National Regional Development Agency.

Although efforts aiming at regional development and regionalism at large, formerly condemned, came to receive the formal support of the government, this did not enhance cooperation on the regional level. With its goal of reducing regional disparities through the stimulation of balanced development, the accelerated development of disadvantaged territories, and measures to prevent the emergence of further imbalances, the law on regional development did not favour better-off areas like Timis. Cooperation within the West development region was thus not really interesting for Timis county council, as its vice-president confirmed in a personal interview. The three other member counties were all weaker in terms of budget and expertise, and two of them were burdened with problems connected with the restructuring of old industrial areas. In the opinion of the vice-president of Timis county council, their leaders were also arrogant, unwilling to cooperate to attract investment, and reluctant to accept the advice of their more experienced and successful colleagues in Timis. Here again, EU funds provided an incentive for cooperation: it was hoped that the EU funds channelled through the Regional Development Agency (RDA) would improve cooperation.

According to the law on regional development, regional development agencies should cooperate with the national regional development agency, prepare and implement the regional programmes, and act as intermediaries for the allocation of projects and funds to institutions on the local level. An evaluation of the activity of the Regional Development Agency published on the Internet site of the Timisoara Chamber of Commerce, Industry and Agriculture revealed that the last function was the most important one for the RDA. From the funding available for 1999 it had attracted over 160 billion ROL earmarked for the development of SMEs, labour force re-conversion, and support of the deprived areas. Although none of the zones supported by these funds were part of Timis County, investors from the county may also have profited, as the support mainly consisted of a scheme of incentives for companies investing in the deprived areas. The programmes financed from the Phare 2000 funds were more attractive for Timis, as they included inter-regional projects on regional innovation and the support of innovative start-ups as well as long-term twinning and cross-border cooperation projects with French and Hungarian partners. The estimated funding of over 5 million euros made available for these projects represented a further incentive.

However, it is noteworthy that none of these projects were concerned with agriculture or rural development. The EU funds allocated for the implementation of the SAPARD programme were frozen as a consequence of infighting between different Romanian ministries for the competency to implement the programme. The programme was finally assigned in 2001 to the Ministry of Agriculture, which will implement it through its own agencies (România libera, 17 April 2001). In a press release issued in May 2001, private and public actors, including the county councils of Timis, Arad, and Caras-Severin, jointly argued that the SAPARD programmes for the Banat area should be implemented through the Center for Rural Assistance in Timisoara. However, decision-making stayed with the ministry.

Cooperation between the city of Timisoara and Timis county council did improve as a consequence of the increased availability of EU funding. The budget of the county's strategic development programme for the year 2002, published on the county council's official website (*http://www.cjtimis.ro*), was made up by approximately equal shares of national and international funding. The share of national funding consisted of transfers from the central budget, contributions from the municipalities' local budgets, and small shares of bank credits and other non-specified revenues. The share of international funding mainly consisted of pre-accession funds from the Phare, ISPA, and SAPARD programmes. It also contained smaller shares of international private investment as well as international credits.

The main priority of the county's development strategy was infrastructure development. In 2002, of a total budget of 129,812 thousand euros, 111,771 thousand euros was directed to this end. Infrastructure development was mainly concentrated on the development of the local, county, and cross-border road network; the rehabilitation and development of the water provision network, both in Timisoara and throughout the county; and the extension of the gas network in the county. With regard to infrastructure development, Phare funding was mainly directed at cross-border infrastructure development, while SAPARD funding supported infrastructure projects in rural areas. ISPA funding was exclusively directed towards the rehabilitation of the Timisoara clearing station.

Development of the SME sector represented the second priority. With the exception of a tourism development project in the proximity of Timisoara, the projects listed under this headline were all concentrated in the city. They included the establishment of a regional business centre, an industrial park, a technology park, a regional logistics centre, Interporto, a regional conference centre, and a wholesale market in Timisoara. The establishment of the regional business centre was to be financed mainly from Phare funds, while the regional logistics centre was to be financed by a private-public partnership created by Timisoara city hall with a group of Italian investors.

The development of social and cultural infrastructure was the programme's last priority. It included centrally financed projects aiming at improvement of housing conditions for young couples, child care projects mainly financed by Phare funds, and small-building maintenance works.

In the budget plan for the 2003–2004 period the share of international funding exceeded the share of national funding. In contrast to the previous period, the shares of additional international funding and international private investment have increased as compared to the shares of pre-accession funds. Infrastructure development, with consideration of environmental protection, continued to represent the main priority of the county council. Almost half of the total budget, including the full amount of SAPARD funding, was devoted to this objective. The second priority, as well as the projects included under the headline of SME development, remained unchanged.

Cross-border cooperation within the Danube-Kris-Mures-Tisza euroregion

Cross-border cooperation and the creation of the Danube-Kris-Mures-Tisza (DKMT) euroregion started from a bilateral cooperation agreement signed between Timis county and the Hungarian county of Csongrád in 1992. This cooperation was gradually extended to other counties from the area. Thus, when the first version of the protocol of cooperation was adopted in 1994, two Romanian counties, two Hungarian counties, and one Serbian province had joined. At present, the euroregion is made up of the Romanian West region, the Yugoslavian region of Vojvodina, and the Hungarian counties of Békes, Csongrád, Jász-Nagykún-Szolnok, and Bács-Kiskún. Cooperation is based on the last version of the cooperation protocol adopted in November 1997.

The euroregion is headed by a forum of presidents, which is made up of the presidents of the member county councils and the president of the executive council of the autonomous province of Vojvodina. The forum elects from among its ranks a an executive president with a one–year mandate. The executive president is responsible for the administrative tasks, which he usually assigns to a branch of the county or regional council administration. The organisational structure of the euroregion further includes steering committees made up of experts from the local or regional administration, whose task is to elaborate common cross-border projects and programmes (Branea 2001: 4).

Most of my interview partners considered cooperation on the euroregional level promising. Even if the cooperation was formally extended to many more entities, the Timisoara – Szeged axis remained the decisive core (Branea 2001: 12). This could also be seen as a consequence of the situation in Yugoslavia, which created many additional legal obstacles to cooperation. The forum of presidents could not hold its meetings for a considerable period of time, as the Serbian representative was prohibited from entering either Hungary or Romania, being considered a close collaborator of the former Serbian president Milosevic. However, there were plenty of contacts on lower levels. A joint survey conducted in both the West region and the Vojvodina revealed that large majorities of the population supported the idea of a common regional identity and regarded cross-border cooperation as a source of future prosperity for the whole region (Branea 2001: 15).

Still, the survey further revealed that in spite of popular support the DKMT was »relatively unable« to become a political, economic, and cultural subject. The absence of a legal framework and local dependency on central decision-making have been identified as the main causes (Branea 2001: 19). There were also serious concerns about the actual influence of cross-border cooperation on the regional partners in the present situation. In many cases, it seemed impossible to overcome both differences in the legal framework and economic disparities. Additional problems were generated by the lack of cohesion on the Romanian side. The joint survey stated that Romanian county authorities were »engaged in a competition for primacy and undermined by political incompatibilities« (Branea 2001: 20). In the same vein, the vice-president of Timis County expressed disappointment with the Hungarian partners, whom he accused of preferential treatment of Arad County to the detriment of Timis. The dominance of regional authorities in the context of cross-border cooperation - even though it was the cities of Timisoara, Szeged, and Novi Sad that actually cooperated - was further regarded as a cause of the failure of the structures thus established to acquire legitimacy and credibility.

Analytical framework: Networks of opportunity, opportunities for networking

With basic civil rights guaranteed and local self-government institutionalised, political action in Timisoara and Timis County was no longer monopolised by the centre. Thus self-government bodies were created on the local and the county level and became decision-making centres for certain domains of public policy. Around these new institutions a plethora of networks emerged, linking various local and regional actors as well as actors from outside the local and regional context. While international contacts flourished and succeeded in inducing a cooperative dynamic between the local and regional actors, due to specific local and regional conditions the links with the central government remained less significant. Both symbolic and economic conflicts with the central government hindered the clientelistic incorporation of the local and regional elite, who preferred to focus on international relations instead. Even though this orientation made it possible to ignore centralist tendencies to a certain degree, it also induced new forms of dependencies and vulnerabilities.

Local self-government bodies can further be regarded as an example of new decision-making centres, which became the focal point for the emergence of associative networks linking together internal and external, state and social actors (Chalmers et al 1997: 544). Associative networks stand for new forms of non-clientelistic organisation and representation within the framework of semi-clientelistic regimes. They represent both »sets of individuals or organisations that make claims« and »mediating entities that debate, reshape and transmit claims and pressures to authoritative decision-making centres« (Chalmers et al 1997: 64). They are able to forge alliances between internal and external partners and can thus become channels for modernising tendencies simultaneously directed at both state and society.

Even if they emerge around particular sets of claims, associative networks are involved not only in demand making and bargaining but also in cognitive politics. Coming together within the framework of an associative network, previously dispersed actors get to know each other, acquire a different perception of one another, and learn to communicate with each other. Associative networks thus provide good conditions, not only for knowledge transfer but also for the generation of trust and the reconfiguration of patterns of thinking and action. The main characteristic of associative networks is the fact that they are issue-specific. Thus the emergence of an efficient network in a certain policy domain cannot be interpreted as proof of an overall growth of citizen involvement and political participation. Flexible and diverse, associative networks can easily adapt to changing issues, decision-making rules, participants, or opportunities. Flexibility is also induced by the personal quality of intra-network links, which leads to less rigid hierarchies favouring open-ended discussions. However, personalisation can also work as an impediment to emerging institutionalisation patterns.

All these characteristics make it hard to distinguish associative networks from »opportunity networks« (Mihailescu 2000). »Opportunity networks« have a conservative orientation, as their members mainly focus on improvement, or at least preservation, of their own status position. Their underlying world-view perceives society as an unstable hierarchy, where everybody's position is endangered by permanent competition for resources. Given the present economic and institutional instability, opportunity networks are perceived as the only providers of both social security and opportunity. Like investment bankers operating in an insecure environment, »opportunist networkers« try to invest their trust and resources in a broad range of social relations. They hope in this way to ensure their access to the »right person« in a decision-making position regardless of what happens.

However, associative networks are more than networks of a »special« – be it Western or democratic or market-oriented – character, aiming only at the acquisition of outside funding or investment. Apart from the opportunity networks, where actions are fuelled by purely personal interest directed towards status preservation, associative networks have a general orientation towards structural change involving society as a whole. While opportunity networks seek to secure scarce resources through competitive and exclusive practices, associative networks stand for open-ended debates, transparency in decision-making, and public access to information. This is in part a consequence of dealings with external partners whose huge financial and institutional resources represent a strong incentive towards building local cooperation networks and pooling local resources.

However, the strong personalisation of intra-network links makes it difficult to distinguish clearly between »opportunistic« and »associative« networks or between »progressive« and »conservative« actors from an outsider's perspective. The functioning of a network is determined by the behaviour of its members, while the behaviour of the actors is determined by the context of their actions. These contexts are partly shaped by external constraints, and it is partly the actors themselves who interactively define these contexts. Both rational choice and soft factors like identity have an influence on these definitions. However, soft factors tend to matter less where basic survival needs are concerned.

Assuming that self-government bodies represent democratic patterns for political institutionalisation and focal points for the emergence of associative networks, in what follows I explore the extent to which these forms of organisation and representation succeed in creating social integration and autonomous political actors on the local and regional levels.

Local strategies and policy models

Despite their visible efforts to establish cross-border cooperation, county governments continued to be regarded as unimportant by their constituencies (Suciu 1997). By contrast, surveys have shown that local authorities, and especially mayors, succeeded in breaking out of the general pattern of rejection and suspicion characterising the population's attitudes towards the authorities (Branea 2001: 15). It has also become obvious that the big cities were further empowered by their financial resources, which enabled them to become engaged in private and public, local and international cooperation structures. I will therefore now focus on the local level, trying to identify the different political and economic strategies employed in the cities of Timisoara and Lugoj and the commune of Ciacova.

The following statements were made by a mayor from a small town in Timis in a personal interview: »I intervened in all the ministries where the officials belong to the same party as I do, because these are the rules of the game between the local and central administration [...] As far as the county level is concerned, the cooperation goes well beyond political clientelism«.

Taking this statement as my starting point, I will consider the local public administration system in Romania as having a clientelistic orientation of a variable degree. In analysing the discourses of the three municipalities' mayors, I will try to describe three different policy models, which I label »progressive«, »pragmatic«, and »opportunistic«. I start from the assumption that the policy choices of local actors are shaped by both

»hard« constraints and »soft« factors. The general framework for the functioning of local public authorities, the economic situation of the municipalities, and their size, location, and population structure are regarded as »hard« constraints. Regional identity is considered a »soft« factor. Political mobilisation is the other soft factor considered in the analysis.

I begin with a short analytical description of the three localities, comprising both local identities and the »hard« constraints mentioned above. I then proceed with the comparative analysis of the mayors' discourses. Finally, I will seek to determine how the different behavioural constraints mentioned above influence local strategies.

»The star«, »the heart«, and the forgotten starlet of the Banat

As already described in Chapters 5.1 and 5.2, Timisoara has always been the polarising centre of the whole region, »the star of the Banat«. It is located in the centre of the county and has a developed transport and telecommunication infrastructure. It contains most of the county's educational resources and economic activity. The city's proximity to the border and its internationally recognised technical university led to the development of the IT sector through the activities of different foreign investors. Thriving business attracted financial services: over twenty banks operate in Timisoara. Out-migration of the old city elites is therefore partly compensated for by the influx of students and young professionals. Thanks to the good employment situation, local revenues are relatively high. Local elites are integrated through a common academic background and the common discourse of a multiethnic European local identity. The reference to the imperial past of »little Vienna« enables the authorities to formulate ambitious local development strategies. Their own revenues could make it possible to implement at least some of their innovative ideas.

The county's second largest city, Lugoj, has always been »Timisoara's little sister«. It is located in the eastern, less developed part of the county. It is farther from the border and its transport infrastructure cannot compete with the Timisoara international airport. Being much smaller and economically less competitive, Lugoj has tried to distinguish itself on the basis of a different identity discourse. Thus, while Timisoara always built on its multiethnic Habsburg inheritance, Lugoj was considered to be the centre of the Banat's »Romanianness«, »the heart of the Banat«. It developed from a small, sleepy Habsburg town into a regional administrative centre after the incorporation of the Banat into Greater Romania (Munteanu/Munteanu 1998: 111–112). Under communist rule it maintained its role as a regional sub-centre.

The discourse on local identity reproduces to a great extent the »regional nationalist« discourse described in Chapter 5.2.1. However, it explicitly states that the superiority of people from Lugoj as compared to other Romanians[12] stems from the competitive situation induced by the presence of the Habsburg colonists. Since almost all of the local German population has emigrated, people from Lugoj regard Timisoara as their standard for »urban civilisation«. This is why they do not resent Timisoara's dominant position in the region. Moreover, they seem content to be outshone by »the star«.

In terms of inhabitants, Lugoj has barely one seventh of Timisoara's population. It also has a lower vitality index and poorer educational resources than the regional centre. A private university was established in 1990 through the efforts of a returned émigré.[13]

As in other Romanian small towns, inefficient privatisation led to a complete breakdown of industrial activity in Lugoj. According to the representative of the Timisoara Chamber of Commerce, Industry and Agriculture in Lugoj, of the 2,000 companies registered in Lugoj, only about seventy were operational. Bad management and the prohibitive prices at which enterprises were offered to potential investors led to a catastrophic decline of traditional industries like silk spinning and wood processing. Corruption mechanisms like the ones described in Chapter 4.3.3 must have been at work. Otherwise it is hard to understand how, for example, an internationally recognised furniture factory employing about 700 persons, equipped with up-to-date production lines, and exporting over 90 per cent of its manufactured products to Western markets could go bankrupt within three years. Confronted with steeply rising unemployment rates, the local

12 The motto of the city hall's official website is: »There is no Romanian like the Banatian and no Banatian like one from Lugoj«; in Romanian: »Nu-i român ca banateanu', banatean ca lugojanu'«.

13 Iosif Constantin Dragan is a controversial character. A prominent member of the interwar »Iron Guard« fascist movement, Dragan returned to Romania after 1990 as an investor in the cultural, educational, and media domains. His investments were concentrated in his native region, the Banat, and Lugoj, his native town. The daily newspaper he founded, »Renasterea Banateana«, is one of the most widely read regional media.

authorities resorted to a desperate search for foreign investors. Investment-friendly local policies were successful and attracted a significant amount of investment, most of it German. A discourse stressing traditional good relations with local Germans, as well as the support of the emigrant German community, proved helpful.

Still, the lack of a coherent development strategy could prove problematic in the long run. Foreign investment was attracted somewhat chaotically, without taking into account educational and training resources or possible local synergy effects. Although some investors opted for Lugoj because they preferred a small-town environment with accessible and cooperative local authorities, others were re-directed from Timisoara because they were mainly looking for low production costs. The result is a fragmented local industrial landscape where every unit represents the final link in a separate, internationally operating chain. There is no integrated local small business structure in any domain, and there is no preoccupation with support for local business. Local small businesses have capitalisation problems and very poor access to banks. Should policy changes on the part of the international investors lead to serious local consequences, there is no way the local community could intervene.

Ciacova is one of the county's oldest settlements. It is located in the south-western part of the county, at a distance of 32 km from Timisoara. The commune's transport and communication infrastructure is a disaster.[14] Although it enjoyed the status of a city, together with Timisoara and Lugoj, as long ago as the Middle Ages (Munteanu/Munteanu 1998: 103), today Ciacova is no more than a commune, albeit the largest commune in Timis County. Its development dynamics are somewhat contrary to the development dynamics of Lugoj. If incorporation into Greater Romania meant a new opportunity for the formerly peripheral town of Lugoj, Ciacova was cut off from its traditional market environment by the new border. Banking and trade activities collapsed and agricultural production declined, as the town was no longer up to its position as a local trade fair. This re-agrarisation continued during communist rule, when the takeover of arable land by state agricultural farms started driving away the local population. In 1900 Ciacova had, together with the neighbouring villages of Cebza, Gad,

14 I could not contact the mayor's office for an interview appointment, because the telephone lines were broken down. The wires had been stolen and sold as scrap metal. It took me three hours, with two changes of train, to get to Ciacova from Timisoara. On my way back I had to resort to hitchhiking, as there were no more trains that day.

Ghilad, Macedonia, Obad, and Petroman, over 15,000 inhabitants, but the population numbers less than 7,500 today.

Apart from its traditional Habsburg architecture, the after-effects of a recent earthquake, and a marble plate commemorating the birthplace of the most prominent representative of the Serbian Enlightenment, there is not much left from Ciacova's past. My local interview partners all stressed that it used to be different, but no one could really tell me how it had been and what was so special about it. Against the background of ongoing in-migration from other parts of the country, local identities are disrupted. Asked to describe their commune, my interview partners either said nothing or started minutely describing the destructive activities of the newcomers.

The economic situation of the commune is just as depressing. After the collapse of the state agricultural farms, there is nothing left. Some small businesses like a bakery or a furniture shop are struggling hard to survive. When I asked about investment, I received the following answer: »Oh yes, we've got a foreign investor, an Italian. I even posted a note on the window that he is looking for women to employ them in a factory for assembling irons«.

Even though there is a local promoter financed by the Open Society Network appointed to Ciacova, the mayor seems to ignore the young man's activities. He also ignores the existence of an emigrant German community and looked quite surprised when I suggested during the interview that it might be helpful to establish some contacts with Germany. Instead, he prefers to get things done using his personal contacts. This approach does not seem very helpful for local development. Although he told me that he personally had found the best and cheapest possible factory location, as well as more than a hundred qualified women for the Italian investor mentioned above, he was neither sure that the investor would actually come nor could he tell me where I could reach him for an interview.

Ciacova's only ray of hope is its youth. Due to the higher natality rates of the in-migrants, the commune is one of the rare rural settlements that is not affected by overaging. Every village has its own elementary school and there are even two high schools, one with a mathematics-informatics profile and one with an agricultural profile, in operation in Ciacova itself. The Tele-Center, a computer-assisted youth community centre financed by the Timisoara-based Center for Rural Assistance, affiliated with the Soros

Open Society Network, offers additional educational resources like computer training, arts and English classes. Given the youngsters' eagerness to get involved, there is hope that new forms of local integration and participation might emerge in the long run.

Types of mayors in Timis County: »The poet«, »the administrator« and the »well-connected«

Before analysing the discourses of the three municipalities' mayors, I would like to introduce them in a few words and sketch their career paths. Most of the information is taken from the personal interviews I conducted with the mayors.

The present mayor of Timisoara is the son of a prominent local family, born and raised in the city. He completed his education in the most prestigious local schools and university departments. After working as a construction engineer and architect, he presently holds a teaching position in the German-language architecture department of Technical University. His political career started with his active participation in the revolution of 1989. Given his Orthodox family background, it was logical for him to join the Christian Democrat National Peasant Party in 1990. He moved up the local party hierarchy and was nominated as a candidate for the mayor's office in 1996. He was elected with a comfortable majority in 1996 and re-elected in 2000.

The present mayor of Lugoj is a mechanical engineer. He started his career as the head of a workshop in a Lugoj mechanical engineering company and slowly rose to an executive position. Due to his position he became a member of the National Salvation Front in 1990, and when the FNS split between the followers of Iliescu and Roman, he opted for the latter. In 1992 he was elected city councillor on the FNS list. His fellow councillors elected him vice-mayor and he held this position until 1996, when his success as a vice-mayor encouraged him to run for the mayor's position. He was elected in 1996 and re-elected in 2000.

The present mayor of Ciacova is an agricultural engineer, specialising in pedology. He came to Timisoara to study and after graduation worked as the head of a cooperative farm in Ciacova. After the dismantling of the cooperatives in 1990, he succeeded in obtaining a teaching position at Agricultural University in Timisoara, where he completed his Ph.D. thesis.

He ran for the mayor's office in Ciacova in 1996. During the election campaign he obtained an academic scholarship from France and opted for research instead of local politics. He ran again in 2000, when he was elected with a comfortable majority.

This brief outline of the mayors' career paths already hints at major differences between the three mayors' approaches to local politics. While in the first two cases we have different but consistent career models, the third case seems quite inconsistent. This becomes even more obvious when we listen to the mayors' different »tales of success«.

In the opinion of the present mayor of Timisoara, a good mayor has to be more than anything else an honest person. He says that there are many temptations in city hall and in public administration generally, so that a mayor can only make his way when he has a solid moral basis, honesty, and correctness. Furthermore, he must be hard-working and communicative, always present when needed. He must, of course, also be competent in the technical, economic, and legal fields. Experience gained in an executive position is a further advantage, but one can learn this by doing it. Apart from honesty, readiness to work hard, and competence, the most important thing is to be locally integrated and to have a vision of what the locality one is heading should become. If a mayor does not have a vision he can make decisions which turn out to be mistakes in the long run, and if he is not locally integrated he can be easily manipulated by the »other interests« that »helped« him into the position.

In contrast to the present mayor of Timisoara, who exemplifies the first–generation, post-communist »ethos politician«, the present mayor of Lugoj openly states that he personally prefers administrative action to political discourse. In his opinion this means solving many small problems, and it was this that helped gradually to gain the trust of the local community. He, too, refers to communication competences, the willingness to work hard, and executive experience as additional advantages. But in contrast to the present mayor of Timisoara, who criticises the corruption of the administration and tries to counteract it through local integration, the present mayor of Lugoj accepts the rules of the game, which he openly calls »political clientelism«. He is proud of some local infrastructure projects he was able to accomplish by mobilising his patrons in the ministries. On the other hand, the present mayor of Lugoj is open to other policy models as well. He is very much in favour of foreign investment and has been more successful than his colleague in Timisoara in combating corruption and establishing a lean, investor-friendly administration. He is ready to learn and cooperate in domains where Timisoara has a competitive edge. Still, he lacks a »vision«, and thus some of his »small successes« may turn out to be failures in the long run.

In contrast to the mayors of Timisoara and Lugoj, whose re-election clearly showed that they were supported by their respective communities, the present mayor of Ciacova was elected because he succeeded in mobilising some VIPs to participate in a village festival. He believes he won the election because »the people saw that personalities come to the village and speak for me«. He complains about the extremely difficult situation in the commune and of the fact that he is getting no support from anywhere »because they all promise before the elections and soon forget after the elections«. In contrast to the present mayor of Lugoj, he is apparently not able to mobilise the support of his political patrons. He is also unable to cooperate with emerging local initiatives. His constant fears that somewhat unpopular decisions might hurt his good relations with persons in higher positions hinder any kind of activity on his part. He seems to have no power base either in the community or in the Liberal Party of which he is a member. He joined the liberals in order to have better access to the county council president, but was disappointed because the liberals did not make it into the county council in the last elections. As an educated person with a good deal of local experience, he should have known what he was doing when he ran for office. His persistent complaints hint at the fact that he might be the type of local office holder who runs for his position not because he really wants to get involved in local affairs but in the hope of extra income.

Although they seem to represent strongly contrasting mayoral types, the mayors of both Timisoara and Lugoj are »good mayors« according to their own standards and according to the standards of their electorate. The present mayor of Timisoara is widely respected as an honest, balanced, and educated person. When talking about him, everybody respectfully mentions that he represents a rare species of post-communist office holder who does not get involved in corruption in office. His successes in attracting foreign investment and EU funding for local infrastructure projects are also appreciated. His constant preoccupation with local integration through the establishment of season-specific local festivals and his concern for public spaces like parks and pedestrian zones further add to his positive record. But he is not perfect. Both local business people and

NGO representatives complain that he is too much of a gentleman, an intellectual, a »poet«, a »dreamer«. This is a way of saying that he is not combative enough, unable to push through local interests at the central level and even uninterested in central politics, preferring to travel abroad instead of going to the capital.

The present mayor of Lugoj seems to be everything the present mayor of Timisoara is not. If the present mayor of Timisoara encourages his staff to attend training courses and get involved in national and international networks and projects, the present mayor of Lugoj is the type of official who »cuts heads and hangs«, inspiring a fearful respect in his staff. He is energetic, even aggressively combative, and his record as a mayor shows that he is able to push through local interests at the central level. He is also preoccupied with the local community, although not on the level of symbolic integration; he is more concerned with down-to-earth matters like communal heating and local unemployment rates. He is flexible and open-minded, ready to learn from his colleagues how to attract international support. And, finally, his less integrated approach – characterised by the lack of an all-encompassing »vision« – seems more efficient in the context of the general insecurity of the Romanian political and economic environment.

»Progressive«, »pragmatic«, and »opportunistic«: local policy models in Timis County

Two concurrent modes of behaviour emerge from the analysis of the local policy models represented by the three mayors. The attitudes of the mayors of Ciacova and Lugoj clearly show that the logic of central redistribution requires clientelistic behaviour. Local budgets can rarely cope with all the tasks assigned to local authorities, so additional funding from the central authorities is needed. The logic of the mayors' own position means that they have to seek access either to the county council or the central body in charge of the specific local issue at stake, and this access can only be obtained through clientelistic party channels. If a small settlement is concerned and the mayor needs to gain access to the county council president first, and if the latter is part of a different clientelistic network than, for example, that of the minister in charge, the situation of the settlement is quite hopeless. It is even more so if the mayor has acceded to his position not by his own efforts and the support of the community but through the support of outside patrons on whom he is completely dependent. This seems to be the case in Ciacova.

By contrast, the mayor of Lugoj acceded to his position with the help of his own former power base and the support of the local community. He »inherited« his position in the clientelistic party network and used it to get involved in local politics, but he gradually won over the support of the local community. On some specific policy issues, like international cooperation, he established good contacts with Timisoara and various other actors. Thus he extended, slowly but steadily, his room for manoeuvre and protected his position against the disruptive effects of the algorithm.

Even though they were probably not nomenklatura members, the mayors of both Ciacova and Lugoj may be regarded as part of the »old« establishment. Bearing in mind that the communist establishment was recruited according to criteria of party loyalty and professional competence, the career paths of the two men seem to point to the two different development dynamics inherent in this model. The present mayor of Ciacova seems to have had difficulties in choosing between professionalization and clientelistic incorporation, though he finally opted for the latter.

His inability to make independent decisions can be interpreted as a sign of extreme loyalty, as he always seems to be waiting for directives. Against the background of his persistent complaints it is hard to say how far his loyalty is rewarded. In contrast, the present mayor of Lugoj's pragmatic approach and adaptability to different policy models suggests flexibility grounded in professional competence. He is aware of all the possible strategies at his disposal and picks the one he considers more efficient for the solution of the specific issues he is confronted with. He accepts party clientelism as the »rule of the game«, but he can also adapt more cooperative strategies if need be.

If the mayors of Ciacova and Lugoj stand for »old« elite survival and reconversion strategies, the mayor of Timisoara represents an altogether new type of politician. Of the three cases studied, he is the only one whose political career started from the momentum of political mobilisation. His active participation in the revolution and his moral perception of the world must have helped him develop his »vision« of all-encompassing change. He uses moral judgement to keep his distance from clientelistic practices and seeks to develop and implement a new model of local policy based on citizen involvement. In order to free himself from central dependency, he tries to rely on both local resources and international funding. The fact that access to external funding requires both cooperation between different local actors and citizen involvement supports and reinforces his own policy approach. Nevertheless, the outcome of this type of policy is contradictory. On the one hand, isolation from the Romanian political issues of the day is necessary to preserve both local and external credibility based on one's high moral standards. On the other hand, internal isolation can lead to high external vulnerability. In a situation where interference on the part of the central state is actively refused and the local community is still fragmented and poor, complete dependency on foreign donors and multinationals can be risky.

Strategies of local actors in Timisoara

Up to this point the analysis has revealed that neither the euroregion DKMT, nor the development region West, nor even Timis County functions as a subject of regional or local development. Although there are many references to a distinct regional identity in cultural terms, this identity is constantly eroded by spatial, economic, and social cleavages. The role of regional self-government structures appears to be ambivalent: although they formally have an integrative function, their actual workings seem more disintegrative. Economic policies designed to generate opportunities for economic participation by attracting foreign investment also have an ambivalent outcome. While high local concentrations of foreign investment are a factor contributing to the empowerment of certain municipalities, it is nevertheless one that at the same time deepens the urban-rural cleavage. The specific modes of integration of certain local industries with the world market make the generation of local cohesion even more difficult.

The analysis has also shown that big cities are in the best position to generate integration on the local level. Urban traditions and intellectual elites able to manipulate the discourse on identity for political and economic ends represent additional advantages for Timisoara. This chapter is therefore concerned with the prospects for local development in Timisoara. Bearing in mind that the establishment of new forms of social interaction and the capacity for technological innovation have been identified as driving forces of local and regional development elsewhere, the analysis will focus on these two aspects. As the case study is concerned with a peripheral region the role of transnational cooperation will also be important.

Organisational »cores« of local policy

With regard to the establishment of new forms of social interaction, local self-government, and the chamber of commerce, industry and agriculture have played a major role as organisational »cores« of the new order based on the market and democracy. In research carried out in Arad County, Suciu found that local power was concentrated in the self-government bodies of the big cities and the chambers of commerce (Suciu 1997).

My interviews conducted in Timis County revealed that local self-government and the chamber of commerce not only had a great symbolic and political importance but were also perceived as the key actors for local and regional development. From a long list of political and economic organisations, the majority of the interview partners selected the city hall and the chamber as being the key actors of local and regional development. They were also named most frequently as organisational cooperation partners. This not surprising as local self-government and the chamber of commerce were the richest local actors in terms of their own revenues, know-how, and international contacts.

Timisoara city hall – organisational structure, tasks and revenues

In the aftermath of the urban uprising in 1989, political power was seized by a spontaneously constituted Romanian Democratic Forum in Timisoara (RDF). The RDF staffed both city and county councils. However, the presidents of both councils gave in to central pressures and tried to merge the RDF with the FNS, which had monopolised central power. Popular protests prevented the merger. Elections for the city council were held under army supervision and an oppositional liberal-democratic city council was established. It dissociated itself from the political restoration tendencies of the central administration and tried to secure both local support and wider administrative competences for itself. In order to win local support, it sought to establish more citizen-oriented, transparent policies. Transparency turned out to be a successful strategy, as a scandal that received wide media coverage prevented the undermining of the council by the appointed mayor, who doubled the size of local administrative staff in order to create a counterweight to the council. The mayor was dismissed on corruption charges and the council elected a new mayor. However, the newly elected mayor was prevented from taking office by the intervention of the local representative of the central government (Leber 1996: 149–150).

Ever since then, liberal-democratic forces concentrated in the RDF and its successor organisation, the local Democratic Convention, have dominated the Timisoara city hall. This can be regarded as a consequence of political mobilisation. Even if this fact was hardly ever mentioned in the interviews, all the mayors elected in Timisoara had been direct participants in the revolution.[15] Despite the disappearance of the Democratic Convention from the national political arena and its loss of significance in the county council, within the city council the Democratic Convention retains its dominant position[16] at present. The mayor of Timisoara was the only Democratic Convention mayor to be elected for a second term in 2000, and the positions of the vice-mayors were taken by the representatives of the same parties that had held them in the previous term.

As far as its competences are concerned, the local government of Timisoara has the right and the effective capacity to settle and manage public affairs in the name and interest of the local community it represents.[17] This right is exercised by the local council and the mayor, who are directly elected by the citizens of the municipality. The members of the council serve on five standing commissions[18] (*http://www.ccctm.ro/cityhall*[19]). The

---

15 Pompiliu Alamorean (21 January 1990–6 August 1990), Liviu Borha (7 August 1990–17 February 1992), Viorel Oancea (18 February 1992–15 June 1996), Gheorghe Ciuhandu (16 June 1996–present).

16 The present local council of Timisoara consists of 31 councillors. Their party affiliation at the time of their election – spring 2000 – was as follows: eight were members of the Democratic Convention, seven of the Party of Social Democracy in Romania (PSDR), three of the National Liberal Party, three of the Greater Romania Party, two of the DUHR, and one each of the Christian-Democratic National Alliance, the Alliance for Romania, the Democratic Party (PD), and the Pensioners' Party.

17 Law on Local Public Administration 215/2001.

18 The commissions are the following: the commission for study, prognosis, economy, budget, finance, and taxation; the commission for urban development, public works, and local public property; the commission for the administration of the public domain, public services, and commerce; the commission for public administration, legal problems, public security, human rights, and problems of religious communities; and the

internal structure of the town hall administration corresponds to the structure of the council's commissions. The town hall administration is divided into five departments[20] (*http://www.infotim.ro/primarie/strdep1.htm*) whose staff carry out the decisions of the council. The staff consists of civil servants. Internal re-organisation and changes in the functioning regulations of the town hall administration, as well as modifications regarding the tasks and competences assigned to staff, can only be carried out with the approval of the council.

As already mentioned in Chapter 5.3, the Timisoara local council has a budget which is more than double the budget of the county council. Timisoara's own revenues – without the city's share of personal income tax – almost equal the county council's total revenues. According to budget execution sheet of September 1, 2000, most of the budget was spent on the operating costs of local authorities, education, health, social protection, public services, and public transport. Additionally, the city of Timisoara received a 24.7 million euro loan from the EBRD for the upgrading of the water and waste-water infrastructure.

The CCIAT – organisational structure, tasks and revenues

As already mentioned, the CCIAT may be regarded as the second basic pillar of the new institutional order emerging after 1989. This perspective is confirmed by the CCIAT's recent history, which reveals it to have been a political project of the democratic elites. Even though the related legal framework was lacking, the Timisoara chamber's activity re-started in March 1990. Its proactive attitude forced the Romanian government to create an institutional framework for the establishment of chambers of commerce through the adoption of Decree-Law 139 in May 1990. This law defines the chambers of commerce as self-financed, autonomous, nongovernmental organisations. The chambers are mandated to promote the economic interests of their members and help them to face the challenges

---

commission for social protection, the environment, health, education, tourism, culture, and sports.

19 This is the official website of Timisoara city hall.

20 These are as follows: the economic department, the technical department, the department for urban development, the department for local public administration, and the PR department.

of the market economy. The budgets of the chambers are made up of membership fees collected from their members, fees for commercial service provision to different economic actors, and the revenues collected from the Office of Business Registry. Membership in a chamber is voluntary.

At present, the Timisoara chamber defines its role as the main promoter of local economic development in cooperation with the local self-government bodies. Its main goals are: domestic and international representation of the members' interests through an efficient lobby and the creation of a modern business environment, development of a wide range of quality services, efficient involvement in local and regional development programmes, and lobbying for the development of a better economic environment (*http://www.cciat.ro*).

The internal structures of the CCIAT involve a high degree of formal differentiation, and its management functions in accordance with democratic procedures. Its membership consists of about 850 enterprises. Broken down by fields of activity, the members of the chamber are organised in different divisions. The first divisions to be set up were the textile and construction divisions in 1992, followed by the divisions for agriculture, food processing, the chemical industry, engineering, the electronics and electrotechnics industry, tourism, and trade and transport in 1993. The wood processing, leather processing, and shoe production divisions were set up in 1994, and the printing, editing, and publicity division was created in 1995. The CCIAT was reorganised in 1997. The agriculture and food processing divisions merged and a new division was set up to accommodate the developing service sector. Additionally, an interdisciplinary division was created; it was dedicated to new production and marketing technologies as well as to achieving and securing higher product quality and environmental awareness. The division for tourism and trade is by far the chamber's largest division, numbering about 180 members. It is followed by the service division with about 130 members and the agriculture and food processing division with about 100 members. This structure reflects the fact that the CCIAT's members are mainly newly created SMEs. The prominent role of the Small Entrepreneurs' Association within the CCIAT's leadership is consistent with this situation.

With a membership of fewer than 1,000 companies of a total of almost 25,000 (Chapter 5.1.2), the CCIAT cannot be regarded as representative of the local business sector. It can, though, be considered an authentic representative of the liberal-minded local business elite and a local actor committed to the market and democracy. As such it sets standards for the operation of a market-oriented local business environment and creates a framework for cooperation for all those who are prepared to adhere to its standards.

Institutionalisation patterns on the local level in Timisoara

Apart from their central position in the local and regional context, these organisations share several other features as well. Both could be regarded simultaneously as traditional local institutions and institutional innovations. On the one hand, local government and the chamber of commerce can look back upon a long history reaching back to Austro-Hungarian times, when these organisations contributed considerably to the development of the city and the well-being of its citizens. But even if historical continuity was symbolically stressed – despite continuous struggles with the other inhabitants, the chamber of commerce was intent on keeping its headquarters in the same building in which it had been located before 1948, while at the entrance to the town hall a white marble plate recalled the names of all the former mayors – in its present form local self-government was established in 1991 and the chamber of commerce took up its activities in June 1990.

Another common feature of these organisations is the fact that they came into being as a result of local initiatives. As a consequence of local mobilisation, the local counter-elites came to power in Timisoara as early as December 1989. In the winter of 1989–1990 they tried to institutionalise the new democratic and market-oriented system they stood for. Thus Timisoara was the only Romanian city with spontaneously established self-government in the winter of 1989–1990. At the same time, Timisoara was the first city to demand the organisation of a chamber of commerce and the first to receive a permit. »We were the first institution typical of a market economy«, the president of the CCIAT proudly stressed in a personal interview.

Nevertheless, neither local political commitment nor the Austro-Hungarian heritage nor ten years of recent history sufficed to give the local self-government bodies and the chamber of commerce internal stability. Both organisations were affected by bureaucratic inertia and the disruptive effects of political clientelism and the algorithm. Comparing the present situation to the situation under communist rule, the mayor of Giroc stated that the major change brought about by the administrative reform was not the separation of politics from administration. Politics and administration were still intertwined; what was new was the division of power between different parties: »Let's take a concrete example: the mayor [of Timisoara], Mr. Ciuhandu, is the president of the county branch of the Peasant Party; Mr. Borza, the vice-president of the Democratic Party, is the vice-mayor; and Mr. Coifan is the vice-president of the Liberal Party and the county council president«.

As perceived by my interview partner, the division of political power on the local level illustrates the perfect reproduction of the »algorithm«, the mechanism by which the members of the party coalition ruling during the 1996–2000 period divided up all the influential positions among themselves.

This situation changed after the last elections in 2000. The county council is now headed by the vice president of the county branch of the PSDR, the ruling party at present, which also has a majority of seats in the council. However, the vice president of the county council, who is in charge of economic development and attracting foreign investment, was re-elected even though his party, the Christian Democratic Peasant Party, is not even represented in the present parliament. The re-elected mayor of Timisoara and one of the two newly elected vice-mayors are also members of the Christian Democratic Peasant Party.

However, neither the city administration nor the chamber seem to be unaffected by political clientelism. Thus the chief accountant of Timisoara noted that putting an end to the influence of politics on the economy was one of the most important goals for regional development. In the same vein, the former president of the county council's economic commission complained about political influence in the chamber, and the president of the Matrix Business Club hoped that company managers would not, in the future, be appointed based on political criteria. If the three interview partners quoted above showed a critical awareness of clientelism, the Democratic Party member of parliament I interviewed openly acknowledged that as an elected representative he cooperated with the chamber of commerce »as they employ(ed) Democratic Party members«. However, it seems to have been a system of reciprocal obligations, as the chamber seems to have profited in its turn from his later appointment as ambassador in Yugoslavia.

Of course, notable efforts have also been made to reorganise and professionalize these organisations. The present mayor of Timisoara stated in a personal interview that he started his work with the reorganisation of the town hall administration, as he found that »even at the local level, many of those who speak about change don't want it in fact«. Confronted with a lot of people unwilling to take responsibility, he had to reorganise the administration and get rid of those who »did not fit into the new spirit«. Instead, he hired young people with whom he felt that he could work better. My observations at the city administration and in informal conversations with young people working in different departments confirmed the emergence of a more dynamic and citizen-oriented attitude among civil servants.

But successive reorganisations also lead to a disruption of routines and an internal destabilisation of organisations. Tellingly, the director of the department for urban development was unable to list the number and the names of the different departments of the city administration. This was also the case with the chamber of commerce, where the director of the department for international relations told me that she had no idea how many departments the chamber had, as it was being reorganised at the time of our interview. From the point of view of their addressees - like the director of the Italian investors' association and honorary consul of Italy - these organisations' conflicting internal logics made them utterly inefficient: »I have met very competent and well-trained people in every institution; of course, there is corruption, too, but also honest people, so this is not the biggest problem. But on the decision-making level I always encounter a great incapacity. [...]«

The fluidity of organisational structures has made personal contacts, generally highly valued in the Romanian context, even more valuable. Thus, when asked how an investment achieved success, the Italian businessman quoted above stated: »It all depends on the contacts of the investor to the administration, in fact to the persons who are in decision-making positions«. Under these circumstances organisations came to be identified with their leaders, and this meant that interview partners were more easily able to name persons than organisations. For the director of the Office for Labour Force Reconversion and Training, the Local Consortium thus became »Mrs. Dragomirescu's«.

Meanwhile, personalisation and the disruption of authoritarian bureaucratic procedures created good opportunities for various outside influences mediated by transnational cooperation. In an evaluation of the performance of Western NGO strategies for democratisation in Romania, Pralong found that cooperation with Romanian organisations was most successful when outsiders were able to identify »the right political entrepreneur« for their issue (Pralong 1999). In a similar vein, the president of the Matrix Business Club explained in a personal interview that if someone wanted to establish a cooperative relationship, the most important thing was to contact »the right person« from within the organisation one wanted to cooperate with. She described »the right political entrepreneur« as somebody who is committed to change and in a position to implement it. According to this definition, both the present mayor of Timisoara and the leadership of the CCIAT seem to embody exactly this type of office holder.

As a consequence, both organisations have established plenty of international contacts. The city of Timisoara has active partnerships with six European cities[21] and cooperates with a series of international organisations on various issues ranging from the implementation of a new sewage system to the rehabilitation of the mentally disabled. Similarly, the chamber of commerce has partnerships with chambers from Hungary, Yugoslavia, Italy, Germany, and Belgium and also cooperates with several European and US organisations on issues ranging from management training to citizen involvement.

When asked about the most successful cooperation, representatives of both local government and the chamber emphasised the case of Karlsruhe in Germany. Launched by an initiative of a Banatian diaspora community and supported by a prominent member of the Karlsruhe city council, over 24 truckloads of humanitarian aid consisting of clothes, medicine, and technical and medical equipment were delivered from Karlsruhe to Timisoara in the aftermath of the revolution in 1989–1990. The first official cooperation contract between the two cities was signed in 1992, and an organisation called »Circle of Friends Karlsruhe – Temeschburg« was founded in 1993. A series of cultural and educational exchanges took place. Officials from the Timisoara city administration had the opportunity to spend time as interns in the Karlsruhe city administration, while students from Karlsruhe joined the Timisoara Chamber of Commerce, Industry and

21 Faenza in Italy, Gera and Karlsruhe in Germany, Mulhouse and Rueil-Malmaison in France, Szeged in Hungary.

Agriculture as interns. The two cities also cooperated on issues of local public transport and local waste and energy management. After an »engagement« period of five years, Karlsruhe and Timisoara became twinned in 1997. With the support of the Karlsruhe city administration, a permanent bureau of the CCIAT was established in Karlsruhe the first non-state-sponsored Romanian economic representation abroad. During its first three months of operation, the bureau provided more than a hundred German companies with information on business and investment opportunities in Timisoara (Stadtzeitung Karlsruhe, 28 November 1997). At the end of his assignment, the first CCIAT representative in Karlsruhe used his freshly acquired contacts and know-how to found his own consulting company in Timisoara in March 1999. His company also works presently as a business contact office for the German state of Rhineland-Palatinate.

Timisoara elites: networks of friends and colleagues

The key positions of the organisations involved in local and regional development are occupied by members of Timisoara elites. And as it has become obvious that people matter more than functions, it is worth examining some general characteristics of the Timisoara elites. Apart from their presence in key institutions, Timisoara elites share a couple of other common features. In political terms the urban elite in Timisoara can be regarded as a counter-elite that came to power in the aftermath of the revolution in December 1989. Significantly, the mayor of the city mentioned in a personal interview his active participation in the revolution as the starting point of his political career. The former prefect of Timis County described himself and his political allies as follows:

»We (are) a group of engaged people, some of them elected, others appointed, who were ready to take over the responsibility and to initiate structural changes in the moral, social, economic and political realms.«

As far as their position in the local social hierarchy is concerned, most of my interview partners belong to the city's »high society«. They were fully conscious of their position and described themselves in terms such as an »elite of people with academic education and a special culture«, or »a relatively homogenous structure of a group of people of a special quality, of a high intellectual standard«. They distinguished themselves from outsiders on intellectual grounds. Thus the competing elites of Arad where described as second-rate intellectuals and the newly-established Arad university was labelled »a university just good enough to train bazaar vendors«. Reputation was highly valued and many efforts directed at modernisation and European integration could be regarded as motivated by the desire to live up to one's reputation.

But in order to gain entrance to the snobbish circles of the city elite, one needed not only education and an academic position but also material wealth. The mayor of Timisoara described his fellow citizens as people who were attached to property and actively sought self-fulfilment, most of all material self-fulfilment. In a similar tone, the spokesman of the county council stated that Timisoara was »a city where money has a very precise value and serves as a basis for the social hierarchy«. The typical representative of this group was born in Timisoara, attended the local German school, and continued his education at one of the most prestigious departments of the local university, where he presently holds an academic position. Simultaneously, he is the owner of a prosperous joint venture that he established together with a former classmate now living abroad.

The local elites are further interconnected by personal and professional relationships. My own observations during a workshop on the elaboration of the local development strategy confirmed this view. Even though they were invited as experts, most of the participants seemed to know each other personally. Some were related to each other, others turned out to be former schoolmates or former students of other participants. Most of the participants addressed each other by their first names, and some even used nicknames.

Communication between organisations takes place not through institutional channels but rather through private conversations. When asked in a personal interview about the emergence of a local consensus on questions of social and economic development, a prominent member of the German Democratic Forum, managing director of the Forum's foundation for economic development and the Forum's representative on the county council, answered that »it results from the private conversations that everybody has the same point of view, as persons, as institutions«. Similarly, when referring to cooperation with the city administration on the elaboration of the local development strategy, the director of the agency for local development said that he was asked to solve some of the mayor's problems. Interview partners further stressed that administrative structures in Timisoara were more cooperative, open, and helpful than elsewhere in the country. This openness and cooperative attitude stemmed from the good personal relationships between the representatives of the different organisations. Thus the manager of the business representation office of the German state of Rhineland-Palatinate mentioned that the prefect had offered to intervene personally should German businesses encounter difficulties with the customs office.

Given their high degree of personalisation, organisations needed to be personally intertwined in order to assure a constant flow of information. This seemed to be the case with the local authorities, the chamber of commerce and the universities. To give just a few prominent examples: the mayor is a university professor, as was the former county council president; the president of the chamber of commerce is a former civil servant from the city administration, and the managing director of the chamber was formerly a city council representative.

Apart from the mutual respect they have for each other as intellectuals and specialists, Timisoara elites are integrated by their discourse on local and regional history and identity as well. When asked to describe themselves, they invariably mentioned democratic traditions, multiethnic identity, and the prominence of a climate of cooperation. At the beginning, no one was prepared to speak openly to an outsider like me about local conflicts. On the contrary, everyone denied that there were any, even if it was obvious that, for example, the economic commission of the county council would not need a mediator if there were no conflicts to mediate. More in-depth conversations revealed that local elites were affected by authority and reputation conflicts as well as by fragmentation and political clientelism. Thus cooperation between the city and county councils was hindered by the personal ambitions of the former county council president, who was involved in personally motivated conflicts with the mayor of Timisoara. The effects of fragmentation and clientelism became obvious when the chamber actively sabotaged the elaboration of the Timisoara area development strategy on the grounds that the mayor would use it in his election campaign, in this way gaining a competitive edge over the vice president of the chamber who was running for the same position.

However, the strategy was finalised, and the final version received the support of members of the whole local political spectrum, who signed written engagements to support it irrespective of future political developments. In the end there was general agreement on goals for local development, especially in relation to attracting foreign investment and development of the IT sector.

History in the discourse of local elites

According to Schöpflin, cultural communities are formed by shared experiences and their transmission from one generation to another. He argues that history and culture merge in this respect. Starting from general agreement on the fact that »history« always consists of a set of choices, one can easily conclude that »the same community in different periods will give saliency to different experiences, according to some contingent need« (Schöpflin 1989: 9).

The revolution is hardly ever mentioned in Timisoara today. Even the present mayor, himself an active participant imprisoned by the secret police, mentioned it only in a short sentence during our interview.[22] In Timisoara history is read through the prism of modernisation. Thus it is that historical periods that can be interpreted as periods of modernisation become relevant. The Austro-Hungarian period, the period between the two world wars, and the revolution gain new relevance as elements of a regional mythology. The founding myth of the Banat is localised in the Austro-Hungarian period. Names like Eugen von Savoyen and Florimund Mercy are emblematic for this period. They are seen as civilizing heroes who created the new order underlying the later development of the region. The founding myth, which celebrates the victory of order over chaos, can be found in the stories of later settlers as a struggle against a hostile outside world. These refer to the acquisition and clearing of the land, the building of houses, and the celebration of the first community festivals. The same elements recur in the discourses of the victims of deportation. The latter also refer to the first settlers, whom they perceive as role models (Vultur 1997: 30–33).

The self-representation of the Banatians as pioneers of civilization is anchored in this myth. This image explains why the uprising against the

22 My questions about the revolution were generally met with evasive remarks like »That was ten years ago«, or silence. When I became more insistent I was told that for the participants the revolution was a deeply personal, quasi-religious experience about which one could only communicate with the other persons who shared the experience. An outsider like me insisting on this issue was considered personally offensive.

communist system started from here and motivates the regional elites to engage in institutional innovations like the establishment of local government, development agencies, strategic development programmes, and cross-border cooperation units.

The Golden Age is described as a chronology of uninterrupted technical progress leading to social and economic well-being. It is also defined in terms of interethnic harmony and mutual respect. The participation of every ethnic group in economic progress is regarded as the basis for interethnic harmony. Statements like »There have never been minorities here, we were all equal«, made by the prefect of Timis County in a personal interview, refer to the equal right to political participation of all the inhabitants of the region. History is viewed as a chronology of technical and economic progress extending from the Habsburg re-conquest to the beginning of communist rule. This view of history makes it possible to ignore the conflicts and tensions that arose following the incorporation of the Banat into the Hungarian part of the Empire and later into Greater Romania. Meanwhile, facts associated with the modernisation that took place later, during communist rule, are shifted to this period.

The period of communist rule is seen as the Dark Ages. It is described in terms of destruction and serves as a screen for a long history of conflicts between a levelling centre and a region struggling for autonomy, between »the Balkans« and »Mitteleuropa«. In this context many problems that arise today are interpreted as delayed consequences of communist destruction.

The return to the Golden Age is the most important goal of regional development concepts today. Development is viewed as economic growth and European integration. Multiethnicity and intercultural communication competences are re-evaluated as important assets.

The specificity of Timisoara within the Romanian context: the relevance of transnational cooperation

Beginning with a general assumption of path dependency, I have so far investigated the possibilities of the emergence of an alternative to the dominant national development path on a sub-national level. I did this by first reconstructing the model of the Romanian development path from a historical perspective. I took into account both the macro- and micro-dimensions of path dependency in the sense of the Braudelian theory. I developed my argument further by reconstructing the history of the Banat region and the city of Timisoara and by analyzing the processes of interdependency between local and regional history on the one hand and local and regional identity discourses on the other. In a subsequent step I linked together these two strands of argumentation by using the concept of the modernizing semi-clientelistic regime developed by Fox.

Using this concept allowed me to view the city of Timisoara as embedded both in the context of the Romanian national transformation regime and the historical region of the Banat. Although I insisted on Timisoara's specificity, I implicitly assumed that Timisoara shared a series of dominant characteristics of the »Romanian model«. However, I was also able to point out a series of relevant differences, which, in my opinion, could have generated a development dynamic different from the national one. I identified these specific resources both on the material and on the symbolic level.

On the material level, I examined the social and economic resources of Timisoara and found that for historical reasons Timisoara's local economy was more suitable for global economic integration than the Romanian economy as a whole. On the symbolic level, I found that local identity discourses were also oriented towards European and global political and economic integration. I further explored the moment of political mobilisation in December 1989, not only as a spectacular political re-enactment and re-affirmation of local identity but also as a cathartic historical moment when creative social energies were set free. Based on this social and political dynamic, institution building on the local level proceeded faster in Timisoara than elsewhere in the country.

Three factors: a less desolate social and economic situation, Western-oriented identity discourses, local political mobilisation and institution-building efforts, as well as the international publicity enjoyed by the city as the starting point of the Romanian revolution, contributed to the establishment of a great number of international contacts and the emergence of various transnational cooperation networks between local and external actors. The relevance of transnational cooperation thus turned out to be the most important characteristic that singled out Timisoara in the Romanian context. I will therefore continue my analysis by presenting three pairs of small case studies, each focussing on different aspects of transnational cooperation.

Transnational cooperation and institutional innovation

The first two cases, the creation of the local development agency ADETIM and the elaboration of Timisoara's local development strategy, address issues from the field of local politics and present local efforts for the creation of instruments for local development. With reference to the findings of Fox (1996) and Chalmers (1997), I suggest that transnational cooperation can contribute to the production of social capital and »societal thickness« in the sense of »the breadth and density of representative societal organisations« (Fox, 1996: 1089). Using the political opportunities created by the modernising, semi-clientelistic regime on the one hand and the social energy and ideas emerging from the momentum of local political mobilisation on the other, local actors gain the capability to develop a series of initiatives, which then become »scaled-up« through cooperation with external actors (Fox, 1996: 1090p.).

Transnational cooperation takes place within the framework of associative networks and is thus not only able to address relevant issues for the specific local situation but also to alter patterns of perception and action. However, associative networks of transnational cooperation do not operate in a field free of power relations, even though they may break through them at certain points. I will reconsider this aspect in more detail after I have presented the cases.

Building institutional capacities: ADETIM – the Economic Development Agency of Timis County

ADETIM, the Economic Development Agency of Timis County, has been described by its first director as the »first Romanian experience in the regional development field« (Balasa 1999: 105). In a personal interview, one of the founding fathers of the agency, a locally born expert working for a German international cooperation agency, recalled that the pioneering experiment began with the visit in 1993 of a leading official from the ministry of economics of the German state of North Rhine-Westphalia. Up to that date, the German state had already invested over 500 million DM in humanitarian aid for Romania and intended to become more involved in economic development. First steps were taken to organise cooperation between the three Banatian counties and North Rhine-Westphalia and to set up a common economic promotion unit. However, these activities were blocked by representatives of the central government in 1994, who accused the initiators of political separatism.

In 1995 the initiators of the economic development agency were instructed by the capital to organise three independent economic development agencies on the county level and then to establish a network for cooperation between them. Consequently, ADETIM, the economic development agency of Timis County, was founded in May 1995. It became the coordination office for cooperation between the three county-level development agencies. At the beginning, ADETIM was managed by the international expert quoted above and financially supported by the German state of North Rhine-Westphalia. Then local staff were hired and trained. The management was taken over by an executive board made up of the president of Timis County council, the mayor of Timisoara, the president of the Timisoara Chamber of Commerce, the vice president of Timis County council, and the president of the economic commission of Timis County council (Balasa 1999: 106). After three years of activity, ADETIM became independent from external support.

However, ADETIM's executive director stated in a personal interview that cooperation on the inter-county level was hampered by poorly functioning economic structures, by a lack of organisational skills, by lack of a common vision, and, not least, by fierce competition for resources within the region. He further complained that the agency's operation was also not without difficulties on the local level. Both the Timisoara Chamber of

Commerce and the city's local government were reluctant to use the agency as an instrument for local and regional development. Ignorance and a lack of recognition for the agency's specific expertise were suggested by my interview partner as possible reasons for this behaviour. The widespread perception of the agency as the personal pet project of the former county council president, a prominent liberal politician, and a stronghold of the local Liberal Party might also have contributed to this situation. ADETIM's executive director admitted that without strong backing by the county council and the personal involvement of the former county council president, the agency would not have had the means to survive independently.

Having the legal status of an NGO, ADETIM was not allowed to make profit. Therefore it was dependent on public funding, which it received from the county council in connection with the commissioning of different projects. The former president of the county council's economic commission stated in a personal interview that a relevant share of the commission's investment budget ended up with the agency. This state of affairs was criticised by the local media as sharing out public funds on the basis of personal preferences (Agenda Zilei, 11 October 2000).

After the adoption of Law 151/1998 on regional development and the establishment of an appropriate institutional framework, ADETIM became part of the national network of development agencies. As an agency established on the county level, it is entrusted with the implementation of local and microregional projects, which are allocated to ADETIM by the Regional Development Agency (Baga/Balasa 1999: 63). Additionally, it acts as a technical advisor to various local government bodies.

In spite of the initial accusations of separatism and later evidence of clientelistic behaviour, ADETIM has developed into an organisation with both thorough knowledge of the social and economic reality of the region and considerable technical expertise in the field of regional planning. Activities centred around the agency gave rise to a group of local experts whose expertise came to be appreciated on the local, regional, national, and international levels. Thus the former county council president had been the representative of the Romanian county governments in the European Assembly of the Regions and the initiator of the euroregion DKMT. As a member of parliament he is at present head of the parliamentary commission for local government. Another former member of the agency's staff headed the Agency for Regional Development in 1999, while yet another staff member acted as advisor to the Timisoara local government on issues of local development. Moreover, through the »Local Promoter« programme the agency has succeeded in attracting and training a dozen young professionals who constitute a county-wide network of local development consultants at present.

ADETIM's cooperation with the Timisoara local government has also improved over time. One of the most important local projects involving ADETIM was the elaboration of a local development strategy for the Timisoara area.

Creating instruments for local development: The Timisoara area local development strategy

The idea for the elaboration of a local development strategy grew out of the need to deal with the growing complexity of the problems local government bodies were confronted with. The gradual devolvement of competences regarding the provision of public services from central government to local government bodies under the conditions of an austerity budget hindered the local government bodies in meeting their redistributive functions and forced them to redefine their aim as support of economic development. However, the ecological consequences of forced economic development under socialist rule created awareness that not simply any kind of economic development would benefit the local community.

The need to have a comprehensive development strategy also arose from intensifying contacts with potential investors and EU bodies. As concerns foreign investment, the strategy paper was – quite realistically – not expected to attract investment to the prioritised domains. However, it could be used as an instrument to prevent unwanted developments, like investment in polluting industries. As far as cooperation with the EU is concerned, the local development strategy was expected to provide a basis for future applications for community development programs sponsored by the EU.

As a pioneering experience in the Romanian context, the elaboration of the Timisoara area local development strategy took place in the form of a transnational cooperation project. The local government's main cooperation partner was the Open Society Foundation, which not only co-financed the project but also had an influence on the choice of the methods to be used and, partly, the choice of the actors to be involved. Thus Timisoara's city administration would have preferred to elaborate a local development strategy only for the city of Timisoara, whereas the donors insisted on the involvement of the neighbouring communes. Also, budget shortfalls made it impossible to delegate the job to a specialised agency, such as ADETIM, which had elaborated development strategies for Timis County and the West Development Region up to that point. Instead, voluntary partnerships with civil society actors were adopted as a working formula. However, ADETIM still played an important role in the project as a technical and management consultant to the project coordination team.

The project, »The institutional and civil society partnership for the planning of the Timisoara area's social and economic development«, represented the first steps undertaken by the Timisoara local government towards a more enabling rather than welfare-oriented organisation. The project description issued by the local government stated that civil society organisations and »every ordinary citizen in the last instance« should be involved in the project in order to facilitate the adaptation of the local public »to the culture of change imposed by the economic mechanism«. Broad public participation was also seen as a chance to reconcile the social and cultural heritage of the city with the economically imposed requirements of »change« (Primaria Municipiului Timisoara 1999: 1).

This description suggests the emergence of new forms of urban governance in the sense of the term used by Bagnasco and Le Galès (2000). Endogenous development was considered the basic principle of the concept. Consequently, the nation state no longer represented the most important point of reference. On the contrary, the main objective of endogenous development was defined as harnessing comparative advantages in competition with other cities and areas. These were expected to be realised through endogenous economic growth, decentralised decision-making structures, and an »area-wide consensus«, as well as through a type of »development compatible with the area, the county and the social and ecological situation« (Primaria Municipiului Timisoara 1999: 3).

Scholars working in the field of urban governance have found that, in a situation where local politics increasingly mobilises support of economic development, the sphere of local political action will expand, with new organisations emerging outside the local authority. The process of coordinating the actors involved in local economic processes gives rise to bargaining systems characterised by a cooperative style of policy-making where the local authority acts as a moderator (Mayer 2000). Such a non-hierarchical style seems to be a precondition for identifying and acting on the intersecting areas of interest of the different actors involved (Hesse 1987: 72, quoted in Mayer 2000). However, this less hierarchical and more pluralist style of policy-making does not necessarily mean that the local negotiation systems thus created will offer an overall openness for democratic influences. On the contrary, the participants of the emerging policy networks may form an exclusive group, and only selected interests may be represented.

These issues also became relevant when it came to elaborating Timisoara's local development strategy. Merely attracting a significant number of local partners, necessary both in order to make up for the limited expertise of administrative staff and to create broad local support for the project, involved considerable efforts. The project manager recalled:

»Then we explained why working in a partnership is thought to bring benefits: because it permits consultancy and the results will be easier accepted. Then we also organized meetings with different professional groups as the press, the NGOs, representatives of the investors, professional organizations and we were trying to bring as many parties in as possible into the project. At the beginning we convinced only 20–30 persons who were willing to work on an honorary basis in this project. At the same time we were trying to involve specialists with a local reputation in this area into the project.«,

The novelty of the task and its pioneering quality within the Romanian context had not only represented a challenge. The wide-spread perception was that government bodies were clientelistic and authoritarian organisations. This perception prevented many people from getting involved. The project manager stated in a personal interview that people were not too enthusiastic at the beginning. She explained that their main fears were concerned with an undemocratic working method and the domination of one group or another. Individual experts were concerned that the city administration would use their time and expertise to elaborate a local development strategy it would then present as the result of its own work, without acknowledging the contributions of other partners. Representatives of competing political groupings were reluctant to participate as they expected that the successful elaboration of the local development strategy would give to the Christian Democrats dominant in the local government bodies a competitive advantage in the upcoming local elections.

Thus the personal qualities of the project manager, her good communication and persuasion skills, as well as her willingness and ability to mobilise her own personal networks for the benefit of the project, contributed decisively to a good start. As the project developed, an increasing number of experts became involved. The involvement of academics also altered the perceptions of the other participants, who believed that »work is being done in professional conditions«. However, it proved impossible to dispel the fear that the overall project could result in a good concept that would never be put into practice.

In addition to referencing academic standards, the presence of external partners also contributed to the acceptance of these new forms of policy-making. By chance, the concluding debate on the results of the first stage of the project coincided with the visit of a group of Danish experts, who were spontaneously invited to participate. Their involvement benefited the project in a twofold way. On the one hand, the Danish experts provided much-needed technical expertise in a situation that was completely new and unfamiliar to the local actors. The discussions with foreign experts, who confirmed most of their perceptions, also gave more confidence to the project team. Feeling more secure, the project team was better able to deal with various criticisms, which, up to this point, it had neglected for reasons of insecurity. The presence of foreign experts in this way strengthened the authority of local government actors, revalorised their expertise, and indirectly contributed to their greater acceptance of divergent opinions. On the other hand, the Danish presence also gave relevance to the desire to rise to international standards. Not least, the presence of the external partners prevented any personalisation of the debate, as it would have been »a shame if they saw us quarrelling like in the market place«.

However, both the »development model« determined by the national transformation regime and the specific shortcomings of associative networks and governance-based new policy models continued to pose problems. I will illustrate them by referring to the workings of a conference organised to validate the intermediary results of the strategy in March 2000, where I had the opportunity to participate personally.

During the discussions there seemed to be a consensus among the participants about the main directions of development defined by the development strategy's mission statement.[23] Nevertheless, when the details were

---

23 The mission statement of the strategy finally adopted defined the aim of the Timisoara area in becoming a strategically competitive European growth pole. In detail, it stressed

examined more closely, it turned out that most of the particular goals for development had more of a wishful-thinking quality, as their realisation far exceeded the means and competences of local actors. Thus a particular set of goals mainly concerning changes in the legislation emerged under the headline »lobby for changes in the legislation«. As far as the strategies for the implementation of this set of goals were concerned, the conference participants hoped that local MPs could be convinced to take over the function of lobbyists with the central government.

As far as the strategies for the goals within the reach of local actors were concerned, there was no general discussion of this issue. However, different points of view were expressed within the working groups. In the working group focussing on the social sector, a point of view was represented that was mainly supported by middle-aged, better-established people who were in favour of administrative reform and the establishment of decentralised, more efficient administrative structures. They invoked early socialist community centres as a model. On the other hand, younger people working in the field mainly stressed that the need to come to terms with the fact that social and medical services will not become a priority in Romania for some time and that no administrative reform could change the misery of the population. They were in favour of a »power-of-the-good example« approach: small projects involving a limited number of people and limited resources, trying to reach out and motivate others to follow.

In addition to the scarcity of resources allocated to the social sector, clientelism re-emerged as an important impediment to development. Thus the chair of the conference got involved at a certain point in the discussions regarding the social sector and stressed that the first need would be to break down the monopoly of a certain group of well-established people who treat public institutions as their personal feudal demesnes. She mentioned the example of certain closed circles of physicians who abuse their dual positions as university professors and chairpersons of the university clinics. Additionally, they are leading members of the chamber of physicians, a strong interest organisation with considerable influence on the ministry of health.

---

the need to create a moral and attractive environment for business and innovation, to create a competitive economic growth pole, to promote both national and European integration, to create a stable and development-friendly social and cultural environment, and to create a friendly ecological habitat as the main directions for strategic development.

Apart from clientelism, elitism also emerged as a problem. On closer scrutiny, one could easily observe that goals for development related to the academic field seemed to outnumber goals for development related to any other field. This was especially striking in relation to the social sector. The strategy included several goals for development such as the organisation of academic conferences and the publication of scientific reviews, which should have remained on the agendas of the universities instead of appearing as goals for local development. In contrast, no mention was made of even one single goal related to the integration of the Roma population.

A returnee from Frankfurt, working as an independent tourism consultant in Timisoara, commented on the situation as follows:

»These people here are all dreamers. They live in a bubble of soap. Timisoara today is a Gypsy city. I live here in the Fabrik neighbourhood and all my neighbours are Gypsies. They're not beggars or poor people, they're merchants and rather well-off. I get along well with them, for me it's no problem. But these people here with their combined Easterner-Latin macho inferiority complex don't even realise what the situation looks like«.

Generally, the interests of the non-academic population were definitely underrepresented as compared with the interests of the academics. This became clear with the emergence of a heated dispute over a proposal from the director of the local office for labour-force re-conversion and training. He suggested implementing training-for-mobilisation programmes in order to fight rising unemployment rates. This suggestion outraged some of the other participants, who argued that it would be foolish to waste scarce local resources on training people who were to leave the region. As the first speaker insisted that unemployment was a severe problem that had to be dealt with, some other representatives from the social sector spoke up, mentioning problems related to crime rates rising along with unemployment and the lack of programmes concerned with the re-integration of former prison inmates.

This bleak picture was completed by the representative of the sanitary administration, who prophesized that the situation would deteriorate in view of the fact that 10 per cent of the county's population aged under 16 were institutionalised children. This figure shocked everybody. Many participants could simply not believe it, and the vice president of the chamber of commerce suggested that this situation might somehow be related to the county's better institutional capacities. His hypothesis being contradicted, he asked whether these children were »our children«, »children of our

Banatians«.[24] It turned out that the institutionalised children were mainly the children of agricultural migrant workers left unemployed after the privatisation of state farms. Still, as persons born and living in Timis, they were part of local society.

Surprisingly, the participants at the workshop hardly reflected o their position vis-à-vis the local society. They perceived themselves as representatives of »civil society« and looked quite bewildered when I dared to mention that they looked rather like the city elite to me. I also mentioned that I considered the presentation of the goals of the development strategy very technical and hardly understandable for a person not familiar with regional planning techniques. Paradoxically, this was taken as a compliment, not as criticism. The authors explained to me at length what a hard job it had been to design the strategy, noting that they were proud it looked »professional« to an outsider like me.

Even so, the partnership was a success inasmuch as it succeeded in bringing together a relevant set of local actors and having them embark on a discussion over the future of their city and the surrounding areas. However, a high degree of personal acquaintance kept the workshop rather informal and personalised. Most of the participants formed small groups and started discussing personal issues, some read newspapers, others gossiped or told jokes during the presentation. Although the event was supposed to be an expert workshop, the tone of the discussions was also very personal and some participants brought up purely personal issues.[25] The chair of the workshop mentioned to me that the most prominent local politicians were present in the room, and yet none of them brought politics into discussion, although some were campaigning against each other during the local election campaign that took place at the same time. She considered this as a big success, noting that people succeeded in overcoming their narrow interests in order to focus on the interests of the city as a whole. She also complained about the general Romanian »backwardness syndrome« (Fonseca 1996), which she described as the eagerness of individuals to block each other's ideas out of envy that somebody else might have

24 The question is not surprising in view of the fact that the dominant family model in the rural Banat has been the one-child family since the beginning of the 20th century. Against this background, the high numbers of abandoned children would have suggested a catastrophic situation in the countryside.

25 Thus, the representative of the water management department campained very emotionally at a certain point for a hospital for palliative medicine, as she could not bear the sight of her mother dying at home without medical assistance.

had a better idea than they themselves; she was happy that the project participants seemed to have overcome this problem as well.

These optimistic assessments were confirmed by the way in which the project proceeded. The final version of the strategy was compiled and published on schedule. The publication was lavishly designed and contained about 200 pages, giving a comprehensive picture of the Timisoara area, which it presented from historical, external, and internal perspectives. The external perspective referred to Timisoara's position in the national and international context as well as to the city's geopolitical location. The internal perspective focussed on geographical data, data about the population and the labour force, infrastructure, the business environment, the social and cultural environment, and the ecological habitat. It also included the general objective of strategic development, the four main directions of strategic development, the 19 central objectives of strategic development, together with 67 specific objectives, which were to be realised through 448 concretely defined measures. Additionally, it contained a complete list of the contributors, as well as written statements issued by all the locally relevant political groupings who expressed their support for the development strategy, irrespective of future political developments.

In his foreword to the publication, the mayor of Timisoara saw the participation of over 185 local actors in the partnership for the elaboration of the strategy as the most important result of the overall process. He regarded this as an important step towards the establishment of more participative forms of local policy-making. He considered the strategy a basic instrument for the coordination and motivation of local action as well as for the pooling of local resources and attraction of additional internal and international funding. He also voiced his hope that this pioneering experience within the Romanian context would transform the Timisoara area into a point of reference for other Romanian cities and would further »consolidate Timisoara's presence in the international arena«.

In turn, the members of the project coordination team were surprised by the participants' strong identification with the final result of their collective work. Feeling that they themselves had done the lion's share of the job, they were slightly amused to see that everybody else claimed the final report as the result of his or her work. However, they were satisfied that the initial fears that the city administration would abuse the participants' time and expertise had vanished and were replaced by an overall feeling of pride for a job well done.

The success of the project has not only changed the outside perception of the city administration. The project team, mostly based at the city administration's urban development department, also mentioned that, as a result of cooperation during the elaboration of the strategy, the relationships between the different departments of the city administration had improved. They felt that even colleagues whom they had considered narrow-minded in the beginning had started opening up and that they had found reliable partners for future projects in most of the other departments.

Transnational integration of the local economy

Attraction of DFI and OPT have already been described as basic preconditions for the economic integration of post-socialist countries (Eichengreen/Kohl 1998). However, despite a positive start beginning in 2000, the Romanian economy's DFI- and OPT -related degree of transnational integration continues to remain low in comparison with other transition countries. Nevertheless, FIEs employed one-quarter of the labour force from the productive sector, and in 2000 they already accounted for almost half of the country's total exports (Dumitriu/Hunya 2002). FIEs were concentrated in and around the capital, Bucharest, as well as along the western border, especially in Timisoara and Timis County (see Chapter 5.1.3).

Scholars working in the field of regional development recommend two distinct strategies aimed at catching-up in the knowledge economy: development of localised capabilities (Maskell/Eskelinen/Hanniballson/Malmberg/Vatne 1998; Berger/Locke 2001) and attraction of leading innovative enterprises, combined with the development of a publicly supported institutional environment for the enhancement of local learning processes (Eraydin 2002). Yet Romanian economists warn that global integration is not an equivalent to economic development, as it is not irrelevant what types of investments are attracted under which circumstances into which economic domains. Although integration inevitably entails economic dependency, there are different forms and degrees of dependency between which local actors have the opportunity to manoeuvre.

Against this background, institutional factors and a clearly defined own development strategy play an important role (Daianu 2002).

In what follows, I will illustrate three different types of integrative dynamics acting upon Timisoara's local economy. The first example refers to the massive delocalisation of Italian district SMEs to the Timisoara area and the local implications of this process. The second and third examples refer to local efforts directed towards upgrading the position of local enterprises within the framework of international production networks.

Timisoara, nuova provincia veneta

It has already been noted that direct foreign investment and outward processing trade represent important levers for local economic development in post-socialist countries. One of Romania's main European partners for these activities is Italy, a country that emerged as Romania's most important partner for outward processing trade during the 1995–2001 period. Thus Romania ranks second only to China as an exporter of clothing to Italy and comes in first as an exporter of shoes (Stocchiero 2002). During the same period, the accumulated figures for Italian FDI reached 13 per cent of the total FDI invested in Romania. These investments, originated mainly from Italy's industrial districts, which are made up of small- and medium-sized enterprises and accounted for the creation of 10,700 new enterprises in Romania (*http://www.grtv.it/2002/luglio2002/17luglio2002/romania7.htm)*. These dynamics seem unbroken up to the present. Thus more recent surveys conducted by the Romanian Commerce Registry Office speak of 13,000 Italian companies operating in the country (*http://www.ccir.ro/ccir/press/rom/mesager/2003/me_32doc)*.

The mainly »small multinationals« investing in Romania are specialized in »traditional« economic sectors with labour-intensive production, such as textiles and clothing, wood processing and furniture production, and leather processing and footwear production. 80 per cent of them are headquartered in the north-eastern Italian regions (Stocchiero 2002). Their delocalisation to Romania was driven by a series of factors. Against the ongoing demographic decline in the northern Italian industrial districts and the culturally rooted reluctance to accept non-European migrant labour, labour availability and low labour costs generally made south-eastern Europe an attractive site for delocalisation (Stocchiero 2002, Mariotti

2003). Another incentive was set by the availability of raw materials such as wood and leather as well as by more favourable environmental regulations regarding their processing. Not least, geographical proximity and low language barriers singled out Romania as especially suited for a business culture characterised by a hands-on management style and less rigid internal hierarchies (Mariotti 2003). And although irrelevant in the initial phase of delocalisation, incentives offered by the Romanian government for foreign investment enterprises and exporting companies may also have played a role in more recent developments (*http://www.grtv.it/2002/luglio2002/17luglio2002/romania7.htm).*

Its location in the westernmost part of Romania, its relatively good transport infrastructure, the presence of an international airport, as well as local tradition in the light industries and the availability of qualified labour, made Timisoara and Timis County a preferential destination for the delocalisation of Italian district SMEs. Of the ca. 10,000 Italian companies registered in Romania in 2000, over 1,000 – totalling 15,000 employees – were located in Timis County, which Italian industrialists started to consider an extension of the province of Veneto (Adesso 7/2001, La Repubblica 05 March 2003). Statistical data also showed that the most important export destination for products manufactured in Timis County was Italy (CSSR 2000).

The empirical study conducted by Ilaria Mariotti in the Italian district of Montebelluna identified four different management approaches connected to delocalisation. The first companies to delocalise were the »pioneers« driven by international competitive pressures. They were usually bigger than the average district SME and had a well-established market presence. Their delocalisation trends started with industrial subcontracting and continued with the transfer of more qualified activities. However, sales, marketing, and qualified production activities were retained at their headquarters. Another type of company were those »born delocalised« as production sites for goods that were directly exported to third-country markets. These combined industrial subcontracting with commercial subcontracting. A third type of company were those represented by the late delocalisers, which consisted generally of producers of quality products specialised in niche markets. Being especially concerned with quality, these companies only delocalised limited segments of less-sophisticated production. The last type of delocalisers was made up by small suppliers that were forced to follow their contractors abroad in order to survive. Re-localisation seemed successful in all cases, as none of the companies investigated intended to withdraw. According to Mariotti, 60 per cent of the companies involved in delocalisation did not plan to change their policies in the next three years, and 16 per cent even planned to increase the number of their local suppliers.

The transition from industrial subcontracting to commercial subcontracting and the devolvement of increasingly qualified activities needed to be supported by upgrading local infrastructure. Thus the general manager of the shoe manufacturing group Geox, one of the most prominent Italian investors in Timisoara, stated in a newspaper interview that if his company had arrived in Timisoara because of a labour shortage at home, it now needed to invest in infrastructure and education and training in order to preserve its competitive edge (Il Piccolo, 19 January 2002). Similarly, Italian regional officials stated that the era of the pioneers was over and that »institutions had to enter the game and build networks with the banking system« (*http://old.lapadania.com/2002/maggio/16/16052002p11a1.htm*). In this context, the development of local infrastructure involved both establishment of a business-friendly institutional infrastructure and upgrading of physical infrastructure, such as the transport and logistics infrastructure.

The establishment of a business-friendly institutional infrastructure involved a number of different aspects. They consisted of reducing local bureaucracy, safeguarding good access to financial resources, and establishing efficient interest representation organisations. As far as the reduction of local bureaucracy is concerned, the expectations of the Italian business community coincided with the aims of local authorities. Thus the »Five Steps« programme designed to reduce bureaucracy for businesses and launched by the US embassy in Romania was successfully completed by the city of Timisoara, which was awarded the title »five-star-city« in 2000. As a consequence, private investment rose more than fivefold in 2000 as compared to 1999 (Embassy of the United States, 29 January 2001).

Reports in the Italian media confirmed the success of the deregulation programme. It turned out that – apart from low labour costs and favourable taxation conditions for exporting companies – the Italian investors most appreciated the improvements of the business environment that resulted from the »Five Steps« deregulation programme. In an interview with the Italian daily »La Repubblica«, the vice president of the confederation of Italian industrialists stated that it was impossible to find a place in

Italy where a company could be registered within five days and a construction permit obtained within twenty (La Repubblica 2001). Another entrepreneur stated in an interview with the Italian magazine *Adesso* that he was able to set up a company producing domestic electrical equipment within a month in Timisoara (Adesso 7/2001).

The improved business environment encouraged Italian companies to seek long-term engagement in the region. Entrepreneurs from the province of Veneto transferred their regional bank, Banca Veneto, to Timisoara in an effort to recreate their familiar business environment (La Repubblica 2001). The only Romanian regional bank based in the south-western part of the country was taken over by the Padova-based Cardine group (Il Piccolo, 19 January 2002).

As far as the establishment of interest representation organisations is concerned, in 1993 Italian entrepreneurs had already set up the Association of Italian Investors in Romania with the aim of lobbying for support in both Italy and Romania as well as the European Union. Their pressure group even claimed to be more successful than the Romanian government in promoting Romania's EU accession through lobbying activities with European organisations (Adesso 7/2001). However, associative dynamics gained a new momentum in March 2001, when the Association of Italian Industrialists, Confindustria, held its annual meeting in Timisoara. The participation of about 400 Italian entrepreneurs, bankers, business people, and public officials created good opportunities for the promotion of local economic development projects. On this occasion, Confindustria announced its intention to create an official association of Italian entrepreneurs in Romania (La Repubblica 2001). The foundation »Sistema Italia Romania« was created in 2002 as a lobby organisation for both Italian and Romanian companies involved in bilateral trade and other types of economic cooperation. The Italian membership of the foundation was composed of the interest organisations of two industrial branches, the Confederation of Italian manufacturers, Confartigianato, and the National Association of Builders as well as three regionally based interest groups, the Association of the Treviso Industrialists, the Association of the Industrialists from the Provinces of Mantova and Reggio Emilia, and the Union of the Industrialists from Padova and Pordenone (*http://www.grtv.it/2002/luglio2002/17luglio2002/romania7.htm*).

In the same year, Antenna Veneto Romania, an information centre for Italian and Romanian businesses interested in bilateral cooperation, was set up in a collaborative effort by the association of the chambers of commerce of the Veneto region and the CCIAT (Agenda Zilei, 17 February 2002). However, the centre's website was hosted by the Italian partner (*http://www.centroesteroveneto.com/romania*) and contained only information in Italian. Its Italian manager also confirmed in an interview with a local newspaper that although the centre offered the same range of services to both Romanian and Italian businesses, only the latter had profited so far, as the former were »not mature enough to penetrate the Italian market« (Ziua de Vest, 6 June 2003).

The involvement of Italian investors in major infrastructure projects also started with the Confindustria meeting. As far as the physical infrastructure in Timisoara and Timis County is concerned, Italian investors became involved in the project of privatising and modernising Timisoara international airport as well as in the establishment of a logistics centre modelled after the Padovan Interporto. Timisoara international airport has been a disputed issue between the local and the central authorities. The director of the Timis county council's economics department mentioned in a personal interview conducted in autumn 2000 that due to political tensions the central authorities had torpedoed local efforts aiming at the establishment of a Free Economic Zone in and around the airport. Moreover, the State Property Fund, the owner of the Romanian airport operator company, has transferred the debts of two other airports to Timisoara airport, in this way making it less attractive for potential investors.

However, one year later media reports announced the completion of a privatisation deal between the Romanian government on the one hand and the Timis county council and the Italian company Save on the other. According to the privatisation agreement quoted in the media, the Romanian government continued to remain the majority shareholder of the company operating Timisoara airport, retaining 60 per cent of the shares. The remaining 40 per cent were to be divided up between the Italian company and the Timis county council. The Italian company obtained 35 per cent of the shares in return for its 60 per cent contribution to the modernisation costs of the airport. The remaining 5 per cent of the shares became the property of the county council. Modernisation work was scheduled to start in 2001 and last until 2005. This work comprised the building of a new maintenance platform, construction of a new access road to the airport, establishment of a business area, and creation of a commercial centre. It was expected that the passenger numbers would increase from 250,000 a year to over one million a year after the modernisation work was completed (L'Arena, 30 May 2002). More recently, in February 2003, the Romanian state transferred the complete share package for the Timisoara airport operating company to the Timis county council (Government Decision 147/2003).[26]

The Interporto logistics centre represents the second most important investment in the infrastructural upgrading of the Timisoara area. In July 2002, local newspapers announced the birth of the commercial company Interporto Romania. The company's most important shareholders were the Timis county council, the Association of International Transport Companies, the Padovan Interporto, and the Padovan Industrial Zone, as well as the company Save, already involved in the privatisation of the international airport, and the Italian company Monlandys, a member of the Padova-based Peruzzo group (Agenda Zilei, 13 June 2002). It was planned to handle about 500 thousand tons of merchandise per year and to offer integrated logistics services ranging from storage and parking to maintenance and restaurants (Newsletter 26/2003). For the first four years, the vice president of the Timis county council and the manager of Monlandys were designated president and vice president of the company's board of administration (Agenda Zilei, 24 February 2002).

However, the Interporto project was contested in both Romania and Italy, and both the Romanian and Italian decision-makers involved were accused by the media of clientelism and rent-seeking (Confidential, 24–30 June 2002, L'opinione, 26–31 March 2003). A major issue of dispute was the location of the future logistics centre.

The idea to create a logistics centre in the neighbourhood of Timisoara was launched in 1998 by an Italian entrepreneur involved in transport and logistics operations in Timisoara for several years. He discussed the matter with several prominent members of the Italian business community, who jointly agreed on to conduct a feasibility study, which they intended to submit to the president of the Timis county council. Having obtained official support from the Veneto region, the support of both local and central authorities in Romania, as well as a favourable opinion from the European Union, the project initiator went ahead by founding a shareholding com-

26 This development might be interpreted as proof of the improvement of the relationship between the central government and the Timis county council as a consequence of the fact that the governing party also has the majority of the seats in the council.

pany and obtaining a concession for 150 hectares of public land located in a village on the northern limits of Timisoara. Meanwhile, another participant at the initial meeting of Italian businesspeople had developed an alternative plan for a logistics centre. He bought 30 hectares of land situated on the southern limits of Timisoara and secured financial support for his plan through discussions with high-level officials from the Italian government.

At this point the initiator of the project intervened by arguing that the northern location would be more favourable for both the city of Timisoara, which would avoid the heavy traffic, and the transport companies, as the logistics centre would be closer to the airport and the roads and railways linking Timisoara to western Europe. Despite its dysfunctionalities, it was the southern project that was finally adopted, obtaining financial support from the Italian authorities (L'opinione, 26–31 March 2003).

Obviously, land-price speculation and mobilisation of high-level political support played a role in the case of the Italian investors. Local political tensions between the city of Timisoara and the neighbouring commune of Giroc also contributed to this outcome. These tensions were created by the reluctance of the smaller settlement's mayor to accept the functional hierarchy between Timisoara and Giroc, by disputes associated with the division of public land situated between the two settlements, and, not least, by the different approaches to local politics and local development represented by the two mayors.

The profile of the mayor of Timisoara and the policy model represented by him have already been discussed in Chapter 5.6.1. The profile of the mayor of Giroc, a graduate of Timisoara Technical University who opted for a career in local politics after the bankruptcy of his personal business, and because of his political affiliation with the party dominating the county council (*http://www.vip2000.banat.ro*), shows a lot of similarities with the profile of the mayor of the other rural settlement described in the above-mentioned chapter. So does his policy model, as becomes obvious from his version of the story of the future Interporto:

»There was a place in the outskirts of the village called ›Schubert's ditch‹. The former owner, a German named Schubert, emigrated to Germany and people used to take their waste there. Until I started thinking on what to do to have the people satisfied and talked to a nephew of mine, who happens to be a real estate agent, and I asked him, what about some propaganda in order to find a buyer for that piece of land.[27] And he told me that he had already tried, but nobody wanted it and I urged him to go on. We both kept looking for a buyer and there was this girl, a former student of mine, [...], who was first involved in the taxi-affair, but then got a job with the chamber of commerce.[28] She put me on the computer with this offer and then some Italians arrived there and said that they intended to build a concrete factory and asked for somebody willing to sell land. Some of the land was owned by a guy who used to work here at the mayor's office as an accountant, and he knew what he knew, so that the land was finally sold to the Italian company Incontro General Beton, and the guy became a partner. And they started building [hangars] and this nephew of mine brought the one and the other and this is how the whole thing came into being. It started developing, but as we didn't want chaotic development we called the whole thing industrial zone. But one cannot just call anything industrial zone, as it is tremendously difficult to get arable land out from agricultural use, and then I thought about a zonal urban development plan, but this was very expensive. But then it turned out that the Italians are willing to pay for it, so we had it done and got through with the change of the land use. ADETIM[29] came with the idea to call the place an industrial park and [...] now we proudly present it to every potential investor.

[...] At present we are about to start a magnificent project, a project never ever mentioned around here, not in a big city and not even on the national level. The initiators are a circle of businesspeople from our commune, what does it matter if they are Italians or locals?! [...] I get on well with the Italians, they adore me, they invite me everywhere. [...] They have all sorts of companies here, constructions, clothing, machine building, construction materials, shoes and other 40 hectares, I don't know exactly what. Anyway, I gave my general agreement, but the urban development certificate is issued by the county council, so I have to pass by, have a beer, have a coke, and find out what's going on there«.

In spite of the controversies associated with its location, the Timis county council and the Timisoara authorities seem to have found a formula for cooperation on the Interporto issue: linking the construction of the logistics centre to the building of a by-pass road for heavy traffic (Ziua de Vest, 03 March 2003). The prestige of the Interporto project and its pioneering quality in the Romanian context may also have played a role. But as the by-

27 Land owned by people willing to emigrate was expropriated by the Romanian state prior to 1989. After the establishment of local self-government, these pieces of land became communal land, and thus the mayor was entitled to look for buyers for them.

28 The »taxi-affair« refers to the attempted MEBO privatisation of the state-owned taxi company in Timisoara. The privatisation process was initiated by the company's chief accountant, who left the company after the failure of the privatisation project and set up his own small business. Later on he became president of the Association of Small Entrepreneurs and vice president of the Timisoara chamber of commerce.

29 ADETIM is the development agency of Timis County.

pass road was planned to cut through the commune of Giroc, the animosities between Giroc and Timisoara continued. The mayor of Giroc initiated a local referendum concerning the status of the settlement, which he wanted changed from commune to city. He also tried to build up stronger political support by migrating from the Liberal Party to the governing post-socialists. At the same time, the Timisoara authorities supported the efforts of the village of Chisoda, now part of the commune of Giroc, which wanted to become an independent administrative unit (Ziua de Vest, 03 March 2003).

The overall development process that led to this final outcome gives rise to a number of questions. Obviously, the delocalisation of Italian district SMEs to the Timisoara area emerged from the districts' internal dynamics and was not a consequence of local efforts to attract DFI. All along the delocalisation process the Italian business community had come up with all the major initiatives, to which the local authorities had only reacted, albeit benevolently. One of the main reasons for this asymmetrical relationship is the lack of funding and competences of local authorities in Romania. The example of the airport privatisation has shown that there had also been local development initiatives, but that they were blocked by the central authorities. As in many other cases, transnational cooperation once again became an instrument of local emancipation from the central state.

However, the example of the Interporto has also shown that local authorities themselves are neither free from infighting, nor immune to clientelistic incentives. Especially within the framework of an asymmetrically constructed transnational relationship, local vulnerabilities can easily be used by the more influential external partner to his or her own ends. The bigger the investments and the wider the range of the contributors – local, regional, national, and European in the case of the Interporto – to their funding, the higher the risks for the creation of fata morgana-like projects used only for rent-seeking, as in the case of the Italian mezzogiorno (L'opinione, 26–31 March 2003).

Another important aspect of this transnational relationship has to do with learning. It is anticipated that during the cooperation process the initially inferior partner will acquire skills and knowledge, so that the initially asymmetrical relationship will become more balanced over time. The delocalisation of increasingly qualified activities by the Italian SMEs serves as evidence for the fact that learning occurs at the level of individual enterprises. However, it is only individuals who benefit from this dynamic. The Italian companies in the Timisoara area form closed clusters. They have established their own support institutions, which they use exclusively. They do not use local suppliers or customers, not to mention local research facilities.

Additionally, newly trained local experts, who could set up their own small businesses and thus build bridges between the expatriate clusters and the local environment, usually opt for different career paths. Research by Italian social scholars shows that Italian investment in the SME sector in Romania has also resulted in strong migratory trends from the receiving to the sending area (Stocchiero 2002). However, the well-established presence of Italian companies and the infrastructure investments involved will continue to provide jobs and opportunities for learning for many individuals in the future. They will also offer the local authorities a model for a development path they could take up, support, and eventually try to imitate.

Technological innovation and localised learning

The example of the delocalisation of Italian district SMEs to the Timisoara area has already pointed up a number of important aspects associated with the integration of a local economy into international production networks under the circumstances created by political and economic transformation. However, the example also makes clear that the dynamic of integration has mostly been determined by the needs of the delocalising companies. The following examples will seek to modify the perspective of the investigation. The first example, concerned with IT development, examines the extent to which local actors are able to attract DFI to locally prioritised domains. The second example, concerned with an industrial branch looking back on a long local tradition, analyses the extent to which localised capabilities create more favourable terms for integration into international production networks.

Local actors in technological innovation

The general aim of the Timisoara area development strategy was defined as the pursuit of prosperity and a high quality of life for the city's inhabitants based on a presentation of Timisoara as a strategic competitive urban centre that adheres to European standards (Primaria Timisoara 2000: 114). To achieve competitiveness, the strategy suggested that scientific research should be stimulated and that support should be provided for businesses engaged in hardware and software development, telecommunications, automation, and development of additional technical equipment (Primaria Timisoara 2000: 118pp.).

Technical education/training and research could look back upon a certain tradition in Timisoara. In 1906, Dr. Ede Telbisz, the mayor of the city at that time, undertook some initial efforts aimed at founding a technical university,. Even though his petition to the government in Budapest was rejected, the intellectual elite of the region enthusiastically supported the idea of a local university, which then materialised when the city was incorporated into Greater Romania. Technical University of Timisoara was founded in 1920. During the inter-war period it trained more than 2,000 engineers and gained a European reputation (Munteanu/Munteanu 1998: 242).

At present, Timisoara is home to four reputable universities and 24 academic research institutes (Chapter 5.5.1). Additionally, Timisoara universities have played a pioneering role in the development and introduction of information technologies. The first Romanian computers were developed at Technical University of Timisoara, and in 1992 West University was the first Romanian university to go on-line and establish an inter-university network. Their capacity to generate solid know-how and technical expertise made the Timisoara universities attractive not only for talented students from all over the country but also for multinational investors. According to the Internet site of the computer and software engineering department of Technical University, the department now cooperates with companies like Siemens, Motorola, Alcatel, and IBM (Ilyes 2001b, 2003).

Despite operating conditions that are often precarious (Primaria Timisoara 2000: 81), the personal and professional standards of the teaching staff and the commitment these persons feel towards the university's reputation have contributed to upholding internationally competitive professional training standards. »I had no single student whom I ›exported‹ come back to me and complain that he did not learn enough in my classes«, a professor from Technical University proudly claimed in a personal interview. Foreign investors agreed with his view. A representative of the largest multinational investor in Timisoara stated in a newspaper interview that his company chose Timisoara as a site for investment because

»there is an excellent technical university producing graduates who are first class, even if their facility is not« (Electronics Time, 15 May 2000).

Under these circumstances, attraction of FDI to the IT sector entails not only the promise of integration into the emerging knowledge-based economy but also a hope for spillover effects and backward linkages. However, in considering the latter aspect, we have to bear in mind the hierarchical stratification of the world-wide IT sector. Thus not only has software production become disconnected from hardware production, the industry's entire value chain has broken down into constituent functions that can be contracted out to independent producers located anywhere in the global economy (Borrus/Zysman 1998: 27).

MNCs like ABB, Alcatel, Philips, Siemens, or Solectron, with investments ranging from 1.5 million to 150 million dollars, were already present in Timisoara (Primaria Timisoara 2000: 58, România libera 20 February 2001). Apart from these investors, over 50 small- and medium-sized software companies were operating in the city (Ilyes 2001: 2). But despite the growing number of IT companies, it would have been misguided to expect the emergence of an integrated IT cluster with an overall positive influence on the entire community.

In view of the country's low degree of penetration by modern technologies, most of these MNCs came to Romania with the aim of opening up new consumer markets (Avery 2000). Impressed by the low labour and production costs as well as by the local staff's competitiveness, these firms started engaging in productive activities as well (Avery 2000, România libera, 16 November 2000). The world's largest - and US-based - electronics manufacturing company started out with operations in Timisoara in 1999, opening a »state-of-the-art manufacturing campus« in 2000 (*http://www.solectron.com*). Even though the company's representatives denied having obtained extra facilities from local and central authorities, and explained that their decision was motivated by »the demand for low-cost, high-volume manufacturing in Europe« as well as by the presence of »a well-educated, highly motivated and dedicated workforce«, the company gained the support of local authorities in purchasing land and obtaining tax privileges from the central government.[30] In turn, the company promised to hire a certain number of people, thus contributing to the local authorities' fight against unemployment.

30 Government Decision 372, published in Official Gazette 207/2000.

This cooperation was initially successful. The company extended its facilities and was planning to develop the Timisoara plant into its eastern European regional centre, while some of its most important customers, like Philips and Siemens, started setting up shop in Timisoara, and others, like Ericsson, announced their intention to follow suit. In an atmosphere of general euphoria, new employees were hired non-stop and the local authorities took the first steps towards founding a technology park to accommodate the growing electronics sector.

But at this point only the MNCs would have profited from the synergies created by a technology park. None of the MNCs worked with local suppliers. This was not surprising because most local start-ups were engaged in software development, while both the world-wide leader and the companies it had attracted moved only their assembly lines to Romania. Of the 4,200 Romanians employed by the leading electronics company, the highest position was held by the manager of the human resources department at the time of my investigation (2000). Neither training and R&D nor marketing and strategy departments were located in Timisoara. Even if most employees were high school graduates, the human resources manager confided in a personal interview that the company's requirements were in fact extremely low: ability to read simple texts and perform simple mathematical operations with up to two-digit numbers, as well as an age between 18 and 35 years. Apart from assembly line operations, there were no other professional training courses or career opportunities available for employees. It was mainly from intra-company exchanges with non-Romanian plants that employees learnt how discriminatory their working hours were – 12-hour shifts and wages of up to 150 US dollars per month, depending on personal performance. A union movement that was formed to fight for a better working environment and higher wages was suppressed by management. The whole local political establishment unanimously supported the suppression of the union, fearing that worker militancy would scare away further investors.

Even though the local authorities supported the company in every possible way, in February 2001 they were confronted with the dismissal of 16 per cent of the work force at the Timisoara plant. The company justified its decision with reference to the general recession in the world-wide IT market. Furthermore, it had lost Ericsson as a customer, which meant that Ericsson also dropped its plans to invest in the future Timisoara technology park. As no Romanian employees were involved in decision-making processes, it was hard to tell from Timisoara whether and to what extent the situation was due to world-wide recession or a result of strategic management mistakes. The local community had no possibilities to intervene either. Like the dismissed workers, some of whom had invested up to 1,000 dollars in bribes to be hired by the company, the local authorities could only hope that the company would stick to its investment plans and start hiring again if the international situation changed.

Operating in a different segment of the IT value chain, local start-ups were not affected by these events. However, prospects for the establishment of independent local software industries were poor. There was no local research institution in the field of software development. Software developers further complained that they were taught only to write code at university, not to develop programmes. As a consequence, the local IT industry lacked the capacity to develop complex systems, and it was therefore used by Western companies only for outsourcing activities (Ilyes 2001: 2). Each company had its own, almost exclusively foreign, clients and operated only in the small market segment it had succeeded in opening up for itself. Although many people engaged in the sector knew each other from the computer high school or the university and informally supported each other when it came to dealing with professional problems, there were no company strategies directed at jointly attracting important customers or helping each other out in cases involving strict deadlines, or even in founding an association to represent common interests.

Even though Timisoara has become increasingly integrated into IPNs, upgrading its position seemed improbable for the near future. There was no integrated approach to technology development or absorption, and there were no institutions to mediate exchanges between industry and academia. Thus cooperation-based relationships remained only ad hoc, mediated by certain professors or graduates. If companies chose to establish a long-term relationship with a university department, the aim was restricted to providing students with specific skills needed by the companies in exchange for equipment.

There was no demand from local industries, either. »Cooperation between the university and the economy is almost nonexistent. The old economy doesn't need us anymore and the new economy hasn't realised how much we can offer them«, stated a professor from Technical University in a personal interview. He could only refer to one case in which his department had done some small research and testing jobs for an Italian company. The cooperation was mediated by former students employed by the company and was mainly viewed as a sideline opportunity for professors. My interview partner summed the matter up as follows: »We were laughing about how much they gave us for it and they were laughing about how little we expected – that's how it is«.The Timisoara area development strategy also stated that academic research was in decline in relation to both the quality and the quantity of the work done. Even more alarming, student participation in research activities had decreased significantly, while academic staff was becoming engaged more in lucrative sideline jobs than in badly paid and time-consuming research activities (Primaria Timisoara 2000: 81).

In my interview partner's opinion, this situation resulted from the authoritarian, centralist, and quantity- rather than quality-oriented Romanian education system. University curricula were generally not in line with labour market requirements. But if the head of a given department wanted to adjust his department's curriculum, he would have to go through never-ending bureaucratic procedures to obtain the approval of the overall »university caste system«, finally failing in the face of the resistance of his colleagues, who would fear income losses as a consequence of curriculum changes.[31]

Even though there may be no lack of professional competence, a coherent research and marketing strategy would certainly help to realize synergy and spillover effects within the computer science department, between the different departments of Technical University, and within the overall academic setting. Instead, the dynamics of an incessant brain-drain have been established. Companies recruit their staff from the lower-level staff of the computer science department, while the department recruits its staff from among the Ph.D. students of other departments. Young professionals emigrate once they have acquired some basic professional experience, thus closing the brain-drain circuit.

31 Their fears were reasonable to the extent that a person teaching at a Romanian university is paid proportionally to the number of his or her students. This regulation makes it almost impossible to reduce the number of students enrolled in obsolete subjects to improve specialisation profiles. Lack of funding for the acquisition of costly laboratory equipment further hinders up-to-date specialisation.

Tradition and modernism in the clothing industry[32]

The development of the textile and clothing industry started in Timisoara in the 18th century, when the mercantilist policies of the Habsburg rulers led to the establishment of the first manufactories. The first felt manufactory was built in 1727. Later it became the centre of a whole chain of manufactories producing foodstuffs, textiles, and various other consumer goods. In 1848 two weaving-mills were registered in Timisoara. At the turn of the century the local textile industry comprised seven big enterprises employing 492 workers. A significant part of the 33,683 individual craftsmen registered were also active in this field.

The development of the sector continued after the First World War. An analysis of the Timisoara Chamber of Commerce and Industry showed that textile industries had the highest investment rates of all local industries in 1938. Twenty-eight big textile enterprises were operating in the city at the time, 26 of them joint ventures with foreign capital participation. It is noteworthy that the high shares of foreign investment involved were not a mere reflection of Timisoara's incorporation into Greater Romania. Czechoslovakian and Canadian investors, who had no traditional links to the region, were present in the sector along with German, Austrian, and Jewish investors.

In 1948 the big textile factories were nationalised. The smaller craftsmen's businesses were either suppressed or incorporated into socialist production units. Both textile and clothing industries continued to account for substantial shares of local industrial production under communist rule (Munteanu/Munteanu 1998: 145–151). The present dynamic of the sector is mostly determined by OPT directed to the European Union.

In trying to understand the local impact of OPT, we have to bear in mind that, as in the case of IT industries, IPNs have also altered the global organisation of textile and clothing industries. The application of modern telecommunication networks in the sector contributed not only to the separation of textile production from garment production but also to the separation of capital-intensive, pre-assembly activities from labour-intensive assembly activities within the garment production process (Graziani 1998: 247). These developments triggered specific relocation trends within the EU's textile and clothing sectors. More capital- and technology-inten-

32 The phrase »tradition and modernism« is taken from the site of the company ModaTim, http://www.modatim.ro.

sive processes that characterise textile production usually remain within the EU. This is also a consequence of the fact that OPT regulations require that the fabrics sent to the subcontractor must be of EU origin. Pre-assembly activities like designing, grading and marking of patterns, and cutting also tend to remain localised. The reasons for this are twofold: some tasks like cutting grow more capital-intensive through automation, while others, like design, draw on localised capabilities in order to remain up-to-date and thus competitive (Graziani 1998: 247–248). It is therefore mainly labour-intensive activities like assembly that are relocated.

This dynamic has a number of negative consequences for the relocation sites. As OPT requires the use of textiles produced in the EU, it prevents the development of local textile industries and makes backward linkages impossible. It also induces a double-edged dependence on foreign partners, with regard to both input and output. Furthermore, it can lead to a lasting downgrading of R&D, financing, and marketing functions, resulting in a lock-in in labour-intensive activities (Graziani 1998: 250).

However, it was also mentioned that IPNs give local enterprises the possibility to move up in the value chain if they succeed in absorbing technologies and upgrading local skills. To illustrate this statement, I will consider the example of the company ModaTim, formerly Bega, which developed into a flagship of local development in Timisoara's clothing sector.

ModaTim, then Bega, was founded in 1959 via a merger of the most important tailor shops in operation at that time in Timisoara. In the following years the company became one of the biggest producers of ladies' garments in Romania. It benefited from Ceausescu's liberalisation policies in the 1970s, which enabled it to raise technological production standards and to enter Western markets as a subcontractor to Austrian, Italian, French, Canadian, and US companies (*http://www.modatim.ro/fisiere_history.html*). A stable and very committed management as well as good cooperation with the local vocational school for textile industries helped to build an international reputation for the company as a reliable and quality-conscious sub-contractor. Thus the company never ran short of contracts and also succeeded in hiring the most competitive local staff, as its good reputation helped employees to set up small, informal tailor shops as sideline businesses.

The revolution did not alter this situation substantially. Given the company's good economic situation, its management had already undertaken some initial efforts to privatise the company through a management-employee buy-out in 1993. After months of bureaucratic struggles with different privatisation bodies, the privatisation contracts were signed in February 1994. Bega was one of the first privatised companies in Timisoara at that time. The near 500 shareholders became full owners of the company in 1998, when payments to the State Property Fund were completed. In spite of political turmoil and severe economic decline, the company showed remarkable stability with regard to management and staff as well as economic output throughout this period. After the death of the general manager, who had held his position for more than 20 years and whose personal commitment had substantially contributed to the success of the privatisation, the shareholders decided to preserve stability by unanimously electing the former director's son to the general manager's position. The young man returned from Sweden, where he was pursuing a Ph.D. in computer science, and took over the company. Thus a formerly state-owned enterprise, created from the forced merger of family businesses, became a family business again.

The new management tried to diversify the company's production with a view to breaking out of the pattern of labour-intensive subcontracting. Still, lohn-operations for prestigious Western brands like Betty Barclay and Gil Brett continued to represent the company's »cash-cow«. But it also moved into more complex operations. Thus ModaTim profited from the bankruptcy of a Belgian client who had made deliveries to a British mail-order business and succeeded in taking over development of the entire product line for the British company. This meant design, procurement, cutting, assembly and delivery. Encouraged by the success, ModaTim upgraded its in-house technological facilities and hired a British agent in the hope of acquiring similar contracts. The company also developed a brand of its own, »Chic&Cher«, which it launched in the domestic market through its own chain of stores. If in 1999 85 per cent of the company's revenues were generated by lohn operations, this share had already decreased to 60 per cent in 2000. In 2000 direct exports to the British market generated 30 per cent of the company's revenues and the remaining share, 10 per cent, was generated through sales of the company's own brand in the domestic market (*http://www.gtz.de/dokumente/AKZ/eng/AKZ_2001_WBF/13–romania.pdf*).

Asked about the company's long-term strategy, the general manager referred to three distinct, strategic directions. His strongest hopes were pinned on direct exports to Western markets. After the initial success in

Great Britain, ModaTim planned to make an inroad into the German markets, where it enjoyed a good reputation as a subcontractor. However, lohn operations were also part of the company's strategy, as long as they generated steady revenues without requiring additional investments or marketing efforts. Most of the difficulties, but also the most challenges, involved were associated with the development of the company's own brand. Although the »Chic&Cher« line has reached its target-group, young professional women in management positions, it proved too expensive for the Romanian market, as it was produced exclusively from imported materials. While hoping that the incomes of Romanian professional women would increase, ModaTim also tried to reach potential customers in the Czech and Hungarian markets.

ModaTim's history and employment patterns alike suggest that the company has a considerable body of tacit knowledge incorporated in its staff. An average ModaTim employee was given his or her first contact with the company while in vocational school. He or she was hired after graduation and looked forward to a steady, life-long career with the company. Staff commitment is additionally generated by above-average wages and by the fact that almost half of the staff are also shareholders in the company. The high wages are justified by ModaTim's good performance. »It's not a good thing if a seamstress comes to the factory preoccupied by how she's going to feed her children or pay her electricity bill. Then of course she won't be able to concentrate on her job«, the general manager stated in a personal interview.

Although both benefits and stable employment prospects helped the company to attract a committed staff, education and training remained the cornerstones of the company's human resource policies. The cooperation-based relations between the clothing factory and the MIU vocational school in Timisoara extend over a period of more than 25 years. At present, ModaTim also acts as an advisor for the development of the school's new curricula, and this enables students to acquire the skills most sought after by the company. Additionally, the company's staff regularly takes part in training courses organised by the local chamber of commerce. ModaTim also participates in a partnership with the German company Pfaff, which offers training courses on the maintenance of sewing machines. The general manager expressed further interest in the establishment of similar partnerships for the training of cutters and graders (*http://www.gtz.de/dokumente/AKZ/eng/Akz-2001_WBF/13-romania.pdf*). Asked about the company's position in the local business environment, the general manager referred to good cooperation with CCIAT, which had helped ModaTim to contact potential new clients and suppliers. The CCIAT was also a valuable source of information on domestic and European legislation, and it had supported ModaTim's participation in international fairs. The management was also involved in the CCIAT's lobbying activities for the improvement of the local business environment and regularly participated in the meetings organised with representatives of local authorities. The general manager was more or less satisfied with cooperation on the local level and regarded his company as only marginally affected by the insecurity of the Romanian business environment. In contrast to other Romanian enterprise managers, who complained that it was nearly impossible to obtain credits, ModaTim's manager complained about an »assault« of local banks seeking to become involved with the company. Thanks to its good performance, the company had no trouble obtaining the re-technologisation credits it needed to expand the company's operations. With a certain degree of financial stability, the company was also able to defend itself in court against exaggerated claims of state control bodies. In the manager's perception, the representatives of these bodies were always seeking to impose taxes and fines on companies, irrespective of the groundedness of their claims, speculating that the company would prefer to pay than to shoulder the burden of an intricate legal case. But if a company can afford the time and money involved, its chances of defending itself in court are fairly good. Cooperation with the customs office was also perceived as improving, though still difficult. However, the main reason for relative satisfaction with the local business environment was not the latter's performance but ModaTim's »position at the periphery of the Romanian economic system«. Only a small share of the company's production was directed to the domestic market, and this share was marketed directly through the company's own stores. The company had neither domestic clients nor domestic suppliers. When asked if the company intended to involve local partners in its operations, the general manager replied by describing a situation very similar to the »communist hell«:

»I can't force them to get involved. If they want to get involved, they should bring their factories up-to-date and produce the quality we require. And not only the quality, also the design and the style that we need and then we will gladly buy from Romanian companies. Right now, our quality requirements are not met. And if the quality is there, the price is too high and if both quality and price correspond, then the people lack seriousness. I ask for a colour and they deliver another, I ask for a delivery date and the delivery is delayed – one cannot build a business relationship this way and we prefer to work with foreign companies«.

Issues like jointly investing in the training of designers, not to mention research or technology centres, with a view to further improving fabric quality was not a concern for ModaTim. When I insinuated that what seemed to be a lack of seriousness in the behaviour of Romanian companies might result from pressures generated by the business environment, ModaTim's general manager briefly retorted that he did not know and that the behaviour of other companies did not concern him.

Under these circumstances it is rather unlikely that ModaTim will become a »technology gatekeeper« (Bell/Albu 1999: 1726) for the local textile sector in the near future. Although the company benefited from extensive counselling from Swiss and German government development agencies and seems to possess solid knowledge, it seems rather reluctant to share it with other local companies, which it perceives more as competitors than as potential partners.

Urban governance in transnational contexts

The last two cases address issues of urban governance and focus on public service and welfare provision. It has already been stated that urban governance is qualitatively different from the small-scale reproduction of the national transformation regime and represents a new form of policy-making emerging on the local level. Different local responses serve to respond to the challenge of transnationalisation, seen as both the option and obligation to act simultaneously in different political, economic, and legal arenas that go beyond the borders and regulatory capacities of the nation state. These depend on the general framework for local action defined by the nation state, incentives set by supranational bodies such as the EU, as well as soft factors such as local identity, local skills in negotiating with supra-local organisations, and locally set priorities. In what follows I will illustrate the risks of and opportunities for local development posed by the context of transnationalisation, using the privatisation of Timisoara's drinking water network and the elaboration and implementation of the city administration's elderly care project as cases in point.

The privatisation of the drinking water network

The most important chapters of Timisoara's history are mirrored in the construction and development of the city's drinking water network. After the Habsburg re-conquest in 1716, Timisoara and the Banat became a test-field for Vienna's mercantilist development policies aimed at administrative inclusion and stimulation of economic growth. Under these circumstances, infrastructure development, mainly road building and hydrological systematisation, became a priority. Canalisation work on the river Bega, which had periodically flooded the city until then, began in 1728. The city of Timisoara was rebuilt from the ground up, becoming »little Vienna«, a small-scale copy of the imperial capital as regards urban development. Beginning as early as 1732, it was equipped with a drinking water network consisting of eight pipes and a clearing station (Munteanu/Munteanu 1998: 62).

For a long time, Timisoara was to remain one of the very few settlements of the region with drinking water provision. The Banat's incorporation into Romania and the establishment of communist rule had hardly any impact on drinking water provision in the region. In 1965 Timisoara was among the three settlements of Timis County that had a drinking water supply system, the largest part of which dates back to Habsburg times. Under communist rule, this system was extended to 91 settlements. At the same time, extensive industrialisation led to severe degradation of groundwater quality. The ambivalence of socialist modernisation also became evident in the fact that newer parts of the pipe network were constructed with materials that - a consequence of the economy of shortage - were not in keeping with technical and hygienic pipework standards.

In 1995, 108 settlements in Timis County benefited from drinking water provision. The length of the network reached almost 1,500 km as compared to only 200 km in 1965 (Munteanu/Munteanu 1998: 96). In 2000, the drinking water provision system in Timisoara consisted of a 552 km long network that supplied 20,780 households in the city (Primaria Timisoara 2000: 51). Although it covered almost the entire population, it was common knowledge throughout the city that the water delivered from taps was not drinking water. A short analysis published by the city administration admitted that one third of the network was in urgent need of rehabilitation. An additional problem was the treatment station, which was unable to handle severely polluted industrial waste-waters (Primaria Timisoara 2000).

This situation resulted in an urgent need for intervention on the part of the city's local government, that is, the authority responsible for drinking water provision on the local level. After the administrative reform of 1991, when local government bodies were created, public service provision at the local level was included among the competences of local self-government. The law on local public administration, Law 69/1991, stated that »the public services of the commune or town shall be organised by the local council, in the principal domains of activity, according to the local character and needs, with observance of the legal provisions, and within the limits of the financial means available to the council« (art. 54, sect. 2).

Starting from this point, the public service provision competences of local government bodies were gradually extended. The law on local public finance, Law 189/1998, stated that local councils were responsible for the financing, establishment, and monitoring of public service provision on the local level. In the most recent step so far, the law on public service provision, Law 326/2001, gives local authorities »the exclusive competence to establish, organise, coordinate, monitor and control local public service provision« (art 12, line 1).

Unfortunately, devolution of competences to the local level was not accompanied by an adequate transfer of financial resources. Since local government bodies did not have any independent sources of revenue until 1998, the building, maintenance, and repair of roads, water supply and sewage systems, heating systems, and public transport facilities continued to be financed by earmarked transfers from the central budget (*http://www sinta.ro/RNE/cartax2.htm*). The situation changed with the adoption of the law on local public finance in 1998. However, most local government bodies were still unable to finance local public service provision from their own revenues. The law therefore gave them the right to concede local public service provision to specialised commercial operators if the concession contributed to increased efficiency and benefited the citizens in the end. This right was further extended. The law on local public service provision adopted in 2001 states that local public services should be provided either by a specialised branch of local public administration or by a commercial operator selected by the local council. The operating costs of local public service provision have to be covered jointly through contributions of end-users and special taxes, which, however, are not further specified. The law also states that all public service operators, be they private or public, need to be certified by a national authority, which can withdraw operating licenses if activities are not in keeping with the standards or do not meet the terms of agreements concluded with local councils (art 23, line 4, point h).

As already mentioned, the treatment station and one-third of the drinking water provision network needed to be rehabilitated in order to improve the quality of drinking water in Timisoara. Obviously, the local budget could not provide the funding necessary for these works. Although central government provided subsidies to support drinking water provision for the population, it did not share out funds for local infrastructure investments. However, it contracted a 28 million US Dollar loan from the EBRD's (European Bank for Reconstruction and Development) Municipal Utilities Development Programme in 1995. It on-lent the funds from this loan to five Romanian municipalities (EBRD 1997). Among others, Timisoara's municipal water-related service provider, Aquatim, received funding from this programme.

Rehabilitation work was started with the help of this loan, but more funding was needed to complete the task. Thus Timisoara had to consider possibilities of attracting foreign direct investment to its drinking water provision network.[33] As EBRD officials were satisfied with Aquatim's performance, the EBRD subsequently provided the municipality with a 24.7 million euro loan in December 1999 under the condition that a controlling stake in Aquatim be sold to a »water operator of international standing«. The reason why the bank introduced this condition was that this was a case without precedent in Romania, »the first non-sovereign loan to a utility that has previously received only a sovereign-guaranteed loan« (EBRD 1999). Additionally, Romanian legislation enabling local govern-

33 Timisoara was no singular case in this respect. The municipalities of Bucuresti and Ploiesti had also concessioned their water and sewerage systems. In both cases, the world-wide market leader, Vivendi, obtained full control over the municipal waterworks after a public tender organised with World Bank support. At present Vivendi holds 100 per cent of the local companies operating in Bucuresti and 80 per cent of those in Ploiesti (Lobina 2001: 34–35).

ment bodies to contract credits on the international financial markets was not completed at that time.

The loan was issued under the Multi-Project Facility programme set up by Suez-Lyonnaise des Eaux and the EBRD in 1995 (Lobina 2001: 34). Therefore it was not surprising that the investor selected by the local council was none other than Suez-Lyonnaise des Eaux, which received a 25-year concession in November 2000. This decision raised many objections. On the one hand, local councillors objected that a public utility company, which was not only generating local income through its successful operations but also receiving government subsidies, should be given away (Timisoara 16. September 2000). On the other hand, it was pointed out that Suez-Lyonnaise des Eaux was »forced upon« the municipality by the EBRD, having been selected without the concession being put out to tender. The mayor of Timisoara countered these objections by arguing that the privatisation was necessary, as the municipality would not have been able to finance the urgently needed restoration work without the private-public partnership thus created. One approach thought to hold promise of savings of time and money was consultations with interested investors instead of a public tender .

Under the contract, Aquatim was transformed into a public-private joint venture, 51 per cent owned by the water multi and 49 per cent by the municipality. In exchange for the controlling stake, Suez-Lyonnaise des Eaux was to contribute 6 million euros to increase the company's capital base. The investment programme was to be financed by an EBRD loan over the duration of the concession (Suez-Lyonnaise des Eaux 2000). These investments were also eligible for additional funding under the European Union's ISPA[34] programme. In August 2002, media reports announced that Aquatim had obtained a 34.1 million euro grant from the European Union, and that a public tender for the execution of the construction and rehabilitation work was to be organised in the following months. The work was scheduled to start in January 2003 and to last until 2008 (România Libera, 6 August 2002). At the same time, there were ongoing discussions between the local authorities and the representatives of the water multinational, who would have liked to fully take over Aquatim under the new circumstances.

34 Instruments for Structural Policies for Pre-Accession.

For the case under study, both transformation and Europeanization have a double impact. As a consequence of the transformation process, local societies were able to become political actors and articulate their interests through elected local government bodies. However, this process took place under the conditions of a global redefinition the role of cities (Bennett 1997; Bagnasco/Le Galès 2000). Cities were redefined as economic actors, with growth and economic success becoming the main goals of local government (Mayer 2000). This new perception of the role of local government brought entailed a tendency to outsource municipal service provision to commercial operators (Lorrain 2000) – a tendency that also left its impact in Timisoara.

The specific – centrally mediated – quality of the opening-up process had additional negative consequences for the case under study. The unilateral retreat of the state from the public service provision sector and its reluctance to provide local government bodies with the local sources of revenue they need to finance their new tasks created conditions that sharply restricted the choices of local actors. The lack of legislation that would have enabled them to act freely in the international arena put further restrictions on their options. Thus, even though the privatisation of the drinking water provision network may be seen as a consequence of global pressures, the unfavourable terms of the agreement have internal causes.

The city administration's elderly care project

Another consequence of globalisation on the urban level is the fact that while urban space continue to be functionally and economically shared, they at the same time become increasingly segregated in social terms and growingly differentiated in cultural terms (Mayer, 2000: 256–258). Under these circumstances, unitary welfare provision by authorities is replaced by more fragmented structures with increased involvement of local businesses and other private and voluntary organisations. Social welfare measures thus become an arena of struggle, and they are implemented in a fragmented fashion, mainly via extractions from investors.

Local struggles over social welfare measures may result either in more divisive or in more responsive and accountable versions of the new local [state. However, in both cases the role of the local authority is changed fundamentally. Instead of being the main provider of social services, it redefines its role as enabler and facilitator of negotiations both between particular departments of local administrative bodies and between local administration and »outside« actors (Mayer, 2000: 261–262).

In what follows, I will illustrate these developments using as a case-in-point the elderly care project developed by the Timisoara local authorities. As already described in the introductory chapters, the Romanian transformation process led to an increasing social polarisation of the population. At the same time, social welfare measures mainly served as a vehicle for populist policies. Analysts point to a massive retreat of the state from the social sphere starting in 1991 (Zamfir 1995). As a consequence, biological survival became a central issue for about 50 per cent of the population, whose main concerns now were how to provide for heating during the winter months and sufficient nourishment. Under these circumstances, state subsidies for basic foodstuffs and central heating came to be perceived as welfare measures (Pasti, Miroiu, Codita 1997: 178–179). However, these measures mainly favoured the inefficient state-owned producing enterprises and not their clients.

One outcome of this situation was child abandonment and the highest mortality rates in Europe for children aged between one and four years (Pasti, Miroiu, Codita 1997: 114–115). Under these circumstances it is not difficult to conclude that adults who could not fulfil their legal obligation to care for their underaged children would be even less able to do so with regard to their elderly parents. However, the latter development did not only apply to adults living in precarious conditions. The transformation of the labour market, which required increased mobility and flexibility from the young labour force, also had an impact. Even if many young professionals fulfilled their legal obligations towards their parents in financial terms, there were prevented from regularly looking after their elderly relatives, not by only geographic distance but also by long working hours.

Timisoara's city administration has been involved in the field of social services from the beginning of the transformation period. Its social services department runs a cafeteria where persons considered hardship cases are provided with warm meals. It is also responsible for severely disabled persons as well as persons qualifying for social housing in buildings under state administration.

A number of mainly church-sponsored NGOs also started to operate in the field of social service provision as early as the beginning of the 1990s. However, the majority of them not only depended almost exclusively on foreign donors, they also had a limited scope, mainly focussing on members of their own church congregations. Nevertheless, they made an important contribution by training and employing specialised staff and implicitly making careers in the field of social services attractive[35] by offering models for the organisation of social services and creating public awareness.

Over time, the retreat of the central state from the social sector and a growing concern for social issues within both the city administration and civil society led to a diversification and specialisation of social services on the local level. The main groups of vulnerable people who came to be supported by local welfare policies were the long-term unemployed, homeless children, young adults leaving children's homes, severely disabled persons, and the elderly. However, in many cases the city administration could not offer financial support due to budget shortages. Thus, for example, payments of welfare benefits to long-term unemployed persons whose entitlements to unemployment support had expired were transferred from the central state to the municipality through Law 67/1995. However, as a consequence of the shortage of funding, only 268 cases had received welfare payments by the end of 2001.

As heating and food continued to represent a central concern for all vulnerable groups, the services of the cafeteria were extended to 731 cases in 2001, and the municipality also took over payment of heating bills for several thousand households selected on a case-by-case basis (*http://orza-raport-2001.netfirms.com)*.

As especially vulnerable groups, children and the elderly received special attention. The Social Office for the Problems of the Third Age was set up by the municipality in 1997. It took over some of the problems associated with social housing to the extent that the office become responsible for evaluating the situation of the elderly requesting admission to old people's homes and geriatric hospitals. The manager of the office recalled in a personal interview that this was the point when she and her colleagues first realised the dimensions of isolation and neglect among aged persons. In order to get a more comprehensive picture, they set up a free-of-charge telephone line where aged persons and concerned relatives or neighbours could call in and talk about their problems. Once again, isolation and ne-

35 My interview partner, the manager of the city administration's office for elderly care, also received her initial training in social service provision in a course organized by a church-sponsored NGO.

glect emerged as a serious concern. Given the shortage of accommodation in specialised homes and hospitals, as well as many aged persons' wishes to continue living in their own homes, the staff of the social services department started thinking about a solution to meet the desires of the elderly while avoiding additional costs for the municipality.

This solution consisted in offering home-care services with the help of long-term unemployed women who were receiving welfare payments from the municipality. Twelve women willing to participate in the pilot programme were selected and trained by the municipality. For the first six months the pilot project obtained sponsoring from the local branch of a multinational corporation that was willing to pay for the home-care staff's wages. A local commercial centre donated the necessary material so that no additional costs emerged for the municipality.

However, this successful model of international private-public partnership only functioned for a limited period. After the first six months, the initial sponsor was unwilling to continue covering the home-care staff's wages, and lack of adequate legislation prevented the municipality from assuming the costs. Still, the project was not discontinued. Some of the women went on working, which was accounted as part of their obligation to perform a monthly 40 hours of public service work as welfare recipients. They were also promised full-time jobs once new sources for funding were secured. A local NGO further agreed to temporarily take over responsibility for the elderly who could no longer be looked after by the municipality.

Under these circumstances the city administration mobilised the contacts it had established through the Assembly of European Regions to Finnish and Swedish partners and became involved in an ECOS Ouverture programme focussing on services and prevention for the elderly (SPE). This step was facilitated by a series of background conditions.

First, the »new spirit« initiated by the present mayor of Timisoara induced the city administration staff to actively seek to overcome citizens' mistrust and hostility towards local authorities. This change of attitude was politically motivated and favoured by the second wave of decentralisation that went along with the implementation of the law on local public finances in 1998. Ongoing conflicts with the centre in Bucharest also made it clear that the Timisoara authorities had no chance to push through local interests as long as they could not rely on the support of local society.

Second, changes to the legislation not only granted the municipalities their own sources of income, the provisions of Law 34/1998 also granted the municipalities the right to subsidise NGOs involved in social service provision on the local level. This finally made it possible for the municipality to employ full-time home-care staff.

Under these circumstances the Timisoara authorities were in the position to set their own priorities and to draft their budget according to local needs. However, assessment of local needs was not unproblematic. The director of the urban planning department described the situation as follows:

»I believe that at a certain stage the town hall went through a transformation process. From a paternalistic and authoritarian institution it became some sort of an Aladdin's lamp. It lacks the necessary authority. It is not clear that the information has to reach the decision-makers and that it has to be directed to them naturally, because if they lack the information concerning you, you cannot expect them to take into account your problems.«

With regard to elderly care, the Social Office for the Problems of the Third Age had already identified some basic problems and designed a network for cooperation in order to overcome them. Once the municipality was admitted to the SPE-project, the office became part of an international network and could thus profit from the other network members' experience. Based on the model of the Scandinavian partners, a local network was created consisting of the Timis County Department of Labour and Social Protection, the Profilaxis Foundation of Medical Aid, and the Social Work Department of West University in Timisoara. The students of the social work department conducted a detailed quantitative and qualitative needs assessment in elderly care and also contributed to fund-raising. Members of the medical NGO instructed both the elderly and home-care staff on issues of accident prevention and offered general medical care. If specialised medical care was required, the office cooperated with the Alzheimer Society and other humanitarian organisations with a religious background.

With the help of this international support, the municipality's home-care project was re-launched and extended. Old and new staff were trained more extensively and offered full-time employment. Existing cooperative relations with local NGOs were strengthened, with new cooperation networks being established. These networks managed to sensitise local authorities to the problems of the socially marginalised by putting issues on the local agenda that otherwise would had been neglected. Meanwhile, they supported and empowered the actors representing the interests of marginalised population segments. Her ability to obtain international funding and to act successfully in an international environment strengthened the position the manager of the elderly care office both within the city administration and the local public arena. She stated in a personal interview that, although she did not feel that her personal authority had increased, she definitely sensed that social issues in general and elderly care in particular had become more than a marginal issue within city hall due to the success of the SPE project. Being the manager of the first Social Office for the Problems of the Third Age in a Romanian municipality, my interview partner also received a lot of media coverage and requests for information from other municipalities interested in setting up similar offices.

However, with a staff consisting of 15 people out of the city administration's 650 employees, the social services department was far from becoming of central importance. Local funding continued to be scarce and could only cover the 20 per cent local contribution requested in most cases for participation in EU-sponsored international partnerships. Under these circumstances, it was difficult to set up an independent agenda or even initiate an project. Local cooperation was also not unproblematic. My interview partner recalled that of about 30 NGOs that were nominally involved in elderly care according to the local NGO coordination office, only five responded to her request to attend regular coordination meetings, and, finally, only three were integrated into a reliable network of cooperation.

Ambivalences also arose from the fact that it was not organisations of the concerned social groups themselves but professional NGOs articulating their needs who gained a voice. Researchers working on NGO development in Romania warned that this situation could lead to a vicious circle: The more local »professional NGOs« claimed to represent civil society, the more empowered they were by Western donors and the more divorced they actually became from local civil society. As a consequence, there was a tendency among NGO professionals to form a separate interest group of »private international civil servants« whose livelihood was directly linked to the amount of international assistance earmarked to support local society. As such they tended to select projects and programmes on the basis of their budgets instead of their overall impact on local society (Pralong 1999).

However, a wide range of international exchanges facilitated contact with different practices in the field of social services, and thorough knowledge of the local situation helped to adopt the best-suited practices. Thus, even though available funding would have allowed for an extension of the home-care services, the municipality decided to restrict their provision to persons in need of special care. The project manager stated in a personal interview that the idea of extending the project was dismissed because it turned out that a stronger outside involvement in elderly care would affect traditional neighbourhood networks. Instead, the creation of a day-care centre offering a wide range of social activities was made a priority.[36]

Given both its formal competences and overall concern with local integration, local self-government in Timisoara could possibly provide an adequate institutional background for the social sector. Thus freely accessible activity reports of the social services department published on the Internet by the vice-mayor in charge of social issues created more transparency, accountability, and trust. Additionally, the transformation of the social services department from a formerly administrative unit into the public Center for Community Assistance, subordinate to the Timisoara local council, in 2002 (Ziua de Vest, 1 January 2002) enlarged the area of political intervention for the local community.

Limitations and ambivalences of transnational cooperation

The limitations and ambivalences of transnational cooperation can be regarded as resulting from the impact of the national transformation regime, and implicitly the »Romanian development model«, from specific features of the local context and, not least, from the relations of dependency imposed by European and global integration.

The national transformation regime maintained its central relevance both as the provider of the dominant identity discourse, i.e. nationalism, and as the provider of the dominant cultural pattern of institutionalisation, i.e. clientelism. The analysis of local efforts directed at the establishment of own instruments for local development, as illustrated by the example of ADETIM, has shown how nationalist identity discourses have been used by the central authorities to block local initiatives. Additionally, the analysis

36 The municipality bought an adequate building, which it equipped with the help of local and international partners. The day-care center for elderly people was inaugurated in autumn 2001 and started receiving clients in 2002.

of local politics has also pointed out that clientelistic incorporation, represented the local authorities' most important mode of access to centrally administered resources. Even if nationalism has less relevance in Timisoara than in Bucharest, local and regional government bodies entrusted with the redistribution of resources that were shared out centrally reproduced quite closely the clientelistic functional logic of the central state. However, clientelism was not exclusively induced by the central state, it also functioned as a pattern of social and cultural organisation inherited from the past and rooted in Timisoara's local society. This phenomenon was illustrated by the case of the Interporto logistics centre, where clientelism worked as an organisational pattern in a transnational context.

Personalism and factionalism were two other features of local society that favoured the reproduction of the clientelist model. The identification of local development projects with their initiators and their perception as personal pet-projects of prominent personalities often limited the circle of the people, and implicitly institutions, willing to become involved. On the other hand, the examples of both ADETIM and the Timisoara area local development strategy have shown that these instruments for development could hardly have been created without the personal commitment of certain personalities. Once established, the instruments for development started to become more widely accepted and if they proved useful, the need for personal involvement to sustain them accordingly diminished.

More specifically, legal and financial provisions gave the national transformation regime the power to limit the impact of transnational cooperation as the factor that defined the room for manoeuvre for sub-national actors. The example of the privatisation of Aquatim has shown that the unilateral retreat of the central state from a series of policy domains, coupled with its reluctance to provide local government bodies with their own sources of revenue to finance these tasks, created conditions that substantially limited the choices of local actors. The lack of legislation that would have enabled sub-national actors to act freely in the international arena put further restrictions on their options. Thus even if local actors sought transnational cooperation, they were often forced to accept unfavourable terms of agreement as a result of home-grown problems.

As already pointed out with reference to clientelism, specific features of the local context also contributed to the limitations and ambivalences of transnational cooperation. Dominant identity discourses in Timisoara were very favourable for international cooperation, even on unequal terms. In reference to the terminology developed by Hannerz (1993), local identity discourses in Timisoara can be regarded as a version of »provincialisms of openness«. Within this context, everything that could be interpreted as »the dernier cri of the metropolis« was enthusiastically taken up. It is therefore not surprising that their pioneering quality and the local prestige derived from their realisation within the framework of transnational cooperation networks contributed to the success of all the projects presented in the case studies.

Under these circumstances, the second scenario referring to local elites' reaction to global integration pressures described by Veltz (2000) comes closest to the strategies developed by Timisoara's urban elites to deal with the need to redefine the city. Politics and culture were not used to recapture the local identity dissolved by economic globalisation. On the contrary, local efforts were directed towards re-establishing the value of local history as a competitive resource. European integration was thus regarded as the reparation of a historical mistake and the terms of integration were not an issue for public debates. The reference to the imperial past of »Little Vienna« enabled local elites to create links to Western Europe and to mobilise for economic development. However, the exclusive use of this identity discourse as a symbolic resource for redefining the city raised some problems. First, it tended to ignore present-day social and economic reality, thus running the risk of losing its legitimacy in the eyes of the local public, which was more concerned with present survival than past glory. Second, it obscured the fact that, unlike the former Habsburg rulers, who promoted local development as a means to increase their tax revenues, global players today may have other objectives in mind.

In spite of their prevalent positive effects, the processes of European and global political and economic integration had their own ambivalences. Thus both the case of the delocalisation of Italian district SMEs and the privatisation of Timisoara's drinking water network showed how transnationally organised economic actors proved able to profit from the dynamic of European integration and extend their sphere of influence vis-à-vis local actors. Still, the higher degree of local involvement made possible by infrastructure investments seemed in both cases to stand for a more favourable pattern of integration than in the case of the electronics company. The city administration's elderly care project also showed that local initiatives had to be brought in line with the agendas of the donors in order to be successful. However, once this definitory task was fulfilled, the local administration was able to use the windows of opportunity created by involvement in an EU-sponsored project to extend its own local sphere of influence. Similarly, the success of the clothing factory in upgrading its position within the framework of an international production network showed that, once the rules of the game are understood and accepted, local actors possessing certain resources are in a position to use them for their own ends.

The explanatory value of the different theoretical approaches and the relevance of fieldwork

Although deterministic at first sight, the theory of path-dependency is not incompatible with institutional change. The analysis of Romania's historical development has identified two moments of institutional revolution: the communist takeover and the urban revolt in 1989. Under communist rule, reconfiguration of overall society under the conditions of external isolation altered several dimensions of the Romanian path to development. However, central dimensions such as nationalism and patterns of thinking derived from an agrarian way of life were reproduced. The urban revolt in 1989 overcame external isolation and re-aligned Romanian society with the dominant institutional trends of the 21st century: liberal democracy and market economy. However, both the political and economic reconfiguration of Romanian society in fact reproduced one of the dominant institutional patterns from before the communist takeover, i.e. clientelism. Still, the openness induced by Romania's desire for European and North-Atlantic integration not only contributed to institutional harmonisation in a number of policy domains such as local government and regional development but also prevented the reproduction of the nationalist and authoritarian tendencies prevalent in the political life of the inter-war period.

However, the theory of path-dependency is only able to identify ex post certain historical paradigms of development and their alterations. It has only a limited ability to recognise alternatives to the dominant paradigms and to anticipate ex ante developments. Therefore it can offer neither hypotheses on how an unproductive path may be changed nor policy recommendations to this end. At this point, the theory of institutional change may prove complementary to path-dependency, as it has a stronger normative character and also offers models for institutional efficiency. However, it does so only within the confines of certain historically created preconditions. In this respect its theoretical applicability is even narrower than that of path-dependency. Thus, when analysing a case that does not fit into the historical frame determined by Western modernity, the theory of institutional change is only able to identify shortcomings and not the alternative resources the case may offer for development.

In such a situation, an empirical approach based on ethnographical inquiry may help, not only to understand the present internal logic of the society under study but also to recognise »hidden« resources for development that may support the emergence of an alternative development path. These resources may be both material and immaterial, such as symbols, discourses, and identities. While the former can be statistically evaluated, qualitative research is needed in order to get a grip on the latter. Moreover, in many cases symbolic reality determines the functioning of a society to a considerable extent, inasmuch as patterns of thinking and action determine how actors relate to their material reality. Depending on the perspective of the actors, deindustrialisation, for example, may be perceived either as a major social and economic catastrophe or as a chance for ecological rehabilitation and attraction of greenfield investments. Resources for local development, even if obvious to the researcher, can therefore only be made productive if they are recognised as such and actively transformed by the actors involved.

To gain an understanding of the thinking and action patterns of the local actors under scrutiny, it is necessary to redefine the subjects of investigation and the relationship between the researcher and the subjects under investigation. I thus regarded the subjects of my investigation as partners in the construction of the research field and tried to include their perspectives and problem definitions in the research design. This approach enabled me to reassess the empirical relevance of the different aspects of the initial hypotheses and to broaden the scope of the initial research design. However, the broad theoretical framework of the overall investigation was not altered and continued to serve as the lens for interpretation and analysis.

The overall methodological approach thus consists of a combination of two different theoretical lines of reasoning: path-dependency and institutional change in the elaboration of the theoretical hypothesis. Additionally, fieldwork and empirical qualitative investigation are used not only for the testing but also for the redefinition of the hypothesis. The innovative quality of the overall approach is therefore given by the possibility to move flexibly between the levels of theoretical and empirical investigation.

The novelty of the approach matches the novelty of the task. No similar investigation has been conducted in Romania before. It was therefore necessary to make the theoretical framework, derived from an empirical reality different from the Romanian, compatible with the object of study. The broad theoretical contextualisation was further made necessary by the fluidity of the field under investigation. The focus of the analysis is on actors in the process of constitution and consolidation and institutions under construction. The results therefore represent only a snapshot of a local society caught up in the process of historical transformation. Further research is necessary to confirm or contradict the systemic traits identified in this analysis.

Acknowledgements

As a teenager growing up in the Romanian city of Cluj, I always wished that my family would move to Timisoara, the town I considered the coolest place in the country. We never moved, but the fascination with Timisoara remained. Many years later, when I finally got the opportunity to spend several weeks in Timisoara, in the framework of an international research project, I was both thrilled and eager to find out what made this place so special.

This book represents an attempt to grasp the special quality of the city of Timisoara the way I came to see it. I would therefore first of all like to thank the people of Timisoara, who shared their time and ideas during lengthy interviews with me, and most of all my colleagues and friends from the Center for Social Science Research at West University.

I owe very special thanks to professor Melanie Tatur, who first introduced me to the field of social research and then also made possible my participation in the project that finally lead me to Timisoara. She further supported me throughout the long years it took to complete this project, carefully reading and commenting on everything I wrote. I would also like to thank professor Gisela Welz, who helped me to gain deeper insight into the cultural and anthropological issues connected with my field, and Dr. Petra Ilyes, with whom I cooperated closely, not only on issues regarding IT development.

I am also indebted to Mr. Paul Knowlton for his patience and thoughtful correction of the present manuscript.

The overall project was made possible by the Volkswagen Foundation and the state of Hesse, which generously supported my research.

Bibliography

ADAR, ADECS, ADETIM: *Investor's Guide. The counties of Arad, Caras-Severin and Timis. Timisoara*: Editura Eurostampa, 1996

ADAR, ADECS, ADEH, ADETIM: *Regiunea economica VEST. Concept de dezvoltare regionala.* Timisoara: Editura Orizonturi Universitare, 1998

ADETIM: *Strategia de dezvoltare economica a judetului Timis.* Timisoara: Editura Orizonturi Universitare, 1999

Amin, Ash: Big Firms versus the Regions in the Single European Market. In: Dunford, Mick/Kafkalas, Grigoris (Eds.): *Cities and Regions in the New Europe: The Global – Local Interplay and Spatial Development Strategies.* London: Belhaven Press 1992, Pp. 127–149

Antohi, Sorin: *Civitas imaginalis: istorie si utopie în cultura româna.* Bucuresti: Editura Litera, 1994

Antohi, Sorin: Cultura româna este o fictiune… In: *Contrafort* 3–6 (2000), pp. 77–80

Augé, Marc: *Orte und Nicht-Orte.* Frankfurt am Main: S. Fischer, 1994

Baboi-Stroe, Adrian/Tiganescu, Oana: Sondaj de opinie la nivelul municipiului Bucuresti privind fenomenul coruptiei. Rezultate principale – raport preliminar
http://www.fdsc.ro/Publicatii (last access: 2000 august 22)

Baga, Enikö: *Regionale Differenzierung in Rumänien.* M.A. thesis, Frankfurt am Main: Johann Wolfgang Goethe University/Social Sciences Department, 1998

Baga, Enikö: Romania's Western Connection: Timisoara and Timis County.Local In: Tatur, Melanie (ed.): *The Making of Regions in Post-Socialist Europe: the Impact of Culture, Economic Structure, and Institutions*, Opladen: Leske+Budrich, forthcoming

Baga, Enikö/Balasa, Sergiu: The Reform of Territorial Administration and the Future Framework for Regional Policy in Romania. In: Tatur, Melanie (ed.): *The Challenge of Regional Policies. Actors and Institutions on the Local and Regional Level in Post-Socialist Europe.* Eschborn: Deutsche Gesellschaft für Technische Zusammenarbeit, 1999, pp. 59–65

Bagnasco, Arnaldo/Le Galès, Patrick (eds.): *Cities in Contemporary Europe.* Cambridge: Cambridge University Press, 2000

Balasa, Sergiu: ADETIM Economic Development Agency in Timis county – the first Romanian Experience in the Regional Field. In: Tatur, Melanie (ed.): *The*

Challenge of Regional Policies. Actors and Institutions on the Local and Regional Level in Post-Socialist Europe. Eschborn: Deutsche Gesellschaft für Technische Zusammenarbeit, 1999, pp. 59–65

Banfield, Edward: *The Moral Basis of a Backward Society.* New York, London: Free Press, 1967

Barbu, Daniel: *Republica absenta.* Bucuresti: Editura Nemira, 1999

Bell, Martin/Albu, Michael: Knowledge Systems and Technological Dynamism in Industrial Clusters in Developing Countries. In: *World Development*, Vol. 27, No. 9 (1999), pp. 1715–1734

Bennett, Robert J.: *Local Government in Post Socialist Cities.* Discussion Papers, No. 2, Local Government and Public Service Reform Initiative, Open Society Institute, 1997

Berger, Suzanne/Locke, Richard M.: *Il Caso Italiano and Globalization.* MIT Industrial Performance Center Globalization Working Paper 00–008, 2001

http://web.mit.edu/polisci/research/berger/ilcasoitalianoandglobal.pdf

Bönker, Frank: The Dog that Did Not Bark? Politische Restriktionen und ökonomische Reformen in den Visegrád-Ländern. In: *Leviathan* Sonderheft 15, 1995, pp. 180–206

Branea, Dorian (ed.): Citizen Participation and Accountability. Report on Cross-Border Cooperation in the Danube-Kris-Mures-Tisza Euroregion. Research report Timisoara, April-September 2001

Braudel, Fernand: Geschichte und Sozialwissenschaft. Die lange Dauer. In: Braudel, Fernand: *Schriften zur Geschichte 1. Gesellschaften und Zeit.* Stuttgart: Klett-Cotta, 1992, pp. 49–87

Bratton, Michael/van de Walle, Nicolas: Neopatrimonial Regimes and Political Transitions in Africa, In: *World Politics* 46 (1993–1994), pp. 453–389

Brucan, Silviu: *Stâlpii noii puteri în România.* Bucuresti: Editura Nemira, 1996

Borrus, Michael/Zysman, John: Globalization with Borders: the Rise of «Wintelism» as the Future of Industrial Competition. In: Zysman, John/Schwartz, Andrew (eds.): *Enlarging Europe: The Industrial Foundations of a New Political Reality*, University of California International and Area Studies Digital Collection Research Series # 99, 1998, pp. 27–62

Capelle-Pogacean, Antonela: Roumanie: l'utopie unitaire en question. In: *Critique internationale* (2000) 6, pp. 101–120

Campbell, Adrian: Local Government in Romania. In: Coulson, Andrew (ed.): *Local Government in Eastern Europe: Establishing Democracy at the Grassroots.* Aldershot: Elgar, 1995, pp. 78–89

Castells, Manuel: *Die Netzwerkgesellschaft*, Opladen: Leske+Budrich, 2001

Center for Social Science Research Timisoara: Consequences of Economic Transformation in Romania. A Decade Reviewed by People. Research Report, Timisoara 1999

Center for Social Science Research Timisoara: Statistical Profile of Timis County. Expertise (unpublished), Timisoara 2000

Center for Social Science Research: Study Case for Rural Areas in Timis County – Romania. Guide for Field Survey, Timisoara 2000a

Cernea, Mihai/Constantinescu, Virgil/Ene, Haralambie/Larionescu, Maria: *Doua sate. Structuri sociale si progres tehnic.* Bucuresti: Editura Tehnica, 1977

Chalmers, Douglas A./Martin, Scott B./Piester, Kerianne: Associative Networks: New Structures of Representation for the Popular Sectors? In: Chalmers, Douglas A./Vilas, Carlos M./Hite, Katherine/Martin, Scott B./Piester, Kerianne/Segarra, Monique (eds.): *The New Politics of Inequality in Latin America. Rethinking Participation and Representation.* Oxford: Oxford University Press, 1997, pp. 543–583

Chelcea, Liviu: Regionalismul banatean înainte si dupa comunism: transformari sociale, relatii etnice si memorie istorica. In: *Altera* 10 (1998), pp. 39–54

Chelcea, Liviu: Nationalism si regionalism în Banat în perioada interbelica: competitie pentru resurse, elite si discursuri culturale. In: *Revista de Cercetari Sociale* 2 (1997), pp. 26–58

Chelcea, Liviu/Latea, Puiu: *România profunda în comunism. Dileme identitare, istorie locala si economie secundara la Sântana.* Bucuresti: Editura Nemira, 2000

Chiribuca, Dan/Comsa, Mircea Ioan: Calea Democratiei. In: Berevoescu, Ionica/Chiribuca, Dan/Comsa, Mircea Ioan/Grigorescu, Narcisa/Lazaroiu, Andra Aldea/Lazaroiu, Sebastian/Pana, Marilena/Pop, Lucian/Stanculescu, Sofia Manuela: *Fetele schimbarii. Românii si provocarile tranzitiei.* Bucuresti: Editura Nemira, 1999, pp. 78–85

Coifan, Viorel (ed.): *Ghid micromonografic al localitatilor judetului Timis.* Timisoara: Editura Helicon, 1996

Commission of the European Communities: Regular Report on Romania's Progress towards Accession, Brussels, 8.11.2000

Commission of the European Communities: Regular Report on Romania's Progress towards Accession, Brussels, 9.10.2002

Cornea, Paul: La democratie roumaine dans l'ère post-totalitaire. Legs du passé et inconnus de l'avenir: In: Gregori, Ilina/Schaser, Angelika (eds.): *Rumänien im Umbruch: Chancen und Probleme der europäischen Integration.* Bochum: Winkler, 1993, pp. 103–108

Crawford, Beverly/Lijphardt, Arend: Explaining Political and Economic Change in Post-Communist Eastern Europe: Old Legacies, New Institutions, Hegemonic Norms, and International Pressures. In: *Comparative Political Studies* 28 (1995), pp. 171–199

Cretan, Remus: *Etnie, confesiune si comportament electoral în Banat. Studiu geografic.* Timisoara: Universitatea de Vest, 1999

Culic, Irina: *Elita politica si democratizare în România*, Ph.D. thesis Cluj-Napoca: Babes-Bolyai University/Sociology Department, 2001

Dahrendorf, Ralf: *Betrachtungen über die Revolution in Europa in einem Brief, der an einen Herrn in Warschau gerichtet ist.* Stuttgart: Deutsche Verlags-Anstalt, 1990

Daianu, Daniel: Is Catching Up Possible in Europe? TIGER Working paper No. 19, Warsaw, May 2002

Dematteis, Giuseppe: Spatial Images of European Urbanisation. In: Bagnasco, Arnaldo/Le Galès, Patrick (eds.): *Cities in Contemporary Europe*. Cambridge: Cambridge University Press, 2000, pp. 48–73

Dumitriu, Irina/Hunya, Gábor: Economic Restructuring Through FDI in Romania. Preliminary draft prepared for the 7th EACES Conference, Forli/Italien, 6–8 Juni 2002

Eichengreen, Barry/Kohl, Richard: The External Sector, the State and Development in Eastern Europe, BRIE Working paper 125, March 1998

http://bis.berkeley.edu/briewww/pubs/wp/wp125.htm

Eisenstadt, Shmuel Noah: *Die Antinomien der Moderne. Die jakobinischen Grundzüge der Moderne und des Fundamentalismus*. Frankfurt am Main: Suhrkamp, 1998

Eraydin, Ayda: Building up Competence, Institutions and Networks: A Perspective on ›Catch-up‹ in the Knowledge Economy. In: Hayter, Roger/Le Heron, Richard (Hg.): *Knowledge, Industry and Environment. Institutions and innovation in territorial perspective*. Burlington: Ashgate Publishing Company, 2002, pp. 49–67

Fonseca, Isabel: *Bury Me Standing. The Gypsies and Their Journey*. New York: Vintage, 1996

Forbess, Alice: Miraculous Transition? Rebellious Nuns and the Local Elections in Romania. Working paper (unpublished) 2000

Fox, Jonathan: How Does Civil Society Thicken? The Political Construction of Social Capital in Rural Mexico. In: *World Development*, 24 (1996) 6, pp. 1089–1103

Fox, Jonathan: The Difficult Transition from Clientelism to Citizenship: Lessons from Mexico. In: Chalmers, Douglas A./Vilas, Carlos M./Hite, Katherine/Martin, Scott B./Piester, Kerianne/Segarra, Monique (eds.): *The New Politics of Inequality in Latin America. Rethinking Participation and Representation*. Oxford: Oxford University Press, 1997, pp. 391–421

Gabanyi, Anneli Ute: *Systemwechsel in Rumänien: Von der Revolution zur Transformation*. München: R. Oldenbourg Verlag, 1998

Gadeanu, Sorin: *Sprache auf der Suche. Zur Identitätsfrage des Deutschen in Rumänien am Beispiel der Temeswarer Stadtsprache*. Regensburg: Roderer Verlag, 1998

Gallagher, Tom: O critica a centralismului esuat si a egotismului regional în România. In: Andreescu, Gabriel/Molnár, Gusztáv (eds.): *Problema transilvana*. Iasi: Editura Polirom, 1999, pp. 100–115

Greenfeld, Liah: Nationalism and Modernity. In: *Social Research* 63 (1996), pp. 3–40

Graziani, Giovanni: Globalization of Production in the Textile and Clothing Industries: the Case of Italian Foreign Direct Investment and Outward Processing Trade in Eastern Europe. In: Zysman, John/Schwartz, Andrew (Hg.): *Enlarging Europe: The Industrial Foundations of a New Political Reality*. University of California International and Area Studies Digital Collection Research Series # 99, 1998, pp. 238–254

Hann, Chris/Dunn, Elizabeth: Civil Society. *Challenging Western Models.* London: Routledge, 1996

Hannerz, Ulf: *Cultural Complexity. Studies in the Social Organization of Meaning.* New York: Columbia University Press, 1992

Hardy, Jane: Cultural Embeddedness, Corporate Strategy and Foreign Investment in Poland: A Tale of Two Firms. In: Hayter, Roger/Le Heron, Richard (eds.): *Knowledge, Industry and Environment. Institutions and Innovation in Territorial Perspective.* Burlington: Ashgate Publishing Company, 2002, pp. 273–289

Hellman, Joel S.: Winners Take All. The Politics of Partial Reform in Postcommunist Transitions. In: *World Politics* 50 (1998), pp. 203–234

Hellman, Joel S./Kaufmann, Daniel: Confronting the Challenge of State Capture in Transition Economies. In: *Finance and Development* Vol. 38 (2001) Number 3, pp. 1–9

Hellman, Joel S./Jones, Geraint/Kaufmann, Daniel: Far From Home: Do Foreign Investors Import Higher Standards of Governance in Transition Economies? Draft for discussion and comments, august 2002

Hitchins, Keith: *România 1866–1947.* Bucuresti: Editura Humanitas, 1996

Hughes, Jim/Sasse, Gwendolyn/Gordon, Claire: The Regional Deficit in Eastward Enlargement of the European Union: Top Down Policies and Bottom Up Reactions. Working Paper 29/01, ESRC »One Europe or Several?« Programme, Sussex European Institute 2001

Hunya, Gábor: Recent FDI trends, policies and challenges in SEE countries in comparison with other regions in transition. Paper presented at the Conference on Foreign Direct Investment in South East Europe: Implementing Best Policy Practices, Vienna, 8–9 November 2000

Iliescu, Adrian-Paul: Tranzitia ca succes – tranzitia ca esec. In: *Polis* 4 (1999), pp. 3–4

Ilyes, Petra: Zwischenbericht. Eine kurze Einschätzung der Situation der IT-Szenerie in Rumänien. Working paper, Frankfurt am Main: Johann Wolfgang Goethe-Universität/Institut für Kulturanthropologie und Europäische Ethnologie, 2001

Ilyes, Petra: Länderbericht Rumänien. Working paper, Frankfurt am Main: Johann Wolfgang Goethe-Universität/Institut für Kulturanthropologie und Europäische Ethnologie, 2002

Ilyes, Petra: *»Technology is Driving the Future«. Informationstechnologie und gesellschaftliche Veränderung aus der Perspektive lokaler IT-Experten.* Ph.D. Dissertation, Frankfurt am Main: Johann Wolfgang Goethe-Universität/Institut für Kulturanthropologie und Europäische Ethnologie, 2003 *http://publikationen.stub.uni-frankfurt.de/volltexte/2003/283*

Institutul pentru Politici Publice/Asociatia Pro Democratia: Bugetele locale între teorie si practica. Project report, Bucuresti 2001

Jowitt, Ken: *The New World Disorder: The Leninist Extinction.* Berkeley, Los Angeles, London: University of California Press 1992

Kideckel, David: *The Solitude of Collectivism: Romanian Villagers to the Revolution and Beyond.* Ithaca and London: Cornell University Press, 1993

Kitschelt, Herbert: Rationale Verfassungswahl? Zum Design von Regierungssystemen in neuen Konkurrenzdemokratien. Antrittvorlesung. Department of Political Science Duke University, North Carolina and Institut für Politkwissenschaft, Philosophische Fakultät III, Humboldt-Universität zu Berlin, 2. Mai 1994

Kitschelt, Herbert/Mansfeldova, Zdenka/Markowski, Radoslaw/Toka, Gábor: *Post-Communist Party Systems. Competition, Representation, and Inter-Party Cooperation.* Cambridge: Cambridge University Press, 1999

Leber, Reinhard: *Politische Kultur und Systemtransformation in Rumänien.* Frankfurt am Main, Berlin, Bern, New York, Paris und Wien: Lang, 1996

Linz, Juan/Stepan, Alfred: Towards Consolidated Democracies. In: *Journal of Democracy* 7, (1996), Nr. 2, pp. 14–33

Livezeanu, Irina: *Cultural Politics in Greater Romania.* Ithaca and London: Cornell University Press, 1995

Lobina, Emanuele: Water Privatisation and Restructuring in Central and Eastern Europe, PSIRU University of Greenwich, paper presented at PSI seminars in Slovakia and Romania, 2001

Lorrain, Dominique: The Construction of Urban Service Models. In: Bagnasco, Arnaldo/Le Galès, Patrick (eds.): *Cities in Contemporary Europe.* Cambridge: Cambridge University Press, 2000, pp. 153–177

Maskell, Peter/Eskelinen, Heikki/Malmberg, Anders/Hannibalsson, Ingjaldur/Vatne, Eirik: *Competitiveness, Localised Learning and Regional Development: Specialization and Prosperity in Small Open Economies.* London: Routledge, 1998

Marcus, George: On the Problematic Contemporary Reception of Ethnography as the Stimulus for Innovation in Its Forms and Norms in Teaching and Research. In: Ina-Maria Greverus (ed.): *Shifting Grounds. Experiments in Doing Ethnography.* Münster, Hamburg, London: Lit Verlag, 2003, pp. 191–207

Mariotti, Ilaria: International Delocalisation of Italian District SMEs: an Overview. Vortrag im Rahmen des Wirtschaftsgeographischen Workshops des Instituts für Wirtschafts- und Sozialgeographie, Johann Wolfgang Goethe-Universität Frankfurt am Main, October 2003

Mavratsas, Caesar: Greece, Cyprus and Greek America: Comparative Issues in Rationalization, Embourgeousment, and the Modernization of Consciousness. In: *Modern Greek Studies Yearbook*, University of Minnesota, Vol. 10/11 (1994–1995), pp. 139–169

Mayer, Margit: The Shifting Local Political System in European Cities. In: Bagnasco, Arnaldo/Le Galès, Patrick (eds.): *Cities in Contemporary Europe.* Cambridge: Cambridge University Press, 2000, pp. 255–277

Meyer, Klaus E.: International Business Research on Transition Economies, Copenhagen Business School, Center for East European Studies, Working paper no. 32, April 2000 *http://www.econ.cbs.dk/institutes/cees/staff/meyer.html*

Mihailescu, Vintila: *Socio Hai-Hui. O alta sociologie a tranzitiei.* Bucuresti: Editura Paideia, 2000

Mihailescu, Vintila: En marge de l'économie-monde: la maisnie diffuse et ses réseaux en Roumanie. Working paper (unpublished), 2000

Mihailescu, Vintila: Sa se revizuiasca primesc! Dar... Ideologie originarista si discursul national românesc. In: *Sfera Politicii*, 91–92/2001

http://www.sfera50megs.com/_private/Arhiva/sfera91–92/articole.htm (last access: 2001 july 6)

Miroiu, Mihaela: *Societatea retro*. Bucuresti: Editura Trel, 1999

Mocan, Marian: *Ghidul judetului Timis pentru investitori.* Timisoara: Editura Marineasa, 1998

Mungiu, Alina: *Românii dupa '89. Istoria unei neînțelegeri.* Bucuresti: Editura Humanitas, 1995

Munteanu, Ioan/Munteanu, Rodica: *Timis. Monografie.* Timisoara: Editura Marineasa, 1998

Negulescu, Oana: *Politische und wirtschaftliche Transformation in Rumänien 1989–1996.* Ph.D. thesis Frankfurt am Main: Johann Wolfgang Goethe University/Social Sciences Department, 2000

Nemoianu, Virgil: Tranzitia si paradoxurile sale. In: *Polis* (1999) 4, pp. 36–46

Nicolau, Irina/Popescu, Ioana: *O strada oarecare din Bucuresti.* Bucuresti: Editura Nemira, 1999

North, Douglass C.: *Institutions, Institutional Change and Economic Performance.* Cambridge: Cambridge University Press, 1990

North, Douglass C.: Institutions and Economic Performance. In Uskali, Mäki et al (eds.): *Rationality, Institution and Economic Methodology.* London: Routledge 1993, pp. 242–261

Offe, Claus: Das Dilemma der Gleichzeitigkeit. In: Offe, Claus (ed.): *Der Tunnel am Ende des Lichts: Erkundungen der politischen Transformation im neuen Osten.* Frankfurt, New York: Campus, 1994, pp. 57–80

Paradis, Paul: Regional Development in Romania. In: *OECD-Observer* 211, (1998) April/May, pp. 40–42

Parliamentary Assembly of the European Commission: Migration Connected with Trafficking in Women and Prostitution. Report of the Comittee on Equal Opportunities for Women and Men, 23.04.2003

Pasti, Vladimir: *România în tranzitie. Caderea în viitor.* Bucuresti: Editura Nemira, 1995

Pasti, Vladimir/Miroiu, Mihaela/Codita, Cornel: *România – Starea de fapt. Volumul I. Societatea.* Bucuresti: Editura Nemira, 1997

Patapievici, Horia Roman: *Politice.* Bucuresti: Editura Humanitas, 1996

Pavel, Dan: De ce nu s-a predat coalitia? In: Sfera Politicii 78 (2000), pp. 2–10

Peristiany, John George (ed.): *Honour and Shame: The Values of Mediterranean Society.* Chicago: Chicago University Press, 1966

Piattoni, Simona: Entwicklungspfade aus der Unterentwicklung. »Königswege« und »Sackgassen« örtlicher Entwicklung und lokaler Politik in Süditalien. In: Heinelt, Hubert/Mayer, Margit (eds.): *Politik in europäischen Städten: Fallstudien zur Bedeutung lokaler Politik*. Basel: Birkhäuser Verlag, 1992, pp. 284–300

Pieterse, Jan Nederveen: Globalization as Hybridization. In Featherstone, Mike/Lash, Scott/Robertson, Roland: *Global Modernities*. London, Thousand Oaks and New Delhi: Sage Publications, 1995, pp. 45–69

Pîrvulescu, Cristian R.: Final de criza? Politic, apolitic, antipolitic – reactii la consolidarea partidocratiei. In: *Sfera Politicii*, 59/1999

http://www.sfera50megs.com/private/Arhiva/sfera59/articole.htm (last access: 2001 july 8)

Pîrvulescu, Cristian: Competitie si transparenta. In: *Sfera Politicii*, 84/2000

http://www.sfera50megs.com/_private/Arhiva/sfera84/articole.htm (last access: 2001 july 6)

Portes, Alejandro/Schauffler, Richard: The Informal Economy in Latin America: Definition, Measurement, and Policies

http://www.jhu.edu/soc/pcid/papers/5(last access: 2000 november 7)

Poznanski, Kazimierz Z.: Teoria comparativa a tranzitiei: Recesiune si redresare în economiile post-comuniste. In: *Polis* 4 (1999), pp. 15–36

Pralong, Sandra: Civil Society and Civic Education in Romania, 1990–1998

http://www.ceip.org/programs/democr/NGOs/Pralong.pdf(last access: 2000 august 22)

Primaria Municipiului Timisoara/Fundatia pentru o societate deschisa: Parteneriatul institutional si al societatii civile pentru planificarea dezvoltarii economico-sociale a zonei Timisoara. Working paper. Timisoara, 1999

Primaria Timisoara: *Concept strategic de dezvoltare economica si sociala a zonei Timisoara*. Timisoara: Editura Brumar, 2000

Putnam, Robert: *Making Democracy Work. Civic Traditions in Modern Italy*. Princeton: Princeton University Press, 1993

Radoslav, Radu: *Topos comportamental. Armonizarea dintre spatiul urban si comportamentul uman*. Timisoara: Editura Marineasa, 2000

Rey, Violette: Questions on Hierarchical Change in Urban Systems in Eastern and Central Europe. In: Braun, Gerhard O. (Ed.): *Managing and Marketing of Urban Development and Urban Life: Proceedings of the IGU-Commission on »Urban Development and Urban Life«*, Berlin, August 15th to 20th, 1994, pp. 49–64

Robertson, Roland: Glocalization: Time-Space and Homogeneity-Heterogeneity. In: Featherstone, Mike/Lash, Scott/Robertson, Roland: *Global Modernities*. London, Thousand Oaks and New Delhi: Sage Publications, 1995, pp. 25–45

Rose-Ackerman, Susan: Democracy and »Grand« Corruption. In: *International Social Science Journal* 48, no.3 (1996), pp. 365–380

Sandor, Dorel: Politics versus Policies: How to Succeed in Blocking Reforms

http://www.worldbank.org.ro/eng/news/conf/sandor.shtml

(last access: 2001 January 14)

Sandu, Dumitru: *Sociologia tranzitiei. Valori si tipuri sociale în România*. Bucuresti: Editura Staff, 1996

Sármány-Parsons, Ilona: Die Rahmenbedingungen für »die Moderne« in den ungarischen Provinzstädten um die Jahrhundertwende. In: Corbea-Hoisie, Andrei/Le Rider, Jacques (eds.): *Metropole und Provinz in Altösterreich (1880–1918)*. Wien, Köln, Weimar: Böhlau, 1996, pp. 180–221

Schöpflin, George: Central Europe: Definitions Old and New. In: Schöpflin, George/Wood, Nancy (eds.): *In Search of Central Europe*. London: Barnes & Noble Books, 1989, pp. 7–30

Shafir, Michael: Alegerile din România: un sufragiu istoric. In: *Sfera Politicii*, 45(1996), pp. 25–31

Suciu, Marius: Quelques aspects de la décéntralisation en Roumanie. A la recherche d'une nouvelle logique gestionnaire de l'espace par la démocratie locale. In: *Caietele tranzitiei* 1(1997), pp. 10–27

Staniszkis, Jadwiga: Dilemmata der Demokratie in Osteuropa. In: Deppe, Rainer et al (eds.): *Demokratischer Umbruch in Osteuropa*. Frankfurt am Main: Suhrkamp, 1991, pp. 326–347

Staniszkis, Jadwiga: In Search of a Paradigm of Transformation. In: Wnuk-Lipinski, Edmund (ed.): *After Communism. A Multidisciplinary Approach to Radical Social Change*. Warsaw: Institute of Political Studies, 1995, pp. 19–55

Stark, David: Das Alte im Neuen: Institutionenwandel in Osteuropa. In: *PROKLA*, 94 (1995), pp. 127 –142

Stocchiero, Andrea: Migration Flows and Small and Medium Sized Enterprise Internationalisation between Romania and the Italian Veneto Region. Working paper, Centro di Studi Politica Internazionale, Rome, June 2002
http://www.cespi.it/pubblicazioni.htm (last access 14.02.2003)

Sterbling, Anton: Historische und aktuelle Fragen der »Bodenfrage« und der Agrarkrise in Siebenbürgen. In: Sterbling, Anton (ed.): *Kontinuität und Wandel in Rumänien und Südosteuropa: historisch-soziologische Analysen*. München: Verlag Südostdeutsches Kulturwerk, 1997, pp. 15–49

Stokes, Gail: The Social Origins of Eastern European Politics. In: Chirot, Daniel (ed.): *The Origins of Backwardness in Eastern Europe*. Berkeley, Los Angeles, Oxford: University Press of California, 1989, pp. 210–251

Sundhaussen, Holm: Institutionen und institutioneller Wandel in den Balkanländern. In: Papalekas, Johannes C. (ed.): *Institutionen und institutioneller Wandel in Südosteuropa*. München: Südosteuropa-Gesellschaft, 1994, pp. 35–55

Szücs, Jenö: *Die drei Regionen Europas*, Frankfurt am Main: Verlag Neue Kritik, 1990

Tanase, Stelian: *Revolutia ca esec. Elite & societate*. Iasi: Editura Polirom, 1996

Tatur, Melanie: Ökonomische Transformation, Staat und moralische Ressourcen in den post-sozialistischen Gesellschaften. In: *PROKLA* 112 (1998) 3, pp. 339–374

Tatur, Melanie (ed.): *The Challenge of Regional Policies. Actors and Institutions on the Local and Regional Level in Post-Socialist Europe*. Eschborn: Deutsche Gesellschaft für Technische Zusammenarbeit, 1999

Thayer, Millie: Traveling Feminisms. From Embodies Women to Gendered Citizenship. In: Burawoy, Michael (ed.): *Global Ethnography. Forces, Connections, and Imaginations in a Postmodern World.* Berkeley, Los Angeles, and London: University of California Press, 2000, pp. 203–235

Tismaneanu, Vladimir: Sfirsitul exceptionalismului românesc: epitaf pentru o a treia cale. In: *Sfera Politicii* 45 (1996), pp. 21–25

Tismaneanu, Vladimir: *Balul mascat. Un dialog cu Mircea Mihaies.* Iasi: Editura Polirom, 199

Turlea, Geomina/Mereuta, Cezar: Markets and Networks in Romania – Life after Disorganisation. Working Paper No.15, Centre for the Study of Economic and Social Change in Eastern Europe, School of Slavonic and Eastern European Studies, University College London, March 2002

Veltz, Pierre: European Cities in the World Economy. In: Bagnasco, Arnaldo/Le Galès, Patrick (eds.): *Cities in Contemporary Europe.* Cambridge: Cambridge University Press, 2000, pp. 33–48

Verdery, Katherine: *What Was Socialism, and What Comes Next?* Princeton: Princeton University Press, 1996

Verdery, Katherine: Fuzzy Property: Rights, Power, and Identity in Transylvania's Decollectivization.In: Burawoy, Michael/Verdery, Katherine (eds.): *Uncertain Transition. Ethnographies of Change in the Postsocialist World.* Lanham, MD: Rowman & Littlefield Publishing, 1999, pp. 53–83

Vilas, Carlos M.: Participation, Inequality, and the Whereabouts of Democracy. In: Chalmers, Douglas A./Vilas, Carlos M./Hite, Katherine/Martin, Scott B./Piester, Kerianne/Segarra, Monique (eds.): *The New Politics of Inequality in Latin America. Rethinking Participation and Representation.* Oxford: Oxford University Press, 1997, pp. 3–43

Vultur, Smaranda: *Istorie traita-istorie povestita. Deportarea în Baragan, 1951–1956.* Timisoara: Editura Amarcord, 1997

Wallerstein, Immanuel: *The Capitalist World Economy.* Cambridge: Cambridge University Press, 1979

Weiner, Robert: Democratization in Romania. In: Stan, Lavinia (ed.): *Romania in Transition.* Aldershot, UK: Dartmouth, 1997, pp. 3–23

World Bank: Diagnostic Surveys of Corruption in Romania

http://www.worldbank.org.ro/ECA/Romania.nsf/ECADocByLink/Economic+Studies+on +Romania?Opendocument (last access 12.01.2003)

Zamfir, Catalin: *Dimensiuni ale saraciei.* Bucuresti: Editura Expert, 1995

Newspaper articles and press releases:
http://www.romanialibera.com/1POL/24s1pape.htm (last access 01.04.2001)
http://www.romanialibera.com/3ECO/28s3emil.htm (last access 10.04.2001)
http://www.romanialibera.com/3ECO/24s3eagr.htm(last access 10.04.2001)
http://www.romanialibera.com/3ECO/07s3erom.htm(last access 10.04.2001)
http://www.romanialibera.com/1POL/26s1ptim.htm(last access 10.04.2001)
Alessandrini, Elisabetta: L' Eldorado in Romania. In: *Adesso* 7/2001, 20–22
Andronescu, Adriana/Boncea, Flavius: Apa din Timisoara nu le da pace consilierilor locali. Trei conferinte de presa politice, o singura tema: »Problema Lyonnaise des Eaux« continua sa încinga spiritele. In: *Timisoara* 16.09.2000
Avery, Bill: Bright Lights, Big City. Philips Romania Comes Back in a Big Way. In: *http://www.moneynations.ch/topics/border/text/philips2.htm* (last access 06.12.2000)
Antica, Andrei/Vilau, Cornel: Contrabanda de stat a fost dirijata de ministrii Taracila si Novac. In: *România Libera*, 3.10.2000
Balan, Eliade: Motorina si arme. In: *România Libera*, 20.11.2000
Balan, Adrian Robert/Vilau, Cornel: In Clisura Dunarii a trecut vremea cand suta de marci cadea din buzunar si nimeni nu se apleca sa o ridice. In: *România Libera*, 2.2.2001
Baranga, Daniela: »Prin asocierea Aquatim cu Suez Lyonnaise des Eaux, bugetul local va avea un câstig de 20% din propria lui valoare«. Interviu cu dl. Philippe Pedrini, directorul regional de dezvoltare al concernului francez. In: *Prima Ora*, 16.09.2000
Boncea, Flavius: Scandal în Consiliul Judetean Timis. In: *Timisoara*, 27.07.2001
Bot, Malin: S-a nascut Interporto. Societatea pe actiuni a luat fiinat, ieri, în fata notarului. In: *Agenda Zilei*, 13.06.2002
Bot, Malin: Cusca administrativa a PSD, din jurul Timisoarei. In: *Ziua de Vest*, 6.06.2003
Brad, Liliana: Garîna, locul unde vin cu placere ministrii cancelariilor occidentale. In: *România Libera*, 25.02.2000
Brad, Liliana: Pentru ca se suspenda cursele de Stuttgart si Ancona investitorii italieni si germani ameninta ca pleaca din Arad. In: *România Libera*, 20.10.2001
Cameron, Ian: West goes East. In: *Electronics Time*, 15.05.2000
Ciobanu, Cristina: Programul SAPARD. Vor primi finantare numai societatile private fara pierderi. In: *România Libera*, 17.04.2001
Condea, Lacramioara: Comisiile Consiliului Judetean Timis analizeaza activitatea din judet. In: *Agenda Zilei*, 11.10.2000
Cu ce se mai ocupa fostii contrabandisti din Clisura Dunarii. In: *România Libera*, 9.2.2001s
EBRD: Press Release. Success in Romania Encourages EBRD to Extend Municipal Lending to an Additional 10 Cities Across the Country, 4.08.1997
EBRD: Press Release. EBRD Supports First Public-Private Partnership. In Romania's Municipal Sector, 22.12.1999

Economia e trasporti. La società del Marco Polo riceverà il 35 % dello scalo rumeno. Timisoara volerà alla veneziana. La Save pagherà il 60 % dell'ammodernamento dell'aeroporto. In: *L'Arena – il giornale di Verona*, 30.06.2002

Epure, Lia Lucia/Bot, Malin: Ordine si Lege. In: *Focus Vest*, June 2001

Embassy of the United States: US Ambassador Travels to Timisoara to Present Plaque Honoring Timisoara for Being One of the First Two Cities to Complete U.S.–Designed »Simple and Fast« Procedures to Reduce Bureaucracy for Business. Press release. Bucharest, 29.01.2001

Fiumani, Piercarlo: A Timisoara la locomotiva produttiva parla la lingua del Nordest. In: *Il Piccolo*, 19.01.2002

Fumi, Alberto: Interporto di Timisoara: storia di un'occasione perduta. In: *L'opinione*, 29.05.2003

Gli imprenditori italiani analizzane loro difficoltà in Romania. In: *Associazione Imprenditori Italiani in Romania, Newsletter* 26/2003, 30.06.2003

I.T.: Timisul risca sa-si compromita cea mai importanta investitie! In: *Confidential*, 24–30.06.2002

Judy, Tim: Raising hopes. In: *Bucharest Business Week*, Vol.5 Nr.5, 12.02.2001

L'assessore regionale Finozzi inaugura a Timisoara lo sportello per le Pmi attive nel Paese dell'Est. Romania, »provincia veneta«. Finita l'era del pioniersimo, le aziende creanu sviluppo e ritorno sul Pil. In: http://oldlapadania.com/2002/maggio

Lera, Ioan: Economia judetului Timis s-a aflat în regres în anul 1999. In: *Renasterea Banateana*, 3.10.2000

Lucaciu, Ileana: Donatii ilegale în campania electorala pentru partide, din... simpatie. In: *România Libera*, 15.05.2001

M. P.: Un pas înainte pentru asistenta sociala din Timisoara. Adrian Orza propune transformarea Serviciului Social al primariei în serviciu public. In: *Ziua de Vest*, 01.01.2002

Medoia, Ion: Firma Philips – investitor la Timisoara. In: *România Libera*, 16.11.2000

Medoia, Ion: Timisoara: Vile luxoase intrate ilegal pe mana tiganilor. Bulevardul C.D. Loga, imbacsit de turnuri si turnulete orientale. In: *România Libera*, 20.11.2000

Medoia, Ion: Ex-directoarea arestata de la ILSA Timisoara – un paravan in spatele caruia se desfasoara afaceri de miliarde. In: *România Libera*, 28.02.2001

Medoia, Ion: Jimbolia, un oras de la granita de vest care vrea sa renasca. In: *România Libera*, 25.05.2001

Medoia, Ion: La Timisoara, investitii directe de 1.028 marci germane pe locuitor. In: *România Libera*, 18.07.2001

Oancea, Ion: Cu peste 7.000 de dolari investitii straine pe locuitor, Sânnicolau Mare este fruntas pe tara. In: *Prima Ora*, 04.10.2000

Opris, M.: Referendum local la Giroc. Aspiratiile urbane aprind spiritele politice. In: *Ziua de Vest*, 03.03.2003

Pantea, Mihaela: Tot impozitele pe salarii sustin bugetul de stat. In: *România Libera*, 18.12.2000

Paulescu, Lucian: Calitatea investitorilor italieni s-a îmbunatatit. In: *Ziua de Vest*, 06.06.2003

Radiografia Agentiei pentru Dezvoltare Regionala: Regiunea V Vest, *http://wwww.banatbusiness.ro* (last access: november 1, 2001)

Radulescu, Dina: Avem nevoie de o strategie a dezvoltarii industriei digitale. In: *România Libera*, 22.11.2000

Radulescu, Dina: Bugetul, facut svaiter de evazionisti.3.164 miliarde lei – valoarea taxelor si impozitelor neplatite. In: România Libera, 13.01.2001

Radulescu, Dina: Politici comerciale- Cu toate ca va concedia 16% din personal

Concernul Solectron isi va continua investitiile in România. In: *România Libera*, 20.02.2001

Solectron Expands Its Low-Cost, High-Volume PCBA and Systems Assembly

Manufacturing Capacity in Europe. Company Breaks Ground for New Facility in Romania and Announces That Its Local Workforce Will Grow by a Factor of Four in Two Years. In: *http://www.solectron.com* (24.11.1999)

Solectron Opens 200,000 Square-Foot, State-of-the-Art Manufacturing Campus

In Timisoara, Romania. Company Announces Plan to Hire 1,000 Additional Associates in the Next Two Years. In: *http://www.solectron.com* (26.10.2000)

Suez-Lyonnaise des Eaux: Press release. Timisoara selects Lyonnaise des Eaux to manage water and wastewater services, 09.11.2000

Synovitz, Ron: Romania: Previous Government Charged with Smuggling Oil to Serbia. In: *RFE/RL Reports*, 21.08.1998

Terciu, Georgeta: Consilierii judeteni s-au dumirit. Legea finantelor publice locale a fost formulata pe criterii politice. In: *Monitorul de Brasov*, 02.03.1999

Timisoara, nuova provincia del Nordest industriale. In: *La Repubblica*, 05.03.2001

Tudorache, Bogdan: Magnet for Investment. In: *Bucharest Business Week*, Vol.5 Nr. 4, 05.02.2001

Zavete, Manuela: S-au aranjat burse, viitoare posturi, locuinte pentru... copii, frati, surori, cumnati si cumetri. In: *România libera*, 10.01.2001

Social Science

Stefani Scherer, Reinhard Pollak, Gunnar Otte, Markus Gangl (Hg.)
FROM ORIGIN TO DESTINATION
Trends and Mechanisms in Social Stratification Research
2007 · 323 p. · ISBN 978-3-593-38411-5

Johannes Harnischfeger
DEMOCRATIZATION AND ISLAMIC LAW
The Sharia Conflict in Nigeria
2007 · 260 p. · ISBN 978-3-593-38256-2

Helmut Willke
SMART GOVERNANCE
Governing the Global Knowledge Society
2007 · 206 p. · ISBN 978-3-593-38253-1

Michael Dauderstädt, Arne Schildberg (eds.)
DEAD ENDS OF TRANSITION
Rentier Economies and Protectorate
2006 · 249 p. · ISBN 978-3-593-38154-1

Magdalena Nowicka
TRANSNATIONAL PROFESSIONALS
AND THEIR COSMOPOLITAN UNIVERSES
2006 · 280 p. · ISBN 978-3-593-38155-8

Sonja Puntscher Riekmann, Monika Mokre, Michael Latzer (eds.)
THE STATE OF EUROPE
Transformations of Statehood from a European Perspective
2004 · 358 p. · ISBN 978-3-593-37632-5